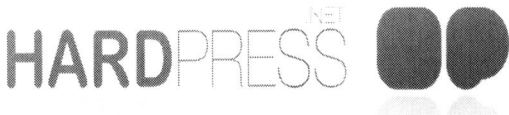

ISBN: 9781407757766

Published by:
HardPress Publishing
8345 NW 66TH ST #2561
MIAMI FL 33166-2626

Email: info@hardpress.net
Web: http://www.hardpress.net

The Scottish Text Society

THE WORKS

OF

SIR WILLIAM MURE

OF ROWALLAN

THE WORKS

OF

SIR WILLIAM MURE

OF ROWALLAN

EDITED

WITH INTRODUCTION, NOTES, AND GLOSSARY

BY

WILLIAM TOUGH, M.A., F.S.A. Scot.

VOL. I.

Printed for the Society by

WILLIAM BLACKWOOD AND SONS
EDINBURGH AND LONDON
MDCCCXCVIII

CONTENTS OF THE FIRST VOLUME.

INTRODUCTION.

ROWALLAN CASTLE.

ROWALLAN CASTLE, the ancient residence of the Mures of Rowallan, stands on the banks of the Carmel Water, about three miles north of Kilmarnock. It is more than probable that at some remote period the stream, widening at this point, altogether surrounded the slight elevation on which the castle stands, and thus formed of it a small island rock or craig—a circumstance to which, it has been suggested, the name Rowallan is due. Several rocks of similar appearance in the Firth of Clyde, in the neighbourhood of the Cumbraes, are called *Allans* to the present day. The promontory forming the approach to the castle would perhaps sufficiently account for the first syllable of the name.[1] The prominence occupied by it is stated by Crawfurd to have been called the "Craig of Rowallan," and the proprietors were sometimes designated therefrom "de Crag." The environs of Rowallan, adorned with many aged trees, some of them of great size and beauty, are delightfully suggestive of poetic musings, while the venerable mansion itself "affords a very perfect specimen of an

---

[1] See note to p. 237 of 'Historie' (p. 301) on etymology of Rowallan.

early feudal residence, progressively enlarged and fashioned to the advancing course of civilisation and manners."

The original fortlet, of which only the vaulted under apartment remains, has been with great probability assigned as the birthplace of Elizabeth More, the first wife of Robert, the High Steward of Scotland, afterwards Robert II. By this marriage—the most important event in the long history of the Barons of Rowallan, and a source of lively discussion to several generations of historians—the descendants of Elizabeth were destined to fill first the throne of Scotland, and afterwards that of Great Britain, and by it the blood of the Mures of Rowallan flows in the veins of our royal family at the present day.

The southern front, the principal and more ornamental part of the building, was erected about the year 1562 by John Mure of Rowallan and his wife, Marion Cunninghame, of the family of Cunninghamehead. This is indicated by the inscription on a small tablet at the top of the wall JON . MVR . M . CVGM . SPVSIS . 1562. In the neighbourhood of this inscription appears the arms of the family and also its crest, a Moor's head. This crest, which seems to be alluded to in the old family tree as the "bludy heid," may probably refer to some feat of arms performed against the Saracens during the Crusades. Unfortunately the building, with its pleasant old garden, is fast falling into decay. With the exception of the part occupied by the ground-officer on the estate, it has long been uninhabited.

LIFE OF SIR WILLIAM MURE.

Sir William Mure was born in the year 1594. As his grandfather was then alive, it is likely that he first saw the light not in the Castle of Rowallan itself, but in the Old Hall, a building situated a short distance from the family seat, and the recognised dwelling of the eldest son after marriage. There is little now to distinguish the Old Hall from the ordinary farmhouse, but in earlier times it was a place of some importance. Before the existence of the village of Fenwick, the smith's and cartwright's shops, and the dwellings of others of the more useful retainers of the family, grouped themselves around it, and in its immediate neighbourhood grew up the first school of the barony.

Of the early life of the poet we cannot speak with any certainty. Whether he received the rudiments of his education in the barony school and afterwards at Kilmarnock, or privately in his father's house, there is no record left to tell us. That he may have attended school at Kilmarnock, however, seems probable. It is true we have no authentic information regarding the parish school of that town until the comparatively late date of 1727. But we know that in 1633 Parliament passed an Act authorising the establishment of a school in every parish in Scotland, "upon a sum to be stented upon every plough or husband land according to the worth"; and, as Kilmarnock had risen to the rank of a burgh long before then, there is no great improbability in supposing it to have had the means of affording rudimentary instruction as early as the period of Mure's boyhood. With greater probability may it be assumed that he finished his scholastic career at the University of Glasgow. His younger brother Hugh, afterwards "preacher at Burstone, in Northfolke in Ingland," was enrolled there as a student in 1618, and his own connection with the university in after-life points to the likelihood of some earlier bond of union. It has been suggested that the sentiment of veneration which he ever cherished towards the eminent Principal, Robert Boyd of Trochrig, may have been due, in part at least, to their early relation as teacher and student; but as Boyd was only appointed Professor and Principal in 1615, the year of Mure's marriage, the suggestion cannot be held to be of much value. Be that as it may, there is no doubt that Mure received the best education the times could afford. There is abundant evidence of this in his writings. The frequent references to classical fable in his earlier poems may not, indeed, prove much. They were probably to some extent due to youthful vanity, and the desire to write "according to the fashion." But his later works, especially his translations from Virgil, and his faithful and vigorous rendering of Boyd's 'Hecatombe Christiana,' prove that he was not only widely read in the classical authors, but also that he was deeply imbued with their spirit and beauty. That with such tastes he should content himself with the exercise of his poetic faculty in his native tongue would be, perhaps, too much to expect, and accordingly we find that the manuscript of his Miscellaneous Poems contains several specimens of his Latin versification. These, however, have not been included in the present volumes, partly because they were considered beyond the scope of the work—partly, perhaps mainly, because of their incompleteness. With one exception,[1] they seem to

[1] The exception consists of the following six lines on the death of his grandfather :—

    " Vir virtutis, homo antiquæ fideique recumbit,
       Quales haud multos tempora nostra ferunt,
    Simplicitas cui cordi et priscæ secula vitæ,
       Sors sine dissidio mens sine fraude fuit,
    Quæ, quia degeneri hoc ævo sunt rara, perosus,
       Ævum hoc indignum dignius ille adiit."

be little more than first drafts. They have many un-
musical lines, and contain defects in Latinity which would
most assuredly have been amended had they had the
benefit of their author's revising hand.

Mure seems to have looked upon himself as a poet by
heredity, and there is no doubt he did his best to cultivate
his hereditary gift. In this endeavour he received every
encouragement from his friends and contemporaries. His
mother was Elizabeth Montgomery,[1] daughter of the laird
of Hazelhead, and sister of Alexander Montgomery, the
author of 'The Cherrie and the Slae.' To this connection
he makes reference in his address to Charles, Prince of
Wales, afterwards Charles I., in the following lines :—

> " Machles Montgomery in his native tounge,
> In former tymes to thy Great Syre hath sung,
> And often ravischt his harmonious ear
> W[t] straynes fitt only for a prince to heir.
>   My muse, q[ch] noght doth challenge worthy fame,
> Saue from Montgomery sche hir birth doth clayme,
> (Altho his Phoenix ashes have sent forth
> Pan for Apollo, if compaird in worth),
> Pretending tytyls to supply his place
> By ryt hereditar to serve thy grace."

In one of two sonnets addressed to him, probably about
the year 1617, the same relationship is also mentioned,[2]

---

[1] See the 'Historie,' p. 256.
[2] The reference is contained in the following lines :—

> " Sprang thou from Maxwell and Montgomerie's muse,
> To let o[r] poets perisch in the West?
> No, no! (brave ȝouth) continow in thy kynd.
> No sweeter subject sall thy muses fynd."

The name of Maxwell which here occurs as that of a then recognised poet
seems to have perished. As Mure's grandmother, however, was a daughter
of Maxwell of Newark, in Renfrewshire, his descent from that branch of the
Maxwells would seem to be pretty clearly indicated.

On the last page of his edition of 'The Historie and Descent of the House

and Mure is urged to continue his poetical efforts. He probably required no encouragement. At all events, from 1611, the date of the first of his poems which has come down to us, till his death in 1657, his pen was rarely idle.

The chief events of Mure's life, as far as possible in their chronological order, may now be given. In 1615, before fully completing his majority, he married Anna Dundas, daughter to the laird of Newliston. It now became necessary for him to set up an establishment of his own, and he accordingly built the house of Dalmusternock. It is prettily situated, and stands quite in the neighbourhood both of the castle itself and of the Old Hall. The arms of Sir William and his wife are still to be seen above the door at Dalmusternock. The date of his marriage, 1615, is shown on a stone to the right of the doorway, and the initials A. D. (Anna Dundas) appeared, until recently, on a stone to the left. The D still remains, but the A has become obliterated within the last few years.

Of this marriage five sons and six daughters were born. The sons were: "Sir William who succeided, Captain Allex[r], slaine in the warre against the Rebells in Irland, Major Ro[t], maried to the ladie Newhall in fyfe, Johne, finnickhill, and Patrick." Of the daughters only one, Elizabeth, reached years of maturity. She married Knox, laird of Ranfurly.

On the death of his first wife Mure married again, choosing for his second wife Dame Jane Hamilton, Lady Duntreth, by whom he had two sons, James and Hugh, and two daughters, Jeane and Marion.

of Rowallan,' the Rev. Wm. Muir curiously enough gives the first part of one of the above-mentioned sonnets, with the omission of two lines, and to this tags on the four lines quoted, which only occur in the other sonnet.

In 1616, the year after Sir William's first marriage, his grandfather died and his father succeeded to the family estates.

In 1617 appeared his 'Address to the King's Maiestie,' which was included in the collection entitled 'The Muse's Welcome,' published the following year, and was thus in all probability the first of Mure's effusions to appear in print. His 'Dido and Æneas' was written before this. In the second stanza of that poem he describes himself as—

"To twyse two lustres scarce of ʒeirs attained,"

so that we shall not probably err in ascribing it to the year 1614. It is now published for the first time.

From 1617 till 1628 we have nothing from Mure's pen ; but in the latter year he issued a small volume containing 'A Spirituall Hymne,' 'Fancies Farewell,' and 'Doomesday.' The first of these is a translation of Boyd of Trochrig's Latin poem, the 'Hecatombe Christiana'; the last is an original poem of considerable length, the nature of which is sufficiently indicated by its full title. In 'Fancies Farewell,' a series of three sonnets, the poet describes the change which had taken place in his views of life since the time when his mind was wholly occupied with his "Amorouse Essayes." He deplores the years of youth wasted in the composition of his "lovelie layes,"—

"Love's false delight and beautees blazing beame
 Too long benighted haue my dazled eyes,"

and resolves to devote his remaining days to the consideration of the only subject worthy of concern to sinful man.

" Hence-foorth fare-well all counterfeit delyte,
Blinde Dwarfling, I disclaime thy deitie,
My Pen thy Trophees neuer more shall write :
Nor after shall thine arts enveigle mee.
With sacred straines, reaching a higher key,
My Thoughts aboue thy fictions farre aspire :
Mounted on wings of immortalitie,
I feele my brest warmde with a wountless fire."

These were no idle words. Mure kept his promise—and wrote very little more that is worthy the name of poetry.

In 1629 'The Trve Crvcifixe' appeared. This is Mure's longest, and, from his own point of view, most important work. It is also his best known, and, whatever we may think of its merits, it undoubtedly deserves the credit of having done more than any of his other writings to preserve his memory from utterly perishing. As a poem, in the true sense of the word, however, it will hardly bear investigation.

The consideration of Mure's remaining works need only occupy a few lines. Between the years 1629 and 1639 he seems to have been engaged on his version of the Psalms, now published for the first time. Next to the 'Dido and Æneas,' this is undoubtedly the most valuable and interesting thing he ever produced. The 'Covnter-bvff to Lysimachus Nicanor' appeared in 1640 under the *nom de plume* of Philopatris. 'Caledon's Complaint,' which bears no date, may, with a fair degree of likelihood, be put down to 1641. 'The Cry of Blood and of a Broken Covenant' was published in 1650. It was the last of Mure's works, with the probable exception of 'The Historie and Descent of the House of Rowallan,' of which we can only surmise, since it was left unfinished, that he was engaged on it at the time of his death in 1657.

On the death of his father in 1639, Mure was at once drawn into the whirlpool of political life. This change, which is immediately reflected in his writings, cannot have been altogether pleasing to one of his disposition and studious habits. Nevertheless, with a conscientious recognition of the claims of his position, he threw himself with vigour into the troublous life of the times, and promptly took his place as the representative of an important county family. In Scotland, as in England, the political atmosphere had long been stormy. The headstrong and bigoted policy of the Court, brought into conflict with the no less obstinate resistance of the Presbyterians, had rendered an open rupture unavoidable. The crisis came in the Assembly held at Glasgow in 1638. There the Covenanters found themselves forced, as a last resource, to decide upon resistance by arms. Early in the summer of 1639, therefore, the forces of the Covenant began to assemble, and, about the beginning of June, they formed the famous camp at Dunse Law. To this gathering Ayrshire sent a contribution of 1200 men, foot and horse, under the leadership of Lord Loudon. Lord Montgomery, the son of the Earl of Eglinton, accompanied them on the march, and the Earl himself, whom a threatened descent from Ireland had kept employed in the west, joined the camp later on. Of this subsidy Mure commanded a company of his own tenants and others from the neighbourhood.

After the assembling of the Scots at Dunse Law we hear nothing of our author until 1643, in which year we find his name mentioned as member of the Scots Parliament for Ayrshire. In 1644 he accompanied the Scottish army into England ; and on July 2nd he was present and

wounded in the memorable battle of Marston Moor. In
August he was engaged in the storming of Newcastle,
where, for some time, he held command of his regiment,
owing to the absence of Colonel Hobart and other officers
who had been wounded in the late battle.[1]

This is the last glimpse we have of Mure in any political
or military capacity. That he did not lose his interest in
public affairs is shown by the publication of ' The Cry of
Blood and of a Broken Covenant' in 1650. But, so far as
we know, the last years of his life were spent in those
peaceful pursuits so suitable to his disposition, and in the
enjoyment of such domestic felicity as the turbulent times

---

[1] The following letter from Sir William to his son may be of interest as
bearing on these events :—

" LOVEING SONE,
                    " We are now lying before Newcastle engaiged anew to
rancounter w[t] new dangers, for we are to adventure the storming of the toun
if it be not quickly rendred by treaty, wherof ther is very smal apearance for
they look very quickly for ayde to releave them. They are very proud as yet
for oght we can perceave, and those that come out to us resolute. For the
most part they are reformer officers under the commandment of the Earle of
Craufurd and Mackay. We have had diverse bowts w[t] them, and on satterday
last, a sound one, wherein we had good sport from the sunryseing till twelve
a'clock, both partyes retreeting and chairgeing by touers w[t]out great losse to
eyther for o[r] gen: Ma: shew himselfe that day both a brave and wise com-
mander, and if it had not been so, we could not but haue great losse, for we
were put back over the water at the last, for their forces grew, and we had
no armes but pistoles and they played upon us still at a very far distance
w[t] muskets and long fowling peeces. I am keept heir now beyond my purpose
upon necessity, haveing the only chairge of the Regiment till Col: Hobert, the
Lieut: Col: and Major come heir, who have bein all in very great danger but
are now pretty well recovered so that I expect them heir very shortly. I am
engadged in credit and cannot leave such a chairge, of such consequence, in
ane abrupt maner, qlk might hazard the breaking of the Regiment notw[t]stand-
ing of the urgent necessity that I know calls for my presence and attendance
upon my owne affaires at this time, which in so far as yee can be able ye must
haue ane ey to.
        " I have writen to Adame Mure to whom yee shall also speak and requeist,
that he must take the whole care and chairge of my harvest and stay constantly at my house for that effect and I will sufficiently recompense his paynes.

allowed. The Rowallan loft in Fenwick church was evidently built by him during this period of retirement, since over the door leading to it is a representation of the Mure arms with the date 1649. Mure's character is excellently, if somewhat quaintly, summed up in the concluding words of the 'Historie': "This S^r W^m was pious & learned, & had ane excellent vaine in poyesie; he delyted much in building and planting, he builded the new wark in the north syde of the close, & the batlement of the back wall, & reformed the whole house exceidingly. He lived Religiouslie & died Christianlie in the yeare of [his] age 63, and the yeare of [our] lord 1657."

MURE'S POSITION AS A POET.

Considering the esteem in which which Sir William Mure was held by his contemporaries, it is remarkable

Yee may be now and then visiting my workers, and hasting them to their dwty as yor owne affaires may permitt. It is very long since I heard from you, and am uncertane whither yee receaved my letters writen since the battle at long marston moore. I know I will hear from you by this bearar, again whose retourne to me I hope to be ready to take a voyage home. Praying heartily the Lord to blesse you, yor bedfellow and children, till o^r happy meeting and ever I rest,

"Youre loveing father,

"S. W. M. Rowallane.

*from Tyne-side before newcastle
the 12 of august 1644.*

"I blesse the Lord I am in good health and sound every way.

"I gote a sore blow at the battle upon my back w^t the butt of a musket, which hath vexed me very much but specially in the night being deprivd therby of sleep, but I hope it shall peece and peece weare away, for I am already nearly sound. I thank god for it."

[*Superscription.*]
"ffor his very Loveing Sone
Sr William Mure
yo: of Rowallane."

b

that no edition of his collected works has appeared before this time. The Rev. William Muir, editor of the 'Historie,' did indeed announce as preparing for publication in 1625, "The Poetical Remains of Sir William Mure, written from the year 1611 to 1635"; but, unfortunately, for some reason the project seems to have fallen through, and Mure was left in undisturbed obscurity. That there has been some excuse for this obscurity and this neglect cannot be doubted. Mure's manuscripts had passed, by some means, regarding which it would be unprofitable now to make any inquiry, into the possession of certain individuals who made use of them simply in so far as it suited their own convenience. Consequently it was only by those works which were published by their author himself that any estimate of his position as a poet could be formed. The grounds for judgment have hitherto, therefore, been insufficient. No wonder, then, that the judgment itself has been inadequate and unjust. The works which Mure considered most important are precisely those which reveal him at his weakest as a poet. A perusal of 'The Trve Crvcifixe,' 'Caledon's Complaint,' or the 'Covnter-byff,' is not calculated to impress the reader with any high idea of the "divine fire" of their author. But as those and a few other similar pieces were almost all by which the reader had to judge, there is little cause for astonishment that Mure's name should long have been—among the comparatively few who were aware of his existence at all—a synonym for all that is dreary and barren in poetry. The criticism is justifiable only so far as it concerns itself with his later writings; applied in a general sense it is unjust, because it is based on insufficient knowledge. That large proportion of Mure's work which now sees the light for the first time contains all of his that is most valuable from a literary, not to mention a poetical, point of view. In his earlier years at least Mure was no mere Dryasdust. In some of his Miscellaneous Poems, in his paraphrase of the Psalms, and particularly in his 'Dido and Æneas,' qualities are shown and excellences displayed which will no doubt materially alter the views of those who have hitherto looked upon him merely as the stern and somewhat gloomy laureate of the Covenanters.

On the other hand, however, it is true that by no possibility can Mure ever be assigned a high rank among poets. His limits are too narrow. Nevertheless, by confining himself to the two great concerns of love and religion, he enjoyed a considerable reputation in his own day as the poet of both. His later poems contain his most serious and original work; but they cannot compare with those of his more youthful days in lightness, grace, and mastery of technique. Much of his earlier poetry, indeed, will bear favourable comparison for smoothness of diction, and purity and delicacy of thought, with the work of his better known contemporaries and immediate predecessors both in Scotland and England.

Whether all of Mure's love poetry is to be taken seriously is open to question. He was apparently well read in the English poets of the Elizabethan period, and much of his work is modelled on their writings. It had become recognised as indispensable to the reputation of a man of blood and breeding that he should offer up homage to beauty; and if he was not touched with a real passion, nothing was easier than to feign one. It was but natural that much of this imitated emotion should be expressed in exaggerated and artificial language. Its main design was to paint the unhappy condition of the lover agitated by doubts and terrors ; to extol the beauty of his lady, and chronicle the means by which she maintained her empire over his susceptible feelings, her looks and gestures, her disdain that froze, and her kindness that thawed again his heart. Hence, while there was considerable scope for variety in the treatment of details, there was little room for originality of conception. Consequently we find the same ideas, the same images, and even the same turns of expression, constantly reproduced. It would be easy to parallel lines of Mure with those of Surrey, Wyatt, and other writers who did much to transplant this fictional love from the sonnets of Petrarch into English poetry. But the mistake must not be made of setting down as artificial all that is expressed in conventional form. The miscellaneous poems numbered viii., ix., and x. seem undoubtedly to have been addressed by Mure to the lady who became his wife. They breathe the spirit of a true and fervent love in the language of genuine passion.

It is not so much in the mere art of expression that Mure falls short of more famous writers. It is because, as a love poet, he has only one string to his harp. Though altogether introspective, his glance penetrates to no great depth. He has but little originality, and is deficient in powers both of reflection and of observation.

Let us examine the last point somewhat in detail, as one which must forcibly strike every reader of Mure's poems. It is not too much to say that for him external nature has absolutely no existence. Apart from the ' Dido and Æneas,' which is mostly translation, there is hardly a reference to outside nature in all his writings. Even in the ' Dido and Æneas ' itself he seems to avoid the merely picturesque as much as possible. To take an example. The happy and restful description of the bay, or inlet, where the Trojans, wearied with the buffeting of the stormy seas, and burdened with the grief of lost comrades, first find refuge on the Carthaginian coast, is entirely omitted. The pictures of the hunting of the deer and of the feasting that followed also appeal to him in vain. These and similar omissions are particularly interesting in the case of a writer like Mure, who, as a man, was evidently not insensible to the charms of wood and stream and flower. Brought up amid the scenery surrounding his ancestral seat of Rowallan, which he did so much to improve and beautify, such insensibility on his part would seem to be impossible. But the sense of beauty, though undoubtedly there, was not strong enough to assert itself in literary form.

From this point of view Mure's "ryt hereditar" to the mantle of Montgomery is open to question. The influence of Montgomery on his young relative was unmistakable, and is remarked on elsewhere ; [1] but, in nearly all that constitutes the true poet, the older man towers head and shoulders above the younger. In vigour, passion, and power Mure never approaches Montgomery. Unlike the latter, he neither sees with the eye nor feels with the heart of the true lover of nature. The " melodious mirth of merle and mavis," the bloom spread over "branche and bewch," the sparkling dew, like diamonds "vpon the tender twists," "the sounding beis," the shadows of the trees in the river,—none of these, or the thousand other equally beautiful sights and sounds with which he must have been familiar from his childhood, had importance, even exist-

[1] Notes to Miscellaneous Poems.

ence, for Mure as a poet. It is true that in the opening lines of his second poem he makes reference to a pleasant spring—

" Wᵗ fairest schads of trees o'rschadoued, wnder "—·

but the description is too general to be effective. It strikes one as accidental rather than as due to any innate sense of beauty. What is perhaps his only other attempt at nature - painting occurs in his 'Address to the King's Maiestie,' lines 97-102 :—

> " Heir plesant plains alongst the crystall Clyd,
> Which in a flowrie labyrinth her playes,
> Heir blooming banks, heir silver brooks doe slyd,
> Heir Mearle and Mavis sing melodious layes,
>   Heir heards of Deer defy the fleetest hounds ;
>   Heir wods and vails and echoes that resounds."

This is not only merely conventional; as a piece of poetical description it is stiff, forced, and utterly hopeless.

The late Professor Veitch, whose own passionate delight in every aspect of external nature lay at the root of most of his writings, has well expressed the condition into which Scottish poetry had sunk in the time of Mure : " With Montgomerie and his contemporaries, Scott and Hume, we bid adieu for a long period to any apparent sympathy with the Scottish landscape. After these men, we have almost no references to outward scenery in the way of description for several generations of poets, and those we have are generally mere imitations. There was, indeed, no true return to nature among the acknowledged poets until the time of Drummond of Hawthornden, to be followed by Allan Ramsay. For the most part it is wholly passed by ; and we find the Scottish muse employed on what are known as sacred themes — seeking to make popular, or throw into recognised popular forms, theological and spiritual conceptions and experience—often with a passionate conviction and enthusiasm which command respect, while it is quaint in its form and eminently national. The very intensity which pervades this kind of composition is perhaps essentially connected with its narrowness, even in the religious sphere, and with its exclusion of what is high, elevating, and refining, alike in the walks of reflection and imagination. It was probably a necessity of the age and time ; it arose partly in the way of reaction from the insincerity, hypocrisy, and unworthiness of life characteristic of the immediately preceding age ; but that it involved a serious loss to the integrity of our human life—to its breadth, its culture, its true vitality and place in the real world of experience— cannot, I think, be doubted. We cannot without harm turn a deaf ear to any side of that world through which God is revealed to us. To sever the twinship of Nature and Revelation, or to break with art for the sake of worship, is a mistake hurtful to the interests of both." [1] It is not difficult to believe, although he makes no mention of him, that while penning the above sentences the writer had in his mind the author of ' The Trve Crvcifixe.'

But although we must deny Mure the divine gift of originality, and not only acknowledge but insist on the limits, both natural and self - imposed, within which he worked, we must grant him the possession of a cultured literary taste and a high power of literary expression. He was in no sense a " Makar," but, on the other hand, he was no contemptible artist. His skill in versification led him

[1] The Feeling for Nature in Scottish Poetry, vol. i. pp. 339, 340.

to the occasional perpetration of a mere feat of rhyming
gymnastics, but his feeling for what was best in literature
was pure and true. Detached examples, such as the
application of Spenser's beautiful line, to Venus, might be
given in proof of this :—

> " Thus having said, she turn'd away her face,
> *Which made a sunne-shine in the shady place.*"

But the best proof is his choice of the story of Dido and
Æneas itself, combined with his selection of Virgil for
translation rather than Ovid. That a Scottish lad, barely
twenty years of age, should undertake the translation of
two books of the 'Æneid' into English verse, one of those
being the fourth, and thus challenge direct comparison
with the famous Lord Surrey, perhaps only indicates the
presence of the usual self-confidence of youth. That he
succeeded so well proves that the confidence was not
unfounded. The performance, indeed, in no small degree
justified the pretension. In his choice of a subject, to
begin with, Mure showed that he was possessed of the
true instinct. Of all the episodes in the 'Æneid,' perhaps
in all Roman literature, there is nothing that appeals to
us—awakens our sympathies, kindles our emotions, and
arouses our feelings of kinship as human beings—like the
story of the unfortunate Dido. In the words of Professor
Sellar, " The only personage of the 'Æneid' which entitles
Virgil to rank among great creators is Dido, an ideal
of a true queen and a true woman. She is the sole
creation which Roman poetry has added to the great
gallery of men and women filled by the imaginative art
of different times and peoples. . . . Dido alone is a life-
like and completed picture. On the episode of which

she is the heroine the most intense human interest is concentrated." In his choice, therefore, Mure showed an unmistakable appreciation, not only of what was best in his author and most calculated to interest his readers, but also of what he himself was best fitted to accomplish. But he had not only the ability to recognise; he had also the power to assimilate and reproduce—in a word, the gifts of the born translator. How great is the pity, then, that he should have buried so much of his talent in the barren field of religious and political controversy!

That Mure should have so tightly bound himself within the limits of verse in his translation was perhaps unfortunate. Into the question of the possibility of doing justice to Virgil in any verse-rendering there is no need to enter here. That is a point regarding which there seems to be no doubt in the minds of those best qualified to judge. In Mure's case the effect of the restraint on the dignity and power of his original is marked; but his attempt, as a totally new departure, may fairly enough look for lenient criticism, and this can be the more willingly accorded in consideration of the truthful rendering, and in admiration of the force and beauty of many of the passages.

Regarding Mure's later works, almost all that need be said will be found in the notes. Perhaps the most valuable, and undoubtedly the most interesting, of them is his paraphrase of the Psalms. Of the esteem in which his other works were held by his contemporaries we can judge from their own utterances. But from the nineteenth century point of view, it seems that little would have been lost, perhaps something gained, had they been composed in good nervous prose. His own standing, and the conditions of his time, seemed to demand their composition and publication as a duty ; but it is perhaps not too much to say, that if all the works which Mure published in his lifetime had remained unwritten, and only those had been made public which appear in these volumes for the first time, his reputation as a poet would not have suffered.

Of Mure as a man, apart from the indirect evidence of his writings, we know little. What his personal appearance was—whether he was tall or short, dark or fair, slender or buirdly—we cannot tell. What we do know is that he was, in every sense of the word, a truly religious and highly cultured gentleman. Upright, kindly, courteous, no word he ever wrote could give offence to the most fastidious taste. He could indeed write strongly when stirred to indignation by injustice and oppression ; but the course ribaldry of the " Flytings " and the witty licentiousness of many of his predecessors were equally distasteful to his pure and modest mind. That he could fight bravely in defence of what he believed to be the right he proved, and that he was a careful and prudent manager of his own affairs his letter to his son shows.

An interesting relic, giving evidence of Mure's musical tastes, is still preserved in the Edinburgh University Library.[1] This is his ' Lute Book,' a small, neatly bound volume, containing a considerable number of pieces, and bearing the quaint inscription : " For Kissing, for Clapping, for Lowing, for Proveing, goe to ye Lute be W. Mure." Several of the tunes have no title, but among those which have are " Corne Yairds," " Battel of Harlaw," " Our the dek [dyke], Davie," " Maggr^t. Ramsay," and " Katherine Bairdie." Most of the pieces in this interesting collection

[1] Laing collection of MSS., No. 487.

have probably been long forgotten — both names and music. None of them are accompanied by the words.

It is believed that the present edition of Sir William Mure's works is as complete as it is possible now to make it. At all events, it contains every writing of his made mention of by the numerous authorities consulted by the editor, with two exceptions. These two, a religious poem called 'The Joy of Tears,' and another called 'The Challenge and Reply,' are mentioned in the Rev. Wm. Muir's continuation of the 'Historie of the House of Rowallan,' but no trace of them has been found. They are probably lost beyond recovery.

I have to record my obligations to the following gentlemen for kindly aid in preparing this book : To Dr Cranstoun and the late Dr Gregor, for assistance in reading the proofs ; to Mr Webster of the University Library, and Mr Clark of the Advocates' Library, for facilities in consulting MSS., original editions, and works of reference ; to the authorities of Glasgow University Library, for permission to copy the MSS. of the Psalms ; and particularly to Mr George Muir, of Kilmarnock, who placed his wide knowledge of all pertaining to the Rowallan family, as well as his manuscript notes to the 'Historie,' entirely at my disposal.

W. T.

E R R A T A.

Volume I.

Miscellaneous Poems, xvi. 6. *For* He *read* I'le.
Dido and Æneas, iii. 13. *For* wals as *read* als was.

Volume II.

Covnter-Bvff, 382. *For* sesam *read* sceane.

EARLY MISCELLANEOUS POEMS

I.

ANE CONFLICT TUIX LOVE AND RESSOUN.

QUHEN Morpheus, w^t his sleepie vaile,
   Apollo's brightnes did assaile,
  And forc'd him chainge his course,
  Towards ye Ocean streamis,
  To coole his burning beimis   5
  In ould Neptunus' source,
And quhen the Night the Stigian caues had schroudit,
And ye Horizons of myne eyes o'rcloudit,

  The Citherean boy in Airmes
  Appeird then, sounding Loues alarmes.   10
    Ane Ensigne displayed
    In sing of ware he bair,
    Quhose colours to declair
    ʒit maks my hert affrayed,
Resolu'd, by force, by subtil slight, or treassoune,   15
To siege, and sack the Rampier of my ressoune.

  His campe was arm'd w^t horrid night
  As one quho lothed to sie ye Light,
    A bow bent in his hand
    He caryed to invaid   20
    All such as durst wpbraid,
    Or contrar his com̃and.
Inventing then all the Ingynes he can,
To brash my breast ye battery thus began.

Cup.   "ȝeeld to his powar quho rules and ringis   .   25
        Both ower mein men, and o're kingis ;
            Quhose schafts hath ay subdued
            Ye most heroick hertis ;
            Quhose flames and deidly derts
            No martiall mynds eschued ;   30
    ȝeild thou and learne how to practize and proue
    The heavinly Joyes, and suggared sweits of Loue.

        "Once taist yat nectared delyte,
        Of all pleasoures ye most perfyte,
            To spend thy tender ȝeiris   35
            In loves lascivious layes
            Sporting thy ȝouthfull dayes
            In Ven[s] wantoune weiris :
    O, so the springtyme of thyne age t'imploy,
    It is to baith in oceanes of Joy."   40

        His speichis beutifully sainted,
        And for ye present purpose painted,
            Mou'd, (by thair chairming power,)
            Against me to conspyre,
            ȝouth, courage, and desyer,   45
            To haist my fatall houer;
    Ressoune alone, to ratifie my right,
    To Cupid then replyed, suolne w[t] dispicht :

R.   "Cease, serpent, seik no to subdue
        And kill ane hert, bot for a vieu ;   50
            Thy pleasour is bot paine,
            A dreame, a toy, a schadou,
            Lyk to a blooming meadou,
            Quhose pryd doth schort remaine.
    Thy sweitest joyes proue oft in end most sowre,   55
    Lyk to a fair sunschyne befoir a schoure."

ȝouth then, with courage and desyer,
All flaming in voluptuouse fyre,
    Wᵗ fervent mynds assayed
    My Sences to suppryse,   60
    Esteiming me wnwyse
    To ressoune to be tyed,
So that, by only his adwyce and will,
My actiounes all must be directed still.

Z. "Fy thou," (quod ȝouth,) "faint is the spirit,   65
Of lytill vertue, worth, or merit,
    Can tolerat to liue,
    Thrall to an oyers will,
    His humour to fulfill,
    As he comand doth giwe.   70
Fy thou, contemne such servile slawischnes,
If any spunk of valour ye possesse."

R. "Peace, peace," (qᵈ ressoune), "stint thy tounge,
No lesse he profits hes bein dumbe ;
    Thoght thine owin eyes be blind,   75
    ȝit woldst thou teach ane oyer,
    To saile wᵗout ane routher,
    Contrair both waue and wind ;
To losse ane Infinit and endles treassour,
In hope to gaine ye fleiting frooths of pleassour."   80

I then perplex'd qᵗ to performe,
To hazard or escheu ȝe storme :
    To suime in sueatned seas
    Now loues delights bereaues me :
    Now feir of falling greeues me,   85
    To such as raschly flies :
Sua, now to loue, now contrairely inclyn'd,
A field of fancies musterd in my mynd.

To flie I long'd, aboue all things ;
3it loth to trust in Cupid's wings,   90
    Tuix danger and desyer,
    Thus howering to and fro,
    3outh newer ceas'd to blo,
    Forging affectiounes fyre.
Bot ressoune, then, perceauing my estait,   95
W^t wraithfull voice did thus begin to threat :

R.   " Art thus thy vertue rock'd asleepe,
    Thy witt dround in a boundles deepe,
      Thy senses so ensnared,
      To sie and 3it miskno   100
      Ane labyrinth of woe,
      For ye (puir wretch), prepair'd ?
Behold h'ill proue, quho now doth ye promote,
Ane monstruouse Minotaur to cutt thy throate.

    " Ane spytfull spidar, ewer spewing   105
    Ye poysonous potioune of late rewing,
      3ouths venemous infectioune ;
      In age, a doating madnes,
      A schort abiding glaidnes,
      A foolisch imperfectioune,   110
A basse-borne passioune schairce rype till rottin,
Tuix hatefull lust and Idilnes begottin."

C.   Quod Cupid then : " Let ressoune raue ;
    Its not his counsell thou must craue ;
      Bot once his 3ock reject,   115
      And proue yat divine pleassour,
      That Joy be3ond all meassour,
      First from aboue direct,
That heavinl[y] vniting of tuo mynds in one,
Quhich nothing can dissolue bot death alone."   120

R.   "Abstract," (q^d ressoune,) " then thyne eares
 Ye chairming Sirenes songs q^{ch} hears,
  Flie ye voluptuouse voice,
  Quhich hes no other scope
  But guyde ye on ye rock   125
  Of thy perpetuell losse.
In tyme tak heid then, least too lait thou mourne,
Ye port is patent, bot w^tout retourne."

C.   " Behold," (q^d Cupid,) " ressounes schifts
 Of false philosophie consists ;   130
  By sophistrie he schaues
  Loues hoñy to be gall,
  A bait only to thrall
  Such as obeys his lawes.
Bot quho into such Rhethorick reposses, 135
Lyfes sueitest joyes, and true contentmēt lossis.

 "Since then, to the, consists our stryfe,
 Of no lesse momēt then thy lyfe,
  Present, befoir thyne eyes,
  Ye cause of our dissentioune,   140
  And ponder my intentioune
  W^t ressounes fenʒied eyes.
Let yen thy hert discern quho best doth merit,
If subtile fraud, or faith, sould the inherit."

 My hert, elected then to judge,   145
 Armies of diverse tho^tis did ludge ;
  ʒit, out of judgments deepe,
  Did loue in end prefer,
  Quhose adversar did erre
  And thus pronunc'd decreit :   150
Hencefoorth contemne, reject and banisch reassoune,
A crocodoil, w^t tears obscuiring treassoune.

"Giue place to loues cælestial force,
  Quhich joynes tuo soules w^tout diworce;
     Quhose vertue and true power   155
     No crosse can oght impaire,
     Bot still growes mair and mair,
     Quhen most it seimes to lowre.
Since then this heavinly essence thus doth proue,
Let death alone put period to thy loue."   160

Finis be me, W. Mure.

II.

MES AMOURS ET MES DOULEURS SONT
SANS COMPARISOUNE.

QUHILL Beutie by a pleasant spring reposes,
    W^t fairest schads of trees o'rschadoued, wnder;
Ye cooling air, w^t calmest blasts, rejoyses
To sport hir w^t hir locks, o'rcume w^t wonder;
    So then, admiring hir most heavinly featour,   5
    I mervel'd much if scho was form'd by natour.

The smyling blinks, sent from hir wantoune eyes,
Had force to robe proud Cupid of his dairts;
Hir schamefast, blusching smyles quho ever sies,
Must pairt perforce, liuing behind yair herts.   10
    I stuid astonisch'd, greedie to behold
    So rair perfectioune as cannot be told.

B.   Scho then, perceauing me in thot perplex'd,
W^t voice angelicall did thus begin:
"Thy gesture doth bewray thy mynd is wexed,   15
W^t crosses compast and invironed in:
    Schau then if loue, or q^t misfortoune else,
    Such sings of sorow in thy saule compellis."

A.   "No crosse at all, fair dame, no force in loue
Can aght disquyet or perturbe my mynde.   20
Ye wonders now ar present me doth moue
To sie heavins excellence in humane kynd."

B.   " No, Cupid the molestis, cease to deny him."
A.   " Fy, treacherouse loue, fond Cupid I defy him."

Evin at this tyme the blindit god arywed,   25
His bow bent in his hand ready to nocke :
Bot q^u he aim'd, of power quyte deprywed,
Himself he band in his awin flattring ȝocke.
    Feeding his eyes on beuties tempting lookes,
    His pain he thot to ease w^t baited hookes.   30

C.   So boyl'd w^t flames, vex'd both w^t feir and teires,
Out of the anguisch of his hert did plaine :
" Ah, mackles dame, quhom all ye world admires,
Pitty, I pray, my never ceasing paine.
    Do not thy rigour wnto me extend,   35
    Quhome once no mortall durst presume t'offend.

" Bot now at last, o'rcume, I humbly ȝeild ;
Save then or sloe ane captiue beggand grace :
Receaue, in sing that thou hes won the field,
Ye bow, ye schafts, ye quaver and ye brace,   40
    Once q^{ch} I bruick'd, bot now w^tout invy
    I yeild to the, more worthie thame nor I."

The homage endit, and ye goddesse airmed
W^t proud, presuming Cupid's conquered spoyle,
He then, remitted, fled away wnhairmed :   45
Bot, (woes me,) left behind his tort'ring toyle.
    Scho, spying me ȝit wnacquaint in loue,
    Hir new got dairts throught my puir hert did roue.

[*B.*]   " Sport now," (scho sayes), " w^t Cupid : boldly try him ;
In loue if any force, no[w] proue, I pray :   50
Too lait, I feir, thow rew thou did espy him,
Thyne insolence 'gainst him or he repay."
    Disdainfully delywring thus hir words,
    No small displeasour to my saule affordis.

I, ȝit ane novice in my new learned airt,   55
Admir'd so quick a chainge from joy to woe ;
Doubted myself ; ewin gif it was my hert ;
My tears, quhich trickling from myne eyes did go,
      Bot (ah) in vaine, for ȝit my wound did bleede ;
      No spaits of teires culd quench ye boyling leede. 60

I flam'd, I fruise, in loue, in cold disdaine,
Dyed in dispair, in hope againe I liued.
All pleasours past agredg'd my present paine,
Hir froune did kill, hir smyle againe reviued.
      Q^{ll} death I wish'd, lyf then refuised to liue me :   65
      Liue q^{ll} I wold, death then propon'd to riue me.

Quhil in this weak estait, all meanes I soght
To be aweng'd on him quhose schaftes did greiue me :
Alace ! ane faint persuit ; I furthered noht.
For he, now Cupid, now a spreit, did liue me.   70
      Thus metamorphos'd fled away for ayde,
      In Beuties lippes, q^{r} I durst not invaid.

Then favour beg'd, pitty moued hir consent
Rendir ye fortresse, and his suirest scheild.
Great searche I maid to mak ye wretch repent   75
His bold attemps, intreating him to ȝeild.
      Bot nather prayers could prevaile nor wisses,
      Then I resolued to kill him euen w^{t} kissis.

Afrayed he fled then in hir eyes to hyde him,
Out of hir eyes into hir lipps againe.   80
"Stay, fond wretch, stay," thus I beguth to chyde him,
" Or chuise hir hert, thou chainges oft in vaine.
      Sua, as by the, our lipps els ar vnited,
      Our herts als to conioyne may be invited."

Bot nothing could ye cruel spidar moue   85
To liue his hold, delichting in my woe :
Sche lykwyse, quhom I serued, bot scorn'd my loue,
Lauching to sie my trickling teirs doune go.
  The more sche did perceaue increase my paine,
  The more sche mach'd my loue w^t cold disdaine.   90

Quhat then, sall I liue off my hope to speid,
And liue no more, cros'd w^t consuming cair?
No ! let hir froune and flit, yairs no remeid ;
I liue resolued neaver to dispair.
  Content I am, (and sua my faith deserwest,)   95
  My spring be toylsume w^t a pleasent herwest.

Finis, 1611.

III.

ANE REPLY TO I CAIR NOT QUITHER I GET HIR OR NO.

TO pleid bot q^r mutuel kyndnes is gain'd,
 And fancie alone quhair favour hath place,
Such frozen affectioune I ewer disdain'd.
Can oght be impaird by distance or space?
My loue salbe endles quhair once I affect.   5
Ewin thoght it sould please hir my service reject,
 Stil sall I determine, till breath and lyfe go,
 To loue hir quither scho loue me or no.

If sche, by quhose favour I liue, sould disdaine,
Sall I match hir wnkyndnes by prowing wngrait?   10
O no! in hir keiping my hert must remaine,
To honour and loue hir, more then sche can heat.
Hir pleasour can nowayes retourne to my smairt,
Quhose lyfe, in hir power, must stay or depairt.
 Thoght fortoune delyt into my owirthro,   15
 I loue hir quither scho loue me or no.

To losse both trawel and tyme for a froune,
And chainge for a secreit surmize of disdaine ;
Loues force, and trew vertue to such is wnknowne,
Quhose faintnes of courage is constancies staine.   20

My loyal affectioune no tyme sall diminisch.
Quhair once I affect my favour sall finisch.
So sall I determine, till breath and lyfe go,
To loue hir quither scho loue me or no.

Finis, 1614, 10 Octob.

IV.

ELEGIE.

ALACE! q^n I begin into my mynd to call
    The tragick end of Icarus and his most fatall fall;
My stait yen worse then his, if any worse can be,
Convoyed w^t duilfull death, ensues to end the fait's decree,
    Lyk as he did presume, too hie w^t borrowed pends,   5
Bot by the raiging force of floods o'rquhelm'd but mercie endis.
    Sua q^u aboue my bounds fondly I did aspyre,
Deceau'd by loues alluiring wingis, I fell in quenchles fyre,
    In quhich alace I boyle but mercie or retourne.
Sche quhom I serue the fornace feeds, quhair my puir hert doth
    burne;   10
    Bot causles is sche blaim'd, in hir no wayt remaines,
Nocht els bot cruell Cupid's ire my martyrdome constrainis.
    In endles pain I liue, in furiouse flams I fume,
Death still doth threat my dayes to end, I sie no other doome.
    My passiounes ar extreame, my hert doth brist for woe,   15
My tears lyk water from a spring doune from myne eyes doth go.
    Consum'd w^t secreit sighs, but confort I remaine;
Ilk thing on earth gainst me conspyre to agravat my paine.
    Bot most of all, alace! that sche by quhom I liue,
Feeling, by simpathie, my smairt, from death wold me reviue.   20
    Bot (ah), the frouning faits, alwayes my fatall foes,
Noch bot our mynds permits to meet, to periodize our woes.
    3it tho^t ane perfyte end in loue ye faits deny,
Still sall I hir adoir and serwe, ewer till death envy:

Resolu'd I am but chainge to loue hir q^{ll} I liue.　　25
Let fortoune froune, the world invy, hir smyle will me reviue.
　And tho^t, against my will, distant we must remaine,
ȝit in a breist sall both our herts no more at all be tuaine.
　Thoght crossis intervein to mak our myndis remoue,
ȝit still sall I most constant liue, death sall dissolue my loue.　30

Finis, 1611.

V.

CHAUNSOUNE.

CALLING to mynd the heauinly featour,
  The baschfull blinks, and comely grace,
 The forme of hir angelick face
Deckt w^t ye quintascence of natour,
  To none inferiour in place,   5
   Oft am I forc'd,
   Altho diuors'd
From presence of my deirests eyes,
   The too slou day
   To steil away,   10
Admiring hir, my smairt quho sies.

Thoght by myne eyes I sould distill,
  And quyt dissolue in tears my hert
 To satisfie hir causles smairt;
Ʒit rather sche delytis to kill,   15
  Then any joy to me impairt.
   Bot since ye faits,
   Q^{ch} ruils all staits,
Such tragick luck to me doth threat,
   Do quhat sche can,   20
   Resolued I am
To loue hir more then sche can heat.

Altho sche froune, sall I dispair?
    Or, if it please hir prove wnkynd,
    Sall I abstrack my loyal mynd?   25
O no! its sche must hail my sair.
    For hir I loth no to be pyn'd.
       Shee, I suppose,
       Lyk to the rose,
The prick befoir ye smell impairts.   30
       Hert-breking woes
       Oft-tymes forgoes
The mirth of murning, martyred herts.

Finis, 1611.

VI.

ANAGRAME.

TO the Cupido ʒeilds his golden dairt,
    Quhoise name aboue both fame and envy flies;
No rair decoirment natour can impairt,
Q^{ch} doth not schyne in those sueit Angel's eyes,
    Heauin's admiratioune, and ye world's terrour,   5
    Earth's excellence, and loue's most machles mirrour.

A machles mirrour of vnstain'd renoune,
Quhair beutie, (by wnspotted puirnes graced,)
Adorn'd w^t chest Dianais sacred croune,
(To tymes amaizment,) from above is plac'd;   10
    So that to the, in nather earth nor heauin,
    In all preferment, any match is giwin.

Na maches giuin to equall thy perfectioune
In diuin rairnes, vertue, worth, or witt.
Euin so, (the heauins doth kno,) in true affectioune,   15
In spotles loue, no maches I admitt.
    Since then on earth machles we liue alone,
    Justly, (sueit loue), we sould be mach'd in one.

                        Finis, 1614, W. Muir.

VII.

ANE REPROCH TO YE PRATLER.

ENVIOUSE wretch, on earth ye most ingrait,
  In Venus Court thy libertie is loissed,
Deseruing punischment as Momus mait,
Misconstruing ladies mirrily disposit.
If proud Ixion, in ye hels incloisit,   5
Doth suffer tortour on ye restles quheele,
Justly from all felicity depoisit,
Junois discredit quho did not conceale ;
And if Acteon Cynthya's ire did feele,
Turn'd in a hert, (thus for a vieu revengit),   10
Much more thou, then, quho ladyes did reveale,
In worse then he demerites to be chaingit :
    Form'd in a doge, to bark at such, most meet.
    As chalmer talk divulgats on ye street.

Finis. 1614.

VIII.

TO YE TUNE OF PERT JEAN.

FAIR goddes, Loadstar of delight,
　　Natours triumph, and beuties lyfe,
Earth's ornament, my hopes full hight,
My only peace, and pleasing stryfe
Let mercie mollifie thy mynd !　　　　　　5
A Saturnes hert sould Venus haue?
Or sould thou proue to him wnkynd,
Quho humbly lyfe of ye doth craue?
Since all thy pairts sum special grace
Decoris, to schau thy heavinly race,　　　10
Vertue thy mynd, and loue thy face,
　　Proportioune braue thy featour,
Pitty then must neids haue place
　　In such a diuin creatour,
　　　　Quhose sueitnes　　　　　　15
　　　　And meiknes
　　Exceids ye bounds of natour.

Quhen first thoise angel's eyes I vieued,
(Tuo sparks t'inflame a world of loue),
My fatal thraldome then ensued,　　　　20
Then did my liberty remoue.
Thair first infected was my mynd,
Loues nectared poysoune thair I drank,
Thy sacred countenance so schyn'd
So far aboue all humane rank.　　　　　25

Let then thoise eyes q^{ch} did insnair,
(Those schyning stares), thair fault repair,
Dispersing by thair beimes preclair
   The clouds of thy disdaining.
Wosdome, vertue, beutie rair,   30
    In the haue all remaining.
       Let not then
       Ye spot then
Of rigour be thy staining.

Sould crueltie, (sueit loue,) ecclips   35
Ye sunschyne of those glorious rayes ?
Or sould thoise louely smyling lips
Breath foorth affectiounes delayes ?
Let mercie countervail thy worth,
And measour pitty by my paine ;   40
Sua, thy perfectiounes to paint foorth
Ane endles labour sall remaine.
Lat beuties beames then thau away,
(Reflecting only on ws tuay),
The ycinesse of loues delay,   45
    And melt disdaines cold treassour.
Natours due so sall we pay,
    Baithing in boundles pleassour,
       Inioying
        That toying,   50
    Quhose sueits exceid all meassour.

Finis, 1615.

IX.

[ANOTHER VERSION OF THE SAME.]

[In this version the first two verses are the same as in the other, with the following exceptions :—

Verse 1, line 2, has " Triumph of nature," for " Natours triumph."
  „   „   „   8, reads—" Quho lyfe of the alone doth craue."
  „   2, „   6, has " potions," for " poysoune."
Verse 3 is given here in full.]

S OULD crueltie, sueit love, ecclipse
    Those eyes quhos smyls seame voyd of wraith ?
Or sould those soule enchanting lips
Pronounce the sentance of my death ?
Banisch disdain, (my deir^t), O spair   5
In guiltles blood thy hands to stayne !
Be bountifull as thow art fair,
Measur thy pitty w^t my pain.
    So shall my Muse rich trophes rayse
    To eternize thy endles prayse,   10
    Q^u heavins haue stars, q^u sune hath rayes,
    W^t light all creatours cheering ;
    Q^u Cupid's scepter earth o'rsweyes
    Nor great nor small forbearing,
        Thy prayse sall   15
        Amaze all
    Things sensible of heering.

Finis, S. W. M., Rowallan.

X.

TO THE TUNE OF ANE NEW LILT.

BEUTIE hath myne eyes assailed,
    And subdued my saulis affectioune.
Cupid's dairt hath so prevail'd,
That I must liue in his subiectioune,
      Tyed till one,   5
      Quho's machles alone,
      And secund to none
      In all perfectioune.
Since my fortoune such must be,
No chainge sall pairt my loue and me.   10

Wosdome, meiknes, vertue, grace,
Sueitnes, modestie, bontie but meassour,
Decks her sueit celestial face,
Rich in beuties heavinly treassour.
      Joy nor smairt   15
      Sall newer diuert
      My most loyall hert
      For paine nor pleassour.
Bot resolu'd, I auou, till I die,
No chainge sall pairt my loue and me.   20

Tyme nor distance sall have force,
(Altho by fortounes smyle invited),
Ws tuo ewer to diuorce,
By such a sympathie vnited.

True loue hates   25
Ye waw'ring estaits
Of such as ye faits
Hath chaing'd or retreited.
But recourse in any degre,
No chainge sall pairt my loue and me.   30

Deir ! Let death then only finisch,
And alter alone our choyse and electioune.
Let no chainge our loue diminisch,
Nor breed from constancie any defectioune.
Time nor space,   35
No distance of place,
Sall ewer deface
Our fervēt affectioune.
Then, (sueit loue), thus let us decrie,
No chainge sall pairt ws q^{ll} we die.   40

Finis, 1615.

XI.

ANE LETTER TO ANE MUSICALL TUNE.

GAISE, eyes, on nocht quhich can content 30^r sight,
 Sad tragoedies behold alone !
Ears, heir no sounds quhich can afford delight,
 Till sight and heiring both be gone !
  Hands, forbeare to tuich   5
  Oght 30^r tuiching can bewitch !
   Ah ! since scho doth disdain,
  Eyes, ears, hands and heart,
  Seing, heiring, feeling, smairt
   All in one consort plain,   10
    Since sche, alace !
   Quhose bright angelick face
  Did sett my woundit hert on fyre,
   Will 3eild no grace,
   Regairdles of my cace,   15
  Bot doth against hir awne conspyre.

Eyes, by 30^r streames of silwer trickling teares,
 Regrait, since sche is butt remorce !
Ears, heir no sweits, since nothing sweit apears,
 Q^n thus the faits do us diworce !   20
  Die, most haples heart !
  Newer cease w^t greif to smairt,
   In tears and sighs consume.
  Sorow, smairt and greiff,
  Be only thy releiff,   25
   Since sche hath giwin thy dome.

Oh, (sueit !) then scho
Compassioun on my woe,
Or lett no longer lyf remain.
Lyf giwes no more   30
To cuir my inward soare,
Bot ȝeilds the greatter sence of pain.

Hatred (alace !) for deirest loue I gain,
(Ay me !) this is my best rewaird,
And, for my paines, reaps wndeserwed disdain.   35
My serwice sche doth thus regaird,
Tho^t I plead in vain
Loue for loue of hir t'obtean,
And humbly begs remorce ;
Thoght my tears doun rain,   40
Q^{ch} my sorowing cheiks do stain,
Such is hir bewties force
To charme my mynd,
To liue, alace, thus pynd
For hir, in such a ruefull stait,   45
Resoluing still
To wait wpon hir will,
And loue hir more then sche can heat.

Bot as the rose, in pulling, oft impairts
The prick, before the smell be found,   50
Sua may my Loue now, w^t disdainfull dairts
Thocht sche my hert but mercie wound.
Sche the stroak did giwe,
Only sche must me reviue,
Thocht reuthles now sche proue.   55
Such ane heavinly face
Can not bot giwe pitty place,
And ȝeild at lenth to loue.
Sueit ! then, the more
Thou heats, I sall adore,   60

And serwe the q^{ll} my breath be gone.
My changles mynd
No tyme sall mak wnkynd,
Bot death my loue sall end alone.

Finis, S. W. M., Rowallan, ʒoungar, 1616.

XII.

HYMNE.

HELP, help, O Lord! sueit saviour arysc,
Giwe ear unto my humble suits, and heir my wofull
cryes,
My sorowing sighes, (guid Lord!), do not dispyse,
Awalk, my sillie saul, in sin q^{ch} too securely lyes.
   Help (blessed Lord!) I pray,   5
   Thy servant in distresse;
   Haist, (sueit Jehova!) schune delay,
   My hynous sins redresse.
   Deir Father, I confesse
   Still yat I ran astray;   10
   Bot now recall me, not.ye lesse,
   Out of ye wandring way,
    In quhich so long
    I have gone wronge,
     Alace!   15
  Accompany'd w^t bluid convoyes.
    One drop afford,
    O heavinly Lord!
    Of grace,
 And cloath my sorowing saule w^t joyes.   20
Thyne ayde, O my creatour, I implore;
Withhold from me thy favour now no more;
   Justly tho^t I deserued thyne ire,
   And nothing bot hels fyre,

Ʒit, Lord, I humbly the requyre, 25
    Contemne not my desyre.
Erect my puir dejected spreit,
    Prostrat befoir thy mercies feete,
Full sore affrayed to pleid for grace,
    Wnworthy to present thy face. 30
        Ʒit suffer not, sueit Lord, I pray,
        My silly saule decay,
        Bot once remitt, w'out delay,
            My sinis for now and ay.

Finis.

XIII.

THE EPITAPH OF THE RY^T VENERABLE, GODLY AND
LEARNED FATHER GEORGE, BE GRACE FROM
GOD, ORDERLY CALLIT, AND BE HIS PRINCE
APOYNTED TO BE GREATEST PRELAT
IN SCOTLAND, ARCHBISCHOPE
OF SANCTANDROIS.

BEREFT of breath, ȝit nocht from lyfe depoised,
    Heir lyes inclos'd Sanctandrois richest treassour,
A pearle but meassour hath ye word ill loossed
Quhoise mynd repoissed in no decaying pleassour,
    A machles Phoenix, quho, from mein estait,   5
    Becam a prelat and a prince's mait.
A painfull pastour, worthy such a place,
Too schort a space his natioune hath decoired;
Quho now restord to earth, doth rest in peace,
Receaued in grace, the heawins in sanctis hath stoired.   10
    Quhoise corps t'intomb, glaid ar ye sensles stones,
    Promou'd to honour by his buried bones,

In Zoilum

Thou then, quho by thy false and fenzied fact,
Strywes to detract this prudent prelat's name,   15
Bewar such schame becum thy suirest hap,
Thrawin from ye tap of fortoune to defame.
    No blot, no blemisch, no defect, no moth
    Presum'd to enter in so rich a cleath.

XIV.

ANE EPITAPH (EFTER YE VULGAR OPINIOUNE) WPON YE D(EATH) OF GEORGE GLAIDSTANES B. OF S. A.

G LAIDSTONES is gone, his corps doth heir duell,
　　Bot q^r be his oyer halfe no man can tell.
The heauins doth abhor to ludge such a ghost,
　　Quho still, q^{ll} he liued, to Pluto raid post.
The earth hath expell'd him, as loathing such load,　　　5
　　Quho honoured Bacchus and no other god.
Since both then reiect him, t' this outcast of heavin
　　In midst of ye furies a place must be giwin ;
Quhose covetouse mynd no richesse contented,
　　Bot heiping wp treassour wnmyndfull quho lēt it,　　10
Till contrarie fortoun, by turning ye dyce,
　　Metamorphos'd his thowsands in milleounes of lyce ;
　　　　Quhich endit ye dayes of this sensuall slaue,
　　　　Wnwordy the earth sould ȝeild him a graue.
By him quho wischeth that this wretches fait　　　　15
May giwe exemple wnto ewery stait ;
That hyer Powares be w^t feir regairdit,
Or by this Athist's punischmēt rewairded.

Finis, 1615.

XV.

THE EPITAPH OF THE WERY VERTUOUSE AND EXCELLENT GENTELUOMAN A. C. SISTER TO ƷE RIGHT HONOᴸᴸ THE LAIRD OF CAPRINTOUNE.

AH ! qᵗ ecclipse, qᵗ night of sad añoyis
    Thus hath o'rschadoued Phoebus' schyning face ?
Art natour's pryde, loue's mirrour, earthis true joyes,
Fled and evanischt in a moment's space ?
    Ah ! art affectioune's florisch, beutie's vigour,   5
    Crop't in the floure, and slain by Clotho's rigour ?

Ah ! art ye sunschyne of those machles beames
In sorowes seas so suddenly gone doune,
Lyk fleing schadoues, and deceauing dreames,
Tomorrou clay, today perfectioune's croune ?   10
    Ah ! art ye world of hir rair Phoenix spoyld,
    And earth's decoirment by death's furie soyld ?

Ʒit nothing straunge, thot Joue chusd such a mait,
This age wnworthy such a braue ingyne ;
And chaing't this mortal's mutable estait   15
For ay in immortality to schyne.
    Thus sche, to quhom belou na mache's giuin,
    Triumphs in endles glorie, mached in heauin.

C

Then happie nimph, quhoise spreit in peace repoises,
Fred of all chainge and to na frailtie thrall,   20
The tomb thryse happie, q'ʰ thy corps incloises,
So happie ay, bot happiest nou of all,
    That, as ye world did learne to liue by the,
    Sua, by thy death, ye world may learne to die.

Be then comforted, ȝe, whom natour tyes   25
Wᵗ weiping eyes this spectacle to vieu.
Heauins did afford, and now ȝe heauins denyes
This staige of toyes sould more retein thair due.
    Since all must die, thē let no mortall froune,
    Thot hyer powers do reclaime thair owin.   30

XVI.

SAX LYNES WPON THE FALL OF SOMERSAIT.

E ACH man w^t silence stopes his mouth, and heares
    Sad newes w^t wonder, bot my barren muse
Fain wold brust foorth, bot ȝit to wryt forbear[s];
Feir to offend must be my best excuise.
    Since malice thrists for braue Ephestion's blood,   5
    Ile wryt no Ill, nor dar I wryt no good.

XVII.

EPITAPH OF THE WERY EXCELLENT, VERTUOUSE AND TRULIE HONOURED LADY, THE LADY ARNESTOUN.

PEACE! wantone Muse, Leave now thy lovelie layes.
    Here, here a sadder subject thou doth fynd.
Hence Helicon, hence Phoebus blooming bayes,
The sorowing Cypres now thy brows must bynd,
Ane Tragick Tokin of a mourning mynd,   5
    Quhich fain wold wtter, (if it could for smairt,)
    Thir latest dutyes of a dulefull hert.

Quhat ey so cruell must no melt in teares?
Q^t flintie hert from sorow can refrain?
Q^t ruthles care, this tragedy q^{ch} heares,   10
Can inward anguish smother and restrain?
O! sence wnsensible q^{ch} feeles no pain,
    And, pittiles, doth not w^t greif regrait
    This ruefull object and wntymely fait.

Death hath subdued Wit, Vertue, Beutie braue,   15
By conquering hir in q^m those all remain'd.
Nane humbler, meiker, modester, more graue,
Mor wyse, more worthy, Natour ewer framed.
Few matches earth hath any quhair retain'd
    So prudent, patient, pittifull, but pryde.   20
    More courtesse, comelie creator newer dyed.

Then nothing strange tho^t Joue chus'd such a mait,
This age wnworthy such a rair ingyne,
And chang't this mortal's mutable estate,
For ay in imortality to schyne ;   25
Quho glorefied amidst the schads dewyne,
    In place of wordlie transitorie toyes
    Reaps now all plentie of Celestiall joyes.

Finis, 1616.

XVIII.

VPON THE DEATH OF THE RICHT WORSCHIPFULL, VERTEOUSE AND WERY WORTHY GENTLEMAN, THE LAIRD OF ARNESTON ȝOUNGAR

THOU, thou, quhose lovelie schaip, of all admyr'de,
 In robs most rich a richer spreit attyrd ;
In quhom true vertue, worth and valour schynd ;
In face a Venus, and a Mars in mynd.
  Too sone, (alace !) in blossome of thyn age   5
  Thy pairt is acted on this wordlie stage.

ȝit happie, happie thou, in earth quho lyes !
Quhose ghost triumphes in azor-volted skyes !
Lou'd q^{ll} thou liu'd, of all, all now regrait
In ȝouthes Apryle thy far vntymelie fait.   10
  Bot ah ! no eyes can render store of teares
  To mourne aneugh thy losse in such ȝoung ȝeares.

Then, (worthy ȝouth,) dear to thy freinds, adieu !
Heawins have reclaimed bot q^t to thame was due.
Ane Angel's place far better doth beseame the, 15
For this inferiour fram could no conteane the.
  For quhy, (braue ȝouth,) basse earth was far wnfitt
  To comprehend such beutie, grace, and wit.

    S. W. M., Rowallane, ȝoungar, 1617.

XIX.

[MUST I WNPITTIED STILL REMAIN].

MUST I wnpittied still remain,
But regaird,
Or rewaird,
Nothing caird,
Bot by my sueitest slain ?   5

Ah ! sall I still contemned remain,
Still, alace !
Begging grace,
Bot in place
Of favo^r reap disdain ?   10

Zit, most sueit,
I must no retreat,
Altho thou froun a quhyle.
Since my pain proceeds of the,
All is sueit it breeds to me,   15
If thou wouchaife bot on smyle.

XX.

TO THE MOST HOPEFUL AND HIGH-BORN PRINCE CHARLES, PRINCE OF WALES.

M ACHLES Montgomery in his native tounge,
    In former tymes to thy Great Syre hath sung,
And often ravischt his harmonious ear
W^t straynes fitt only for a prince to heir.
    My muse, q^{ch} noght doth challenge worthy fame,   5
Saue from Montgomery sche hir birth doth clayme,
(Altho his Phoenix ashes have sent forth
Pan for Apollo, if compaird in worth),
Pretending tytyls to supply his place
By ryt hereditar to serve thy grace.   10
Tho the puir issues of my weak ingyne
Can add smal luster to thy gloryes schyne,
Q^{ch}, (lyk the boundles oceā), swels no moir,
Tho springs and founts infuis thair liquid stoir ;
And tho the guift be mean I may bestow,   15
3it, (gratiows prince,) my myt to thee I owe,
Q^{ch} I w^t 3eale present. O daigne to vieu
Those airtles measurs, to thee only due ;
    Q^n thy auntcestors' passiouns I have schowne,
    Iff, (but offence,) Great Charles, Ile sing thyne owne.   20

The most vnworthy of 3or hy : Vassels, S. W. M.

XXI.

THE KINGS MAIESTIE CAME TO HAMILTON ON MONDAY THE XXVIII IULY [1617].

BURST furth, my Muse, Too long thou holds thy peace.
  Paint furth the passions of thy new-borne joy :
Forbear to sing thy lovelie layes a space ;
Leave wanton Venus and her blinded boy.
    Raise vp thy voice and now, deare Muse, proclaime   5
    A greater subject and a graver theame.

Since our much lov'd *Apollo* doth appeare
In pompe and pow'r, busked with golden rayes,
More brigt heir shyning on our hemisphearc,
Nor that great planet, father of the dayes ;   10
    With boldnes offer at his sacred shryne
    These firstlings of thy weake and poore ingyne.

GREAT IAMES, whose hand a thre-fold scepter swayes,
By heavens exalted to so high a place,
Both crown'd with gold and never fading bayes.   15
Who keps three kingdoms in so still a peace,
    Whose love, cair, wisdome, grace & high descrts
    Have maid thee Monarch of thy subjects' harts.

Thogh thou by armes great empyrs may'st emprise,
Mak Europ thrall and over Asia reigne,   20
Yet at thy feet despysed, Bellona lyes :
No crownes thou craves which bloodie conqueis staine.

Whill others aime at greatnes boght with blood,
Not to bee great thou stryves, bot to bee good.

Whome snakie hatred, soule conceav'd disdaine,   25
Hart-rooted rancor, envy borne in hell
Did long in long antipathie detaine
To eithers ruine, as they both can tell.
 Uniting them thou hast enlarged thy throne,
 And maid devyded *Albion* all bee one.   30

O heavenlie vnion !   O thryse happie change !
From bloodie broyles, from battells and debait,
From mischeifs, cruelties and sad revenge
To love and peace thou hes transformd our stait,
 Which now confirmed, by thee before begunne,   35
 Shall last till earth is circuit with the Sunne.

Jov's great vice-gerent, Neptun's richest treasure,
Earth's glorie, Europ's wonder, Britann's pryde,
Thy wit (lyk heaven) in such a divyne measure
This litle world so happilie doth guyd,   40
 That Caesar, Trajan, Pompey, Alexander,
 If now they liv'd, the place to thee might rander.

What wants in the (O king) heavens could impairt?
Or what is in thee not of highest pryce?
A liberall hand, a most magnifick hart,   45
A readie judgment, and a prompt advyse,
 A mynd onconquered, fearcest foes to thrall,
 Bright eye of knowledge : singular in all.

Thy waitchfull caire, thy ʒeale, and fervent love,
The Church, the laye, each high or low estaite   50
Long-since by many worthie deeds did prove ;
Bot most of all by these effects of laite.
 For thou affects amongst thy high designs
 To build the Sanctuarie of the King of Kings.

Heavens therefore did thy royall grandeur guaird ;   55
Thy Royall person from the cradle keap'd
From thousand plots t'eclips thy Sunne, prepair'd
By these who horror vpon horror heap'd
  Their barbarous hands into thy blood to bathe
  And mak thee (guiltles) object of their wrathe.   60

Thogh Anak's cursed children did repyne,
Yet heavens made Josua over them prevaill :
Thogh hellish harts envyd'd thy glories shyne,
Yet in the practise their attempts did faill.
  But loe, thy mercie still to be admir'd !   65
  Thou spared them against thee who conspyr'd.

For as in all thou second art to none,
To thee all kings in clemencie give place.
Thryce happie people rul'd by such a one,
Whose lyfe both this and after-tymes shall grace :   70
  Long may thy subjects, ere thy glasse outrunne,
  Enjoy the light of thee, their glorious Sunne.

What Load-stone strange had such attractive force
To draw thee home-ward to these northerne parts ?
Whill Mars the world affrights with trumpets hoarse,   75
Broyls inhumaine devyding humane harts ;
  Whill Belgium braine-sick is, France mother sick,
  And with Iberian fyres the Alpes doe reik.

Most lyk that fishe, whose golden shape of late
Was to thee given, thy love to represent,   80
Which in the Ocean thogh she doe grow great,
And many foraine floods and shelves frequēt ;
  Yet not vnmyndfull of her native Burnes,
  Thogh with great toyle, vnto them back returnes.

Rejoyce then, Scotland ; change thy mourning weed ;   85
Now deck thyselfe into thy best attyre :
And lyk a bryd advance thy chearfull head ;
Enjoy with surfet now thy soules desyre ;
  Uncessantlie with sights importune heaven
  That thou may long enjoy this gift new given.   90

Welcome, O welcome thryse, our glorious guyd ;
A thousand tymes this soyle doth thee salute ;
Welcome, O welcome, Britann's greatest pryde,
By thee which happie doth it selfe repute.
  Thogh all-where welcome ; yet most welcome heir ;   95
  Long haunt thir bounds, ere thou from hence retire.

Heir plesant plains alongst the crystall Clyd,
Which in a flowrie labyrinth her playes,
Heir blooming banks, heir silver brooks doe slyd,
Heir Mearle and Mavis sing melodious layes,   100
  Heir heards of Deer defy the fleetest hounds ;
  Heir wods and vails and echoes that resounds.

Stay then, O stay, and with thy presence grace
That noble race, which famous by thy blood,
Long toyle and trouble glaidlie did embrace,   105
And wounded oft gusht furth a crimson flood,
  In hazards great defending with renowne
  The liberties and glorie of thy Crowne.

But leaving more to entertaine thyn ears
With airie accents, hoarse and homelie songs,   110
My solitarie Muse her selfe reteirs,
Un-usd abroad to haunt such pompous throngs.
  Sua renders place that after emptie words
  Thou may partack such as this soyle affords.

    Sr. William Mure, younger : of Rowallan.

SONNETS

I.

[TO MARGAREIT.]

M ORE chest then fair Diana, first in place,
    From quhose fair eyes floues loue's alluiring springis
Secund to none in bonty, beutie, grace,
Quhoise heavinly hands holds proud Cupidois stingis;
Endles repoirt, wpon aspyring wingis,
Thy hie, heroick verteues hath stoired.
Admir'd, but maik, euin in a thowsand thingis,
To eternize ye fame hath endeuoired.
Miraculous, machles Margareit, decoired
With all preferments natour can afford!
Favourd from heauins aboue, in earth adoir'd,
Extold by treuth of thy most loyall word,
    With vertue grac'd far more yen forme of face,
    Ʒit Venus in ye same doth ʒeild ye place.

II.

[TO THE SAME.]

MAIRGRAIT then I can any wayes deserue,
   Mair rair then fair, ȝit machles in ye same.
Quho with thy eyes, (least my puir lyfe sould sterue),
Wouchaiffes to look w^t pitty on my paine.
Heir I avou thyne ewer to remaine,   5
To serwe ye still, till breath and lyfe depairt,
Reviu'd by vertue of thy sacred name.
Cum death or lyfe, in loue I find no smairt.
Let Cupid wreck him on my martyred hert;
Let fortoune froune, and all ye world invy;   10
Gif I be thyne, no greiff can death impairt
Sall mak me seime thy service to deny.
    I liue mair weil contented thyne to die
    Then cround w^t honour, and disdain'd by the.

III.

[TO THE SAME.]

CAN any crosse, sall ewer intervein
  Mak me to chaunge my neuer chaunging mynd?
Can oght, yat my puir eyes hath ewer seine,
Mak me to hir quho holds my lyfe wnkynd?
O no! euin tho^t ye worldis beutie schyn'd,   5
To try my treuth and temp my loyall loue,
I more esteime for hir to liue still pynd,
Then any other be preferd aboue.
My constant hert no tortour sall remoue,
Thoght duilfull death and frouning fortoune threat. 10
No greif at all, no paine that I can proue,
Sall mack me ewer loath of my estait.
  I glaidly ȝeild me; let hir saue or kill,
  I heat to liue except it be hir will.

IV.

[TO THE SAME.]

ALACE ! (sueit love,) yat ewer my puir eyes
   Presum'd to gaize on yat most heauinly face.
Alace ! yat fortoune ewer seimd to ease
My endles woes, but now wold me deface.
Alace ! yat ewer I expected grace,   5
To snair myselfe in hope to be reliued.
Alace ! Alace ! that loue wold now disgrace
My loyall hert, q^{ch} once to serwe him liued.
Alace ! Alace ! yat ewer I surviued
Ye fatall tyme, quhen first appeir'd my joy :   10
For now, alace ! I die : bot ȝit reviued,
In hope thy love my luck sall once injoy.
     Still to remaine, resolued then sall I liue,
     Thy humblest servant, ewin till breath me liue.

V.

[TO THE SAME.]

L YK as Actaeon fand the fatall boundis
    Q^r as Diana baithed hir by a well,
Quhich hie attempt, punisch'd by his awin hounds,
Turn'd in ane timorouse hert, he fled, bot fell.
Sua, q^n my Cynthia, quho doth hir excell,   5
I did behold, cruell Cupid invyed,
And myne awin eyes to crosse me did compell,
Still gaizing on ye goddesse they espyed.
At liberty befoir, alace ! now tyed,
I live expecting my Dianais doome ;   10
Ather to be prefer'd, or die denyed,
Wnworthy of ye honour to presume.
    3it tho^t I die, (for sua I ewer doe,)
    Had I mo lyfes, tham sould I hazart too.

VI.

[TO THE SAME.]

SINCE fame's schril trumpet equal'd w^t the skyes
    The rair perfectiounes and miraculous art,
Natour and educatioun did impairt
To mak the wondrouse to amazed eyes,
Thy beutyes did my sensses suire suppryse,   5
Or eir thy sight my ravischt eyes did blesse.
Bot now I fynd Fame too, too niggard is,
Or thy deserts above hir reach aryse.
All loue, all joy, all sueitnes, all delight,
The heawins into thoise angel's eyes haue plac'd.   10
Thryse happie he quho may the rosis taist,
And pull the lilies of those cheeks so quhyt.
    But those fayre brests' rype clusters quho myt presse
    W^t Jove may weel compair in happines.

VII.

[TO THE SAME.]

A DIEU ! my loue, my lyfe, my blesse, my beeing,
 My hope, my hape, my joy, my all, adieu !
Adieu ! sueit subject of my pleasant dying,
And most delichtfull object of my view.
Bright spark of beutie, paragon'd by few ;   5
Wnspotted pearle, q^{ch} doth thy sex adorne ;
Loadstar of loue, quhose puir vermilion hew
Makes pale the rose ę stains the blushing morne ;
That zeale to the q^{ch} I haue ewer borne,
Sole essence, lyfe and vigour of my spreit,   10
By tract of tyme sall newer be out worne ;
My secund self, my charming syren sueit.
  And so, my Phoenix ę my turtle true,
  A thousand, thousand tymes adieu ! adieu !

VIII.

[TO THE SAME.]

SOME gallant spreits desyrouse of renowne,
    To climb w^t pain Parnassus do aspyre.
By Natour some do weir ye Lawrell croun,
And some the poet proues for hoip of hyre.
Bot none of those my spirits doth inspyre,   5
My muse is more admird then all the nyne,
Quho doth infuse my breast w^t sacred fyre
To paint hir foorth most heavinly and dewyne.
Hir worth I raise in Elegiak lyne;
In Lyricks sueit hir beuties I extoll;   10
The brave Heroik doth hir rair ingyne
In tyme's immortal register enroll:
    Since thou of me hath maid thy poet, then
    Be bold, (sueit Lady), to imploy my pen.

IX.

[THE POWER OF BEAUTY.]

IN bewty, (loue's sueit object), ravischt sight
   Doth some peculiar perfectioun pryse,
In which most worth ę admiration lyes,
The sensses charming with most deir delight.
Some eyes adoir, lyk stars, cleir glistering bright ;   5
Some, wrapt in blak, those comets most entyse ;
Some ar transported w^t pureayn dyes,
And some most value greene about ye light.
Awrora's flaming hayre some fondly love.
Quhyt dangling tresses, yallow curls of gold,   10
Wthers in greatest estimation hold.
All eyes alyk, each bewty doth me move ;
    Eyes lovely broun, broun chastnut color'd hayre
    Enflame my hart, and sensses all ensnair.

X.

[ON A VILE PRIEST.]

FAITH, now, (wryt all falsifyed ar found
   By one, quho must be faithles, fals, perjur'd ;
Quhose othe (promeis ar a slidrie ground
To build wpon, to make a man assuird.
My modest muse must keip his name obscur'd ;   5
His epithets do sound the same a-loud.
A drunkin divin, by the devil obdurd,
A preacher, oh ! a persecuter proud,
To Bacchus great, quhose knees ar oftest boud.
Devoirs tabacco, Cupid's plagues to quenche ;   10
Quhose paralytik lips and tounge vntrou'd
Hath oft intrappit many a wanton wench;
    This Priest, or beist, doth weir a fylthy fame,
    A blotted conscience, and a spotted name.

XI.

[THE SAME.]

NAME spotted, fame defyld, saule fraucht w^t sin,
    Too long in such a carioun vyle inclois'd ;
Presumptuous, puir, aspyring for a pin,
Adulterous, double, deuilischly disposit,
A sensual slaue, quho sence of schame hath loosit ;   5
False, flatt'ring, fickle, and defamed for ay,
Quhose doating and deceat ar oft discloisd ;
Earth's excrement, heavin's hatred, Plutoes pray,
A parlage cur, a brokin staffe for stay ;
A Turk but treuth, a Pagane for a preist,   10
Quho, for his faults, sall render count one day,
Q^{ll} wormes wpon his filthy fleche do feast.
    Sua, till the feinds this fyre brand fetch, I . . .
    W^t such a subject loath to stain my . . .

XII.

[THE SAME.]

PUIR, perjurd palliard, plaged w^t the parls,
   By quick repentance heavin's just wrath prevēts,
Of paine to come the gallouse is but arles,
Q^{lk} for the gaips, and laiks but ones consent.
Thy epitaph sall then be putt in prent,   5
To blaize abroad how leudlie thou hath liued ;
Religioun's foe, against thy brethren bent,
Quho one and all, (and not but cause), ar greeued
. . . the rape hath no^t thy lyfe berewed.
. . . thy calling, to the churche a curse   10
. . . thou thy birth had not survived
. . . . no conscience for to fill thy purse.
   Adieu till death ; to die a slauchterd oxe
   How punisht w^t the palsie ꝑ the poxe.

DIDO AND ÆNEAS

Aetas prima canat veneres

TO THE READER.

SONET.

3OW Heliconian witts, with arte who viewe
The pain-borne brood of heaven-enspired spreits ;
3owr presence, humbly, (loe), my muse invites,
To taist of her fore-rypened fruits a few.
Though meane and small desert for such be dew,   5
Her strenthles pinneouns and vnhardned plume,
As 3it in blood, no hyer dar presume,
Till ryper 3eirs her infancy subdue.
Accept what she doth painfully impairt
With toyle and travell to begyle the time ;   10
And let, in her minority and prime,
Her tender age excuse her slender airt ;
    Not darring things of importance to write,
    With humble 3eale, (loe), she presents her mite.

S. W. M.

DIDO AND ÆNEAS.

THE FIRST BOOK.

I ISING Aeneas fortunes, whil on fyr
   Of dying Troy he takes his last farewell ;
Queen Didoe's love, and cruell Junoe's ire
With equall fervor which he both doth feell.
     Path'd wayes I trace, as Theseus in his neid,   5
     Conducted by a loyall virgin's threid.

But pardon ! Maro, if myn infant muse
(To twyse two lustres scarce of ʒeirs attained),
Such task to treat (vnwisely bold), doth choose,
As thy sweit voyce hath earst divinly strained.   10
     And in grave numbers of bewitching verse
     Ravisht with wonder all the vniverse.

Rap't with delight of thy mellifluous phrase,
Thy divine discant, and harmonious layes,
Whose sugg'red accords, (which thy worth do blaze),   15
The hearers' senses, at thair ears betrayes.
     O then I stowp as one in airt too shallow
     Thy never matched monarch muse to follow.

But, ravisht with a vehement desyre,
Those paths to trace which ʒeilds ane endles name,   20
By the, to climb Parnassus I aspyre,
And by thy feathers to impen my fame :
     Nothing asham'd thir colours to display,
     Vnder thy conduct as my first assay.

Sacred Apollo! Lend thy Cynthia light,   25
Which by thy gloriows rayes reflexe doth shyne,
That I, partaking of thy purest spright,
May grave (anew) on tyme's immortall shryne,
     In homely stile, those sweit deliciows ayrs
     In which thy Muse admirable appears.   30

And ȝe Pierian maids! ȝe sacred nyne!
Which haunt Parnassus and the Pegas spring,
Infuse ȝour furie in my weak ingyne,
That (mask'd with Maro) sweetly I may sing,
     And warble foorth this Hero's changing state,   35
     Eliza's love, and last, her tragick fate.

Now bloody warre, (the mistres of debait,
Attendit still with discorde, death, dispair;
The child of wrath, nurst by despightfull hait,
With visage pale, sterne lookes, and snaiky hair),   40
     By Groecian armes, old Troy had beatne downe,
     And rais'd the ten-ȝeirs siege from Priam's towne.

Whose brasen teeth her walls did shake asunder,
And staitly turrets levell'd with the ground;
Insulting Greeks, with fire and sword, did thunder,   45
And both alike the sone and syre confound,
     The maid and matron, striving to compence
     Fair Helen's rapt, and Paris' prowd offence.

When Venus' sone, got by Anchises great,
The noble prince Æneas re-units   50
His scattered forces, dissipate of laite
By Graecian furie on Troy's bloody streets,
     And sweetly chearing their dejected hearts,
     By sugg'red words he stryves to ease their smarts.

"Lo ! (champions bold," quoth he), "quha fyr and sword,
And thowsand dangers have with me eschewed,   56
Courage and comfort let my words afford
To 30w, though now by sad mischaunce subdued.
  Blind Fortune favoures oft th'ignoble parte,
  But he is free keeps ane vnconquered heart.   60

"Banish base sorrow, raise 30wr drowping heids.
Vertue oppressed brighter still doth blaze.
Let wonted valour, by 30wr worthy deids,
Reconquere credit, and the world amaze ;
  That ritch with spoiles and praise, 30wr prowes hie
  May be renoun'd with fame and victorie.   66

"Learne, (noble warriours !) Fortunes storme to beir ;
And let 30wr valour be by vertue back't.
The golden sunne-shyn of her count'nance cleir
On vs againe may shyne, though Troy be sack't.   70
  Palmes, whil prest downe, ar loathest to give place,
  And Phaebus lowest showes her broadest face.

"Since heir owr countrey, by the foe possest,
And conquer'd kingdomes small content can 3eild ;
Since honour seldome is acquir'd by rest,   75
But wonne by awfull armes in open field :
  Let vs a navie then prepair with speid
  With wings displayed the seas to overspreid.

"In perill praise, in hazard honour lyes.
Hiest attempts ar worthiest of renowne.   80
And who do most death's bitter stroake despise,
Fortune doth such with glory soonest crowne.
  Let vs resolve to suffer all assayes,
  To purchase fame, or perish all with prayse."

Thus said, their hopes half dead ar now revived ;   85
Their troubles calm'd : his speaches so prevaill.
Their hearts of sorrow's heavie load relieved,
Off suddaine joy strange passiouns do assail ;
    All cry alowd : " Quhair ever thow dost leid,
    We follow the, owr prince, owr guide, owr heid."   90

Thair valiant chiftane speidily gives charge,
With sayles display'd, to turne their backs on Troy.
Now many a gailley, brigandine, and barge
Rid ov'r the roaring billowes ; whil with joy
    The Trojane fleet in armes to seas ar gone.   95
    Great Neptune with the burthene greiv'd doth grone.

Their speedy cowrse amidst the maine they ply,
And ways vnknowen search out, twixt foame and flood.
Now scarce the soyle, with bleeding hearts, they spy,
Quhair Troy, (Rome's stately rival whilome), stood ;   100
    Whose ruines poore, which low in ashes lye,
    Doth force a teare from every gaizing eye.

The pleasant plaines of Thracia then they coast,
Which doth their eyes of native land deprive,
Thence through the Ocean speedily they poast,   105
Till now in sight of Delos they arrive.
    The Ile no sooner to their eyes appear'd,
    Till thither Palinure their pilote steir'd.

Apollo there, in dark responses, told
Of things to come the ʒit-vnknowne event ;   110
And did in dowbtsome oracles vnfold
Hid mysteries the curiows to content :
    Where now arriv'd their prince setts foot on land,
    His fortunes of the God to vnderstand.

"Behold!" (quoth he) "before thy sacred schrine,   115
Divine Apollo, the distrest estate
Of Troy's poor remnant, servants all of thine ;
Brought lowe by Graecian furie, and by fate.
    Show to quhat soyle owr cowrse sall be addrest,
    Which after toyle in end, may ȝeild vs rest."   120

"Renowned Prince ! of heavinly issue sprung,"
The God replyed, "Jove doth for the provide !
Thy trophe's sall, (by after-ages sung),
In times immortall register abide.
    Spread foorth thy sayles, to Italy repair ;   125
    Thow and thy race sall swey the scepter thair."

Ravish'd with joy, with clamoures lowd they loose,
And smoothly through the silver waves do slide.
A gentle gale sweet Zephyrus bestowes,
Which streight their cowrse to Italy doth guide.   130
    The azure face of heaven's broad looking-glasse
    With cannowse wings they quickly overpasse.

But scarce the floods had ȝit depriv'd their eyes
Frome sight of shoare, and viewe of neirest land,
Quhen angrie Juno, frome the christall skyes,   135
Vpon ye seas the Trojane navie fand.
    Her deadly hatred and deep-rooted ire
    Inflams her minde, and sets her all on fire.

But say ! my muse, what crime so hynows hath
Commoved the Goddes, who in furie fryes?   140
Showe thow the source of her vindictive wrath :
Why she this Prince so singulare envyes,
    Him tosses to and fro, deprives of rest ?
    Are heavinly mindes with such despight possest ?

E

The Goddes heiring that demolish'd Troy   145
Out of her ashes should a Phoenix raise,
A natioune fierce, who Carthage should destroy,
Her stately towres ov'rturne, and city raise ;
     A martiall people far and neir to reigne,
     In warre invincible, so the Fates ordaine ;   150

This towne above all others to extoll
Her native soyle at Samos Ile she leaves ;
Throughout the streets her hurling chariots roll ;
Her armes heir places, and great honors gives :
     And heir she mindes, (if Fates do not withstand), 155
     To found ane empire shall the world command.

His kinde she hates, which should the same supprise,
And Ganimedes rapt vpbraides her minde ;
And how her beauty Paris did despise
The golden fruit to Venus who assign'd ;   160
     Which most her heart with malice doth incense,
     No mends can expiat this hie offence.

Her forme disprais't ingenders such disdaine
As never female heart could ȝit forgive.
Beauty can not abide to beir a stayne,   165
And with a rivall doth abhorre to live.
     Quhat can so loathsome be a woman told,
     As say she lookes deformed, fowl, or old ?

O cruell sexe ! whose hate no time can change,
Nor furyowse minde with sugg'red words be meased. 170
As Hyrcane tigers, greedy of revenge,
Bellona[s] fury far easier is appeased.
     For one man's caws no Trojane finds a shield.
     Who may resist whil heavinly broode doth ȝeild ?

But what strange furie thus transportes my pen, 175
Those creatures sweit of cruelty to taxe?
Who now-adayes do prove so kinde to men,
Apt for impression as the ȝeilding waxe.
  Of this sweit sexe my muse doth pardon crave,
  Which thus misledde with Juno's rage did rave. 180

The Trojane fleet now being vnder saile,
Whil smyling Nereus with cups is crown'd;
And mariners, glaid of the prosperows gaile,
Their chearful whisles meryly do sownd.
  Enraged Juno, full of discontent, 185
  Thus doth apairt by words her passion vent:

"Thus must I ȝeild? thus my designes forgoe?
And sall the Trojanes save arive on shoare
Maugre my will? Have Fat's ordain'd it so?
Of such a conquest justly [lose the] gloir? 190
  By Pallas earst for Ajax caws alone
  The Graecian fleet was sunk and overthro'ne.

"Devoiring flames downe from the clouds she threw,
Thunder and fireflaught, to avenge her ire.
Waves threat the skies, a fearfull tempest blew, 195
The rageing seas against the Greeks conspire.
  Himself, with fire transfixt, against a rock
  She dasht with whirlwind, quhair his corps did smoake.

"But I, first Goddes, first by birth and place,
Jove's spowse, and sister, heaven's arch-empresse great, 200
With one poore nation never ȝit at peace!
What do availl my dignity, my state?
  Who Juno's godhead, thus contemn'd, sall feare?
  Or who sall offrings on my altar reare?"

With heart inflam'd, from clouds with furie fleeing,   205
The Goddes at Æolia doth arive ;
A land where tempests dwell, stormes have their being ;
In caves inclos'd, where murm'ring winds do strive.
    But Æolus, their king, with mace in hand,
      Theire rage restrains, and fury doth withstand.   210

At such impresonement they oft, repining,
Lowd bellowing all break out, with blust'ring noyse ;
But he in chaines more stoutly them confining,
Tempers their ire, and calmes their roaring voyce ;
    For if they were vnbridled and vnbound,   215
      Heavens, earth, and seas they should anone confound.

The thunder great this fearing, then inclosed
In caverns dark, fast bound with brazen bands :
With hills supprest them, and a prince imposed
To let or loose their rains, as he commands ;   220
    To whom these speeches Juno fierce directed,
      With gesture sad, and ey's on ground dejected :

"O Æolus ! at whose imperiows word
The storms arise, and swelling seas give place ;
My mortall foes, new scaip't the Graecian sword,   225
The Trojans crosse the seas to my disgrace.
    Let louse the winds, thy rav'nows postes imploy,
      Disperse their navie, and themselves destroy !

"Of all my nymphs, in beauty most excelling,
Fair Diopeia sall be thy rewarde ;   230
Who, all her lyf in thy subjection dwelling,
The as her lord and husband sall regarde ;
    With the who many happy dayes sall have,
      And mak the parent of a bairne-tyme brave."

"Too many words, (great Goddes !)," he replyes, 235
"Are spent in vaine, thy servand to entraite.
My self, my scepter, and in me what lyes,
Boldly command to execute thy haite.
    Jov's love by the I find, by the I reigne,
    By thee the stormes I raise, and tempests straine." 240

Butt more, him turning to the hallow hill,
With silver scepter open passage made ;
The winds owt gushing heavens and earth do fill
With hiddeows noyse, none in the cave abaide :
    They roar, they rush, and with a murmuring sownd, 245
    The elements all threatne to confound.

To seas anone all furiows foorth they flew ;
'Gainst East and West are Sowth and North opposed.
Waves climb the clouds, a deadly tempest blew ;
Gray Proteus' flocks through foamie floods ar tossed, 250
    Which present death to sailing Trojans threatne.
    Men cry, and caibles crack by Boreas beatne.

The day grew dark, night shew her sable face,
Ane hoste of clouds did overcast the skies ;
Ane mist obscure did light of day displace, 255
And load starre rest frome woefull sailers eyes.
    With lightning flashes thund'ring heavens gave light ;
    Each where pale death vpbraids the Trojanes sight.

Æneas now, (sad prince), in minde dismayed,
With hands heav'd vp first having heavens implor'd : 260
"Thrise happy ʒe, my mates !" sore sighing say'd,
"In Troyes defence who died by Graecian sword.
    O Diomedes, would to God that I,
    Kill'd by thy martiall hand, at Troy did ly !

"Quhair noble Hector by Achilles spear,   265
And stowt Sarpedon both their breathes did ʒeild ;
Whose live-lesse bodyes Simois' floods did bear
With bloody armᵉs and many a woundit sheild."
    Thus whil apairt he speiks, a contrare blast
    Doth force his saile against the trembling mast.   270

Now helme-les, oar-les now, the shippe doth saill ;
Her ribbes do roare, her tacklings all are torne ;
The tumbling billowes fast her syddes assaill,
She sinking sippes the seas, by weight downe borne.
    The fleet disperst, some to the heavins are throwne,
    To some the bottomes of the seas are showne.   276

Thus tos't with stormes, the poore remaine of Troy
Each to some speciall office him betaks :
Some sailes pull in, others the oares imploy,
Some the maine bouling hale, some tacklings slacks ;   280
    Some hold the helme, some caibles cut in twaine,
    Some at the pumpe powr seas in seas againe.

But all in vaine they strive 'gainst angrie heavin ;
In shallow shelves some vnawares ar cast ;
Some 'gainst a rock are violently drivin ;   285
And some in Syrtes sinking sands are fast ;
    Some, (being robb't of ruther, mast and oares),
    With gaiping mowth the whirling poole devores.

The remnant past all hope, now neir ov'rthrowne,
Their leiking seames drink in the floods so fast,   290
Whil Neptune wond'ring by what charge vnknowne
The swelling seas their limits have ov'rpast ;
    By what strange pow'r they have ov'rflow'd the plains,
    And who, (by his command), hath loos'd the raines.

At which emov'd, his hoarie head he reares 295
Above the waters, toss'd by Juno's wraith.
The Trojane fleet soone to his eyes appeares,
Some drown'd, some dying, some scarce drawing breath ;
 Whome pittying, in the twinkling of ane eye
 The storme he stills, and calm's the rageing sea. 300

Even as a rude concurse of people swairmes,
A heidles multitude misledde by rage,
Do fight confus'd ; furie doth furnish armes ;
No meanes can their ignoble ire asswage.
 But if some man of eminence appeare, 305
 They quit their strife, and to his words give eare.

Even so, no sooner Neptune show[s] his face,
Till bello'ing Boreas calmes his roaring voyce.
The striving stream's are suddenly at peace,
And rageing tempests still their blust'ring noyse. 310
 With trumpets hoarse the Trytons sownd retrait.
 Waves war no more against the scattered fleet.

Cymothoe applies her helping hands,
With many a sea-nymph Neptun's cowrt frequenting ;
Who free the shipp's frome shoalds and sinking sands, 315
To Trojan's pittyfull themselves presenting.
 The storme allay'd, they saiff away do slide.
 On smooth-fac'd seas the God by coatch doth ride.

Now weary sailers with desired sight
Discerne afarre the long-long wissed land ; 320
And thither plying, on the coasts do light
Of Africk, where Queen Dido bears command.
 Frome Italy, a contrare cowrse, which driven,
 Of all the sailes none find the porte but seven.

Soone as the rosie-fingered morning fair   325
Left Tython's bed, and glaid good-morrow gave
To Phaebus, blushing red, with golden hair,
Ariseing from the Orientall wave :
    Wher Æneas early go's abroad,
    And leaves the shipp's at anchore in the roade.   330

To see the soile he slumber sweit forsakes,
Longing to learne what people thair do stay ;
Achates only he his convoy makes,
Swa journey taks where fortune guides the way,
    By paths vnknow'n, perplexed much in minde,   335
    They travell long, but people none can finde.

Till Venus last, disguised in shape, appears,
Most like a Spartan maid in armes and weed ;
The gesture of Harpalice she bears,
To whom the light-foote horse gives place in speed.   340
    Owt runnes swift running Heber's rav'nows streames ;
    With bowe on shoulder she ane huntres seames.

The heavenly treasure of her golden hair
Was toss'd by sweet-breath'd Zephyr heir and thair ;
Her rayment short, her lovely knees wer bair,   345
With which no snowe in whitnes might compair.
    Her eyes shin'd favour, courtessie, and grace,
    No mortall ever saw more sweet a face.

"Stay, stowtly ȝowthes !" (she sayes), "who heir resorte,
And showe me if by chance ȝe have espied   350
Heir any of my sister nymphs at sporte,
With bowe in hand, and quaver by their syd,
    The footsteps of a foamie boare who trace,
    And hallo'ing lowd, fast follow on the chace."

"None such we saw," (quoth they), " O nymph divine !　355
Or sall we rather the a Goddes call?
Such heavenly beautys on thy face do shine,
Thy gloriows rayes owr mortall eyes appal ;
　　But O ! thrice happy Goddes, nymph or maid,
　　Quhat e're thow art, we humbly crave thine aid.　　360

"Teach vs what soile is this, what countrey strange,
What fields so fair heir to owr sight are showen,
Vnder what climat of the heaven we range,
Where neither man nor place to vs are knowne.
　　We crave " (sweit lady), " if a stile so lowe　　365
　　Beseeme thy state, this let thy servants knowe."

"To me such honors," she replies, " forbeare ;
For this the fashion is for virgins heir
A bowe and quaver by their thighs to beare,
And rayment short above their knee to weir.　　370
　　Of fertile Africk heir the soile ʒe see,
　　And those the walls of famows Carthage be.

"The scepter Dido swayes, heir fled of late
For horroʳ of Pigmalion's cruell crime,
Against her mate in privy perpetrate,　　375
Which sad discowrse requirs a longer time.
　　But things of greatest moment to discover,
　　All circumstance I breefly sall runne over.

"Sicheus was her lord and loyall mate,
With many gifts of minde and body graced,　　380
Who her espous'd into her virgin state,
A spotless maid, ʒoung, beautyfull, and chaste.
　　Her bloody brother over Tyrus raigned :
　　No fiercer monster on the earth remained.

"He, blind with greid, to gaine Sicheus gold   385
Him vnawars before the altars slew,
And forg't inventiounes to his sister told,
Cloaking his cruelty with airts anew.
    But murther, though it ly a space conceal'd,
    By meanes vnlook't for, ay at last's reveal'd.   390

"Himself, vnburyed ʒit, Sicheus shew,
Before this wofull lady's sleeping eyes,
With visage wan, pale looks, and deidly hew,
Whom, fearfull lyk, she trembling fast espyes,
    With gapeing wound, from whence a crimson flood 395
    Ran gushing downe his breast, begor'd with blood.

"'Flie! flie! my dearest half,' quoth he, 'from hence
Expect no better at thy brother's hands,
Flie him who kill'd thy husband but offence,
And cruelly dissolv'd owr nuptiall bands;   400
    Whose cursed weapon Hymen's solemne knote
    Disjoin'd, which joined was so long by lote.

"She, (wofull soule), appalled with the sight,
Her fainting hands three times stretcht owt in vaine
The shadow to embrace; but sadly sight   405
When nought but air her folded armes containe.
    Three times againe, thus in her sleep misse-led
    Three times his ghost her kinde embraces fled.

"Awak't, the charge she speedily obeyes;
Prepares for flight, conveining such as hate   410
This monster, who with fear the scepter swayes,
And tyrannizing reignes with terrour greate.
    Whom spoiling, hence they fled with wealth vntold:
    Their shipps they ballast with the traitouoris gold.

"Heir they arived, where now the walls arise   415
Of stately Carthage, reaching to the skies.
The soile she bought, along the coast which lies,
Within the reach and compasse of ʒowr eyes:
    First Byrsa call'd, as much in length and breid
    As she could with an oxen hide ov'rspreid.   420

"But whence be ʒe, (my freinds), who seame so sad,
Whose ruethfull looks ʒowr inward sorrows showe ?
Frome what far coast have ʒe ʒowr journey had ?
Or whither further purpose ʒe to go ? "
    To which, with wounded heart and watrie eyes,   425
    Sore sighing, thus the sea-toss'd prince replies :

"Ah lady ! if I should at length relate
And of owr bitter sorrows showe the source ;
Owr adverse fortune and estrang't estate
Requires a longsome dolorows discowrse :   430
    Day should departe and Phoebus bright descend,
    Long ere owr wofull tragedy should end.

"Frome Troy we come, Troy was owr haples soile,
(If ever Troy into thine ears fand place),
By wind and wave heir toss'd we are with toile,   435
Of heavenly issue and immortall race.
    Frome Jove I sprang ; brought lowe, before thine eyes
    Æneas stands, whose fame surmounts the skyes.

"To Italy Apollo did exhorte
My cowrse : I follow'd where the Fates did guide ;   440
With twentie sailes, (alas !) I left the porte,
Of which scarce seven saiff frome the stormes abide.
    Myself in neid heir strayes, to all vnknowne,
    Far, far from Europ, and frome Asia throwne."

But such regrates vnable more to hear :   445
" Brave Trojane, be encourag'd," Venus sayes ;
" Raise vp thine heart, such sad complaints forbear,
Heavens guide thy footsteps and direct thy wayes.
    Hold on to Carthage, where Quein Dido reignes ;
    Thy shipps ar save ; thy mates alive remaines.   450

" Even as those swanns, by six and six which flye,
Doung by ane eagle in the skies of late,
For joy of perill past all mounting hye,
With wanton wings the ȝielding air they beat :
    Even so thy shipps, long toss'd on seas, in end   455
    With mirth and noyse all to the porte intend."

Thus having said, she turn'd away her face,
Which made a sunne-shine in the shady place,
With rosie cheeks and cheirfull smiling face,
Such as Adonis earst she did embrace,   460
    Her sweet ambrosiall breath and nect'red hair,
    With musk and amber did perfume the air.

He ravish't both with wonder and delight,
" Ah ! mother, stay thy cowrse ; " sore sighing sayes,
" Why, masked thus, dost thow delude my sight ?   465
Pitty thy childe, heir comfortles who stayes."
    Ne're word she spak, but as they walk't in dowbt,
    She with a cloud encompast them abowt.

The subtle air, (a wondrows thing to showe),
In solide substance did the self congeale,   470
With wonder rapt, environing the two,
Themselves with mists enfolded thus to feel,
    To whome alone the cloud transparent bright,
    With thick'ned damps debarr'd all others sight.

They, subject now vnto no mortall eyes,   475
Hold foreward, where the Goddes them commands.
She to her soile, by skies, to Paphos flyes,
Wher consecrate to her a temple stands,
    Whose altars, which in odowrs sweet excell,
    With cassia, myrrhe, and cynamome do smell.   480

They meanewhile to a mountaines toppe intending,
From which the towne lies subject to their sight;
The stately work with walls to skies ascending,
The pompows ports with gold all glist'ring bright,
    The towres, on Porphyr pillars which arise,   485
    And mabre streets feed with delight their eyes.

The workmen earnestly do their hands applie;
Some dig the earth and search a solide ground;
Some found below, some build amidst the skie;
With noyse of hammers hollow heavens resownd.   490
    Some stones do roll; some vnder burthens grone;
    Some grave in brasse; some kyth their craft in stone.

Lyk as when Phoebus, father of the ȝeir,
With warme reflexe the frosted flowrs revives,
When natur's alchimists from rest reteir,   495
And to the sluggarde life and courage gives.
    Whil some at home, some in the fields abroade,
    Their tender thighs with waxe ę hony loade;

Assail'd by stormes, some litle stones do beir,
And ballast thus do contrepoyze the winde;   500
Some waxen pallaces with paine do reir;
Some search a field the fragrant flowrs to finde;
    Some, bussied in the hyve, great murmure mak,
    Whil others of the brood the charge do tak.

All wisely for the winter do provide,   505
And empty combs with liquours sweet do fill;
Parte at the ports, as sentinells abide,
Vnloade their mat's and drowsie dron's do kill;
  The work doth prosper, Nectar-plenish't cels
  With thyme and cammomile most sweetly smels.   510

Even so the Tyrians, some a stately stage
On arches rais'd for comedyes ereck;
For judgement some a place prepare more sage,
Establish lawes, and magistrats eleck.
  Each with a sev'rall work employ'd tak paine: 515
  None sluethfull in the citty do remaine.

"Happy! O happy ȝe!" Æneas sayes,
"Whose fortun's floorish, and whose walls arise."
No longer he vpon the mountaine stayes,
But, ent'ring at the porche, seene by no eyes,   520
  Bereft with wonder he abroad doth range,
  Apparell'd with this airy rayment strange.

A shaddy groave amidst this citty grew,
Of amrows myrtles and immortall bayes,
Which, heavenly sweet, deliciows odowrs threw,   525
Whil Zephyr breath'd among the palme-trie sprayes,
  Whose topps, entwyn'd, a pleasant arbor made,
  Which ȝeelded a delightsome cooling shade.

Amidst this groave, to Juno sacred, stood
A church with all choyse rarities enriched,   530
Which, of no humane industry denude,
All eyes with admiratioune bewitched,
  Who viewe what arte hath in this work devis'd,
  With curiows pencill, cunningly compris'd.

Heir she to nature not inferiowr much,   535
In shapes admir'd her excellence hath showne,
The live-les pictures seeme to see, move, touch,
With wondrows colours by the painter drawne :
  The statues stand, wrought with exceeding coste,
  By cunning craftsmen carved and embost.   540

Æneas wond'ring at this temple's glory,
And, with those sights, his sorrowing eyes delighting,
Neir by, abr[i]g'd, he viewes Troyes tragick story,
Drawen with such life as seem'd he saw them fighting :
  Great Ilion by triumphing Greeks suppris'd,   545
  Their bloody rage who prowdly exercys'd.

Before the towne did stand the woodden horse ;
Whilas the ramme the walls is vndermining.
The Trojans val'rowsly resist their force,
In plumed caskes and glitt'ring armour shining.   550
  Now frome the ports the Greeks they seeme to chase,
  And now retreating, to the foe give place.

Heir sent to death by Diomedes' hand,
The breathles body of prowd Rhesus lyes.
Heir Troylus, vnable to withstand   555
Achilles' stroak's, by gloriows conquest dyes.
  Heir Priame doth his strenthles hands vphold,
  Sueing to ransome Hector's corps with gold.

There, 'mongst his foes, himself anone he viewes,
Acting his parte vpon this bloody stage,   560
In Graecian blood his blaid who oft embrues,
Arm'd with trew valowr, not misseledde with rage.
  There Memnon, there the souldiers of Aurore,
  Distill their dearest blood to conquere glore.

But see! see how Penthesilea leads 565
Her Amazonian trowpes to Troye's supplie!
To all her valour admiration breids,
But death and horrour to the enemy.
    All other women with their tongues mak warre,
    She, by her hands, more famows is be farre. 570

But in this age such Amazons ar rare,
Now strange Hermaphrodites supplie their place,
Whose cloths, whose cariage, curlings, cutted haire,
Complexiounes, coloures, ar their cheifest grace :
    Whose greatest study's foundlings to abuse ; 575
    The mystery of painting how to vse.

Viewing at last those vnexpected sights :
"Ah, deir Achates!" sighing sore, he said :
"In owr mishapps what nation not delights?
What place doth not owr infamies vpbraid ? 580
    Betwix the fyrie and the frozen ʒone
    Our sad misfortunes are vnknowne to none."

But as no joy's so great as lasteth ay,
So no mis-hap's so hard, but once may end.
Dark night o'rpast, succeedes the pleasant day, 585
Heavens, after sorrowes, joyes and solace send.
    So now, the lustre of Eliza's eyes
    Cheirs vp his spreits ꝑ calmes his miscryes.

Her presence soone gives respett to his teares ;
Her milde aspect him with assurance armes ; 590
Her beautyes peace proclaime vnto his feares ;
Her gratiows countenance his anguish charmes.
    For, loe, as Cynthia 'mongst the stars doth shyne,
    She comes attended with a stately tryne.

Fair Iris in her choisest colowrs clad,   595
Arayed in robes of pure blew-golden-green,
Should in this cowrt have look't but pale and sad
Amids the pompows throng which guarde the Queen,
  Who might have put a period to the strife
  'Twix Juno, Pallas, and lame Vulcan's wife.   600

More lovely creature never mortall ey,
More ritch in beautyes, ever ʒit did viewe,
Whose lips of corall, cheeks of yvorie,
Where lillyes sweet ℮ budding roses grew,
  The smothest pearle, and ritchest rubies stain'd,   605
  Still kissing and still blushing which remain'd.

Her fore-head full of bashfullnes and state,
Where Venus' babe did bend his Heben bowe,
Of majesty and mildenes seam't the seate,
Whose native white made pale the purest snowe.   610
  Two stars are fixt into this beautyes spheare,
  Smile-frowning, stormie-calm, and cloudie-cleare.

Each glance alone of those celestiall lights
Dairt foorth a living death, or deadly wound,
And by allurements strange insnare the sights,   615
And do beholders' senses quite confound,
  Whose silent rhetorick far more perswade
  Then all the airts enchaunting Circe hade.

Each beawty, to attract the curiows eye,
Hath something rare, peculiar, and alone,   620
Which most the face with forme doth beautyfie,
And leaves impression in a heart of stone.
  Some, sweetly smileing, kindle Cupid's fire,
  And, blushing, some adde fewell to desire.

F

Some with the cherryes of sweet lips ensnare ;   625
Some with the dimples of a vermile cheek ;
By wanton looks some leave a lasting care,
And others most do move by seeming meek.
　　But heir, all beautyes in this object meit :
　　O miracle of nature thus compleit !   630

Even as Diana, by Eurota's banks,
Or Cynthus' tops, with many a nymph attendit,
With deep-mowth'd hounds the fleeing deir disranks ;
Some fall, by flight some have their lyves defendit.
　　The Goddes egerly the chace doth follow,   635
　　Cheiring her hounds with a harmoniows hallow.

The wanton wod-nymphs fast abowt her throng,
Both at her sport and heavenly shape amazed.
She joyfully them traines the plains along,
Still more admiring, more on her they gazed.   640
　　For loe ! she shynes amids this crew more bright
　　Then clear Aurora, parting frome the night.

So ent'red Dido : such her princely port,
A sweit, majestick, and heart-moving creature,
With pompows splendour, far above report,   645
But airt adorn't, with beautyes choysest feature,
　　Whose gracefull gesture, whose enchanting eyes,
　　Æneas' sorrows seam't at once to ease.

Magnifickly thus mounting to her throne,
Weiring a costly coronet of gold,   650
The sword of justice to her subjects showne,
The scepter her imperiall hand doth hold ;
　　Where, guarded with a groave of awfull armes,
　　She sitts secure frome spightfull traitors' harmes.

There, like that nymph who fled from earth to heaven, 655
So much by all for equity renown'd,
Of justice she doth hold the ballance eaven,
And solidly doth lawes and statutes found,
    Wherby good subjects easily are rain'd,
      The viciows sort by fear and force restrain'd. 660

The Queen scarce plac't into her yvorie throne,
Whil suddenly a companie arives
Of souldiers, as it seam't to all vnknowne,
Which preassing, as perplex't, for presence strives :
    Sergestus, Antheus and Cloanthus strong, 665
      Were leaders of this vnexspected throng.

Three Trojane captanes with their trowpes attendit,
New scaipt the furie of the boyst'rows king,
Heir last on shoare, whil otherwise intendit ;
Heaven's angry Empresse hindred their designe, 670
    Their ships assailing on the wattrie plaine,
      Till Neptune calm'd the swelling seas againe.

Their prince, his people heir at cowrt espying,
In Thetis' bosome whom entomb't he trowed,
Amaz'd he stood, with deep attention trying 675
If visions false his eyes did overcloud,
    If apparitions or chymercœs vaine
      Appear'd, illudeing his distempered braine.

But finding heir his followers in effect,
Sick with a surffeit of excessive joy, 680
He long'd himself vnmasked to detect,
That mutuallie they comfort might enjoy ;
    But, seasouning this passion with feare,
      Their sute to Dido first resolves to heare.

Meanwhile Ilioneus doth humbly kneel,   685
And thus the Queen with reverence doth greet :
"Great Princes ! we, (poore strangers), do appeale
To thy protection, prostrate at thy feet,
    Embold'ned by thy virtewes to draw neare,
    And in thy sacred presence to appeare.   690

"We, wofull Trojanes, wand'ring in exile,
Long toss't abroad vpon the troublows seas,
Do humbly crave to rest with the a while ;
Let not owr sute thy patience displease ;
    But, (gratiows Princes !), pitty owr distres,   695
    And over vs thy people's pride repres.

"To raise thy cittyes and returne with spoile,
To no such end we did vs heir addresse ;
We, being objects of disgrace and toile,
No such prowd thoughts owr conquer'd mindes possesse.
    Whil first we did on foamie seas ascend,   701
    To Italy we did owr cowrse intend.

"Scarce did the floods owr sight from shoar divorce,
Whil mad with furie, and inflam'd with rage,
Lowd bellowing Boreas prowdly offers force,   705
And maid owr navie of his pride the stage.
    The elements, all intermixt in one,
    Owr ships were soone disperst and overthrowne.

"A Prince we had, (O had !), word full of grieff !
By name Æneas, great in armes and fame,   710
Whom, if the heavens preserve for owr relieff,
Feir no ; thy fortoune thow shall never blame,
    That we by the ar favor'd for his caws."
    Thus, with a sigh, the Trojane maide a pause.

Her waxen heart, touch't with a trew remorse,   715
And sympathie of their distrest estate,
Did her compassion in such sort enforce,
As, sweetly smileing, from her regall seat :
    " Cheer vp ȝoᵣ mindes, (brave Trojanes)," she replyed ;
    " Exile base sorrow, be no more dismayed.   720

" What people are so barren of engine,
As have not heard of great Æneas' name ?
Troyes ancient splendour ? of her gloryes shine ?
With longsome warre how Mars did her inflame ?
    To vs ȝour vertewes admiration breeds,   725
    Amazed much by ȝowr heroick deeds.

" If hence ȝe minde, free pasport I will give,
And, with a lib'rall hande, ȝowr wants supplie.
Or, if my kingdome can ȝowr woes relieve,
Welcome ! thrise welcome, heir to stay with me !   730
    If Trojanes can submit them to my throne,
    Trojane and Tyrian sall to me be one.

" And O ! I wish ȝowr brave, illustruows prince,
With whose renowne the earth's seaven climats rings,
Were heir ; if heavens have not him ravish't hence,   735
But do reserve for some vnknowne designes,
    Happy, how happy should Queen Dido bee,
    To succour him in his extremitie."

Scarce had she endit till the airie cloud,
Which him encompas't, vanisht owt of sight,   740
And he, deliv'red of his sable shroud,
With sudden wonder, shyn'd into the light,
    More lyke a God then any earthly creature,
    So perfect he appear'd in every feature.

With stately shape, a smileing awfull eye,   745
A piercing look, a sweet majestick face ;
The golden treasure of his locks which lye
Adowne his shoulders with celestiall grace,
    In heavenly hew excell'd that far sought fleece,
    Gain'd with such hazarde by the ȝowth of Greece.   750

Now see how Dido narrowely doth eye him,
Into her heart great things of him divining ;
With admiration all the cowrt espye him,
Vpon his royall brow true vertue shining.
    No dame so chaste but, spite of all defences,   755
    Must ȝeeld to love, him viewing with right senses.

"Behold," (quoth he), "great Princes, in thy sight,
The man for whome thow kindly dost enquire ;
Thy humblest servant, if a sea-tost wight,
Infolded in misfortune's sad attire,   760
    Can be thought worthy the, (dear Queen), to serve,
    Who dost so infin'tly of vs deserve.

"Thow onely with owr miseryes art moved ;
By the alone we comfort do enjoy ;
Thow only kinde and pittyfull hast proved   765
To vs, the poore distrest remaine of Troy.
    We only by thy gratiows favour breath,
    Near ent'red at the frozen gates of death.

"Thow, feelingly enflam't with ȝealows fire,
Our indigence dost vndeserv'dly aid,   770
The wofull objects of proud Æol's ire,
Whom heavens each where, by sea, by land, invaide ;
    The scorne of time, the mirrour of mishap,
    Of deepest grieff the most expressive map.

"Can e're thy bountyes be by vs repayed? 775
All-vertuouse princes! Africk's gloriows starre!
We straying Pelerins will ne'r assay't,
Thy great deserts exceed owr pow'r so farre.
    Jove, dowbtles, Dido duely sall rewarde,
     If Jove doth rueth or equity regarde. 780

"Whill night's clear torches in true measure daunce
To heavenly accords of harmoniows spheares,
Whil Phoebus' steeds abowt the Poles do praunce,
Earth's pond'rows masse whill giant Atlas beares;
    Thy fame, praise, glory, and thy partes divine, 785
     Shall last, enrol'd on times immortall shrine.

"And, whill the heavens dissolve owr bodyes frame,
Thy kindnes no oblivion shall blot owt."
Thus having said, burnt with affection's flame,
His subjects he embraces all abowt. 790
    Hands join'd in hands, joy hath their hearts transfixed,
     Both smiles and teares at once ar intermixed.

"Great Cytherea's sone!" the Queen replied,
Ravish't with wonder of this object strange;
"What fortune heir thy wand'ring steps doth guide? 795
How coms't thir costs thow solitare dost range?
    Art thow that Prince, by progeny divine,
     Whom great Anchises gote on beautyes Queen?

"My father Belus, (well I do record),
Whil wasteing Cyprus with victoriows hand, 800
To Teucer's aide, who by the dint of sword
Most violently was expell'd the land;
    Their first thy fame did sound into mine eare;
     Their Troyes distres and ruine I did heare.

"Like bitter fortunes als myself have proved ;   805
But, greiff digested, sweet content redowbles.
Afflicted wights to pitty I am moved,
Not inexpert in woe and saddest troubles.
    Rest heir, Æneas, in thir partes a space,
    For bloody broiles enjoying blessed peace."   810

Butt more, descending frome imperiall seate,
Her ghuests she guides into a pompows hall,
Then holy-dayes proclaim'd with triumph great,
In honour of th' ensewing festivall :
    A Hecatombe is offered, beasts are slaine   815
    To Neptune, ruler of the glassie plaine.

The regall palace, royally prepar'd,
With hangings ritch is sumptuously decor'd ;
In midst the tables, on ritch pillars rear'd,
With silver plate are plentifully stor'd.   820
    On which, laboriowsly engraven in gold,
    The Princes' royall pedegrie's enrol'd.

Æneas now discharg't of heavy care,
Preparing to refresh his fainting sprights,
Ascanius' absence only doth empare   825
His perfect joyes, enless'ning his delights.
    Such was the tender, fatherly respect
    Whereby his child he dearly doth affect.

" Achates, haist," (quoth he), "at length relate
To that sweet Boy, who in the ships doth stay,   830
The period of owr paines, owr present state,
How calme a night hath still'd owr stormie day.
    Be thow a guide vnto his footsteps weake,
    That of owr pleasures heir he may partake.

"And those few tokens, which alone do laste   835
Of all the treasures of demolish't Troy,
Bring with that hopefull childe to vs in haste;
The costly jewells Helen did enjoy,
    Her ritch embroid'red robes, the scepter rare,
    And crowne, which fair Ilionea bare.   840

"With these the Queen I purpose to present,
Small pledges of these duetyes to her due.
Whill smoothest words to no effect are spent,
Gifts, (strange perswadeing oratours), subdue,
    And force the firmest mindes, do still prevaill,   845
    Whil complements and kindest speaches faill."

But whill Achates for Ascanius hyes
With winged pace: Loe! frome the cristall skies,
The Cyprian Goddes suddenly espyes
Th'event of all; who doth anone devise   850
    That Cupid shall assume the shape and face
    Of sweet Ascanius, and supplie his place,

And so the Queen with furie strange enspire,
Into her bosome breathing love's infection,
And kindle in her breast a boyling fire,   855
A quenchles flame of violent affection,
    Whose deadly poyson, once infused deep,
    May peice and peice through all her arteirs creep.

And whill he doth present the ritch propyne
Of Trojan reliques, in Ascanius' shape,   860
He may, (vnwarre), the Princes vndermyne,
And craftily her liberty entrape;
    So, being once enamor'd on her sone,
    May free his danger her suspition.

"Cupid, my sone," saith she, (for Cupid still's   865
Attending Venus), "thow my strenth, my stay,
Whose trophes great both heavens and earth do fill,
O'r gods, o'r men, who dost thy scepter swey,
  Behold before thy sacred Deity,
  Thy mother Venus comes entreating the.   870

"With what despight, (thow knowes), Jove's jealows wife
Thy brother, dear Æneas, hath persewed,
Whom, nixt to the, I tender as my life,
My joy, my cheifest care, and neir subdewed
  On Neptun's azure bosome, to my smarte ;   875
  Thow of my woes hast oft made vp a parte.

"Him Carthage now containes ; Loe ! how the Queen,
With sugg'red speaches, much his stay importunes,
And royally her ghuest doth entertaine,
With kinde compassion on his former fortunes.   880
  But what these gloriows guilded sho's portend,
  It's hard to constre : O ! I fear the end.

"In Junoes citty, since by Juno hated,
How can he draw secure one minute's breath ?
Since no where saiff, but by her furie threated,   885
Heir, at her pleasure, she may plot his death.
  No place more oportune, no time more fit,
  Such inhumane a murther to commit.

"But hark ! deir infant, Loe ! I have devis'd
A policie all perill to prevent.   890
Queen Dido, by thy slights, must be suppris'd ;
A secret flame must frome thy forge be sent
  To boyle her breast, her minde to fancie move,
  Æneas only object of her love.

" Now fit occasion favors owr designes. 895
The lovely boy Ascanius goes to cowrt.
Lay thow aside a space thy shafts, thy wings,
Put on his person, and his princely porte.
    A child, thow mayst a childe in shape resemble,
    More subtilly with Dido to dissemble. 900

"That whil embraced, cherish't, entertain'd,
The nectar of thy balmie lips she seiks,
And whil she clasps the in her armes enchain'd,
Redowbling kisses on thy rosiall cheeks,
    Thow privily may in her veines enspire 905
    A pleasing poyson, a deceiving fire."

Cupid obeyes the Goddes' charming voice.
An humane shape him instantly investes.
Of sweet Ascanius' shadow he maks choise,
And of his wings himself anone devestes, 910
    Layes downe his bow and arrowes, one by one,
    So with Achates to the cowrt is gone.

But, least Ascanius should the guile disclose,
To Ida wods the Goddes him doth beare,
Where pleasant slumber, rest and sweet repose 915
Lock't vp his eyes ; and Morpheus drawing neire
    Seas'd on his senses, in the cooling shade
    Which lillyes sweet and budding roses made.

So now, whil Dido doth her ghuests entreat,
With choisest cowrses and deliciows faire, 920
Loading the tables with all sortes of meat,
Which ȝielded are on earth or liquid aire,
    An hundreth groomes, with diligence and skill,
    Giving attendance on the strangers still.

And whill Iöpas sweetly doth expresse   925
With warbling voice, and yvorie instrument,
The motion, order, cowrse of great and lesse,
Fires fixt and straying, in the firmament ;
    How Phoebus eyther hemi-spheare enflames,
    And how his thunders Jove, and lightnings frames. 930

How Mars and Venus Vulcane did ensnare ;
How stars' aspects benigne or froward bee ;
How Iris bends her bowe amids the aire ;
How rolling spheares resound harmoniowsly :
    Lo ! suddenly amids this joyfull throng,   935
    Ascanius, comming, interrupts the song.

For, as he ent'red, all with greedy eyes
Gaze on the beautyes of the lovely boy.
Resplendant rayes his visage beautifyes,
His chearfull countenance augments their joy.   940
    Smiles grace his gesture, which in them doth move
    Amazement, wonder, joy, delight, and love.

They mervell at Æneas ritch propyne.
They mervell at the boy the gifts doth bring.
They muse a mortall's face so bright doth shyne,   945
Mistaking him to be a God, a king,
    A mighty monarch, whose imperiows hand
    Bears over all the vniverse command.

But none, so much as Dido, him admires :
In this sweet object such delight she fand,   950
She, in his breast, (as fixed starrs), ensphears
Her sparkling lights, which still butt motion stand.
    But, still the more, her starving eyes she feeds,
    Desire encreasing still the greater breeds.

The silver beames abowt his locks of gold,   955
The heavenly lustre of his shining face,
Her more and more still in amazement hold.
Within her breast she finds no rest nor peace,
    But, surffeitting on such vnusuall sights,
    Although enflam't, she in the flame delights.   960

Thus, whill she feeds, she pynes herself away,
(An harmeles flie allured by the low) ;
Her self, vnwar, thus doth her self betray,
And feels the force of this small archer's bowe,
    Whose eyes alone, sweet, cowrtes, voide of ire,   965
    Dairt lightnings foorth, a world of love to fire.

But now the Syren, by enchantments false,
The senses charmes of his supposed syre,
Now sucks his lips, now hings abowt his halse,
With kinde embraceings kindling his desyre.   970
    He tenderly his child doth intertaine,
    Mistaking whome his folded armes containe.

His cowrse, anone, vnto the Queen he takes,
Whose marrowe boyles already in her bones.
She, for the cherries of his lips forsakes   975
All other daintyes, and in love suppones
    A sweeter issue, nor experience bad,
    In end expressed, in characters sad.

Within the prison of her yvorie armes,
The infant clasping closely, she confines ;   980
And to her foe's assaultes herself disarmes,
Vnwar, her liberty who vndermines,
    And ignorant she holdeth on her breast
    So great a God, so dangerows a ghuest.

He, peice and peice, the dear remembrance kills 985
Of late Sicheus, who her love enjoyed,
And empty veines with living fire he fills,
Her former flames which quickly have destroyed ;
 Her heart, long disaccustom'd now to love,
 Affections strange and passions new doth prove. 990

Now is the Queen ensnar'd with Cupid's airts,
By love led captive to a suddaine change.
She feels the poyson of his deadly dairts
To work in her by operation strange.
 But none her trembling pulses neids to finde. 995
 Her eyes bewray the sicknes of her minde.

O love ! how many are thy subtle snares,
To conquer beauty and to climb her forte ;
Vowes, protestations, prayers, sighs and teares,
And cowrting strange in many a sundry sorte, 1000
 Betray poore women. Nature beauty made
 Both to be loved and proved, nought die and fade.

Now silent night spred foorth her sable wings,
And broad display'd her spangled cannopye.
In fire, air, sea and earth, all living things, 1005
Which moving, flying, creeping, breathing be,
 Did rest, in pleasant slumber buryed deep,
 Save she whose wakeing thoughts impeacht her sleep.

Heir endeth the First
Book.

.

THE SECOND BOOK.

THE quein, sore sick of love, surcharg't with care,
   In wounded veines a secret flame doth feed.
Æneas' vertue and his stemme preclare,
Still, in her ravisht minde, a place doth pleed.
     Both voyce and eyes one onely object hold,   5
     A masse of cares her restles thoughts enfold.

If slumber sweet vpon her senses sease,
Her troubled braines, with visions new acquainted,
Present her lover still before her eyes,
The object which by day they most frequented.   10
     Awak't againe frome her vnquiet rest,
     She finds her spreit with passions strange possest.

Her beating pulses and her panting heart
Showe the distemper of her troubled minde.
No practise, humane industry, nor airt,   15
For her infection a remeid can finde ;
     Whose spreading poyson wholly hath ov'rrunne
     Her veines, ere scairce she knew her grieff begun.

With purpure blush, soone as the morne displayes
Heaven's cristall gates, (dayes golden beames recall'd),   20
" Deir sister Anna," sighing sore, she sayes,
" What dreames, by night, my senses have appal'd !
     What apparitions did vpraid my sight !
     And broken sleeps, with sudden fears, affright !

"What ghuest so strange hath heir ariv'd of late?   25
How brave of gesture! and in armes as great!
Whose eyes, of humble majesty the seat,
With grave-sweit looks, imperiowsly entreat.
    What broyles, what battles, what enconters bold,
    Hath he ov'rpast with courage vncontrol'd!   30

"If most advis'dly I did not resolve,
Myself to none in nuptiall bands to joine,
Since death my first affection did dissolve,
And sacred Hymen's solemne knot disjoine;
    To his assault, (if vnto any one),   35
    I might be moved, (perhaps), to ʒeeld alone.

"To the, (dear Anne), to the I must reveale,
Since death frome me Sicheus did divorce,
Who prowd Pigmalion's cruelty did feele,
This man alone my fredome did enforce.   40
    He only hath enflam't my dead desires;
    I feel the footsteps of my former fires.

"I feel within the fornace of my breast
A secret flame, a close confined fire;
What hope is left to smother and supress't?   45
Which bred my sight, is fostered by desire;
    O how I frye and freize, I faint and feare.
    How great a loade, (alace), is love to beare!

"What passion strange, (poore Dido!) thus transports the?
Love bids the ʒeeld the in a stranger's will.   50
But honor tells how highly it imports the,
With headles haste thy pleasures to fulfill.
    Since flying beauty most enflames desire,
    And sweet deniall kindles Cupid's fire.

"Love bids the runne where sweet delight doth leade,   55
And prove those pleasures which to ʒowth belong ;
But honor doth advise the to tak heade,
Thy spotles fame and princely partes to wrong.
    Since vertue's field is easily laid waste,
    And meates vnwholsomest most please the taste.   60

"Nay, rather earth devore me first alive,
And, Erebus' dark shad's enclos'd among,
Let thund'ring Jove me of my life deprive,
O sacred modesty, ere I the wrong !
    Or ever prease the statutes to eschew,   65
    Of shamefastnes which to my sexe is due.

"He, he, (alace), to whome I first was fast,
My soules affection hes frome hence transported ;
O let it with his ghost for ever last,
Entomb't with him, where first my love resorted."   70
    This said, her eyes a cristall flood foorth powre,
    And on her cheiks distill a pearlie showre.

"Sweet sister," Anna then at lenth replied,
"Dear as my life, more then my self affected,
Still shall thy ʒowth to mourne alone be tied ?   75
Are childrene deare, by the, no more respected ?
    Hatst thow so much those joyes which Venus brings ?
    And think'st thow soules departed care such things ?

"Although, when sade melancholie of late
Seas'd on thy minde, all sutes thow didst reject ;   80
No Lybian husband, not Hiarbas great,
Nor Africk captaine couldst thow then affect ;
    But canst thow now resist, and not approve
    The sweet effects of such contenting love ?

G

"Thow weyes not well what bounds thow dost ·possesse;   85
Heir the Getulianes and Numidians stowt,
Heir Syrtes sands, famowse in barrennesse,
Heir the Barceans compas the abowt;
    What shall I speak of Tyrus' new debates,
    Which now arise, and of thy brother's threats?   90

"By heaven's assent, (I hope), and Junoes aide,
The Trojane ships have heir the cowrse intended;
What citty, (sister), sall of this be made,
If such alliance prosperowsly wer ended?
    What reignes arise, if Troy with vs wer one?   95
    With what triumph should Africk shine anone?

"Plead first, frome heaven, protectione divine,
Pretending cawses to thy ghuest of stay,
Till stormes be still, the seas to smile incline,
Ships saiff may saile, and heavens their furie lay."   100
    Her kindled breast thus Anna did enflame,
    Swa hope she caught, exiling dowbt and shame.

How easily do women women move,
To whome they truste the secret of their heart!
By her perswasion, O how quick doth love   105
Disperse the self, and spreed in every parte
    A furiows flame, a fumeing fever fell!
    No antidote this poyson can expell.

To church they haste, and first heaven's peace entreate,
On altars off'ring to the gods above,   110
To Ceres, Phaebus, and to Bacchus great,
To Juno chiefly, who hath care of love.
    With cuppe in hand, the Queen herself doth syne
    Powre foorth vpon the sacrifice the wyne.

Or at the altars off'ring gifts she spaces,   115
Observing what new Fortunes do ensue;
Marking the bowells, and the breathing places
Of every beast, with most attentive viewe,
    Which open to her sight; with narrow eyes,
     She gaz'd and guess'd; what all doth boad she sies. 120

Ah fond conceits! What do her vowes availl?
Or what do temples sought her rage empare?
Whill as her marrow doth already faill,
With soaking flames consumed, dry'd vp with care,
    And whill enclos'd into her breast profound,   125
     She nourisheth a deadly feast'ring wound.

Like as the dear, which wounded vnawar,
With hunter's shaft fast fix't into her side,
Runnes headlongs heir and their, both near and far,
But still the dart doth in her breast abide,   130
    So Dido, poyson'd with a deadly head,
     Butt rest doth rage, sore martyr'd but remeid.

Through stately Carthage now her ghuest she guides,
With gloriows shows to entertaine his sight;
Now sumptuows banquets painfully provides,   135
With variows objects surffeiting delight.
    Then Trojane toyles with burning minde to heere,
     Oft she entreats, and gives most watchfull eare.

But whill she speaks, her speach confus'd doth faill,
Whill frome her minde her wav'ring tongue debordes; 140
With looks anone she doth anew assaill,
Dumb oratours perswading more then words;
    Whose silent language doth most lively teach,
     How meane a messenger in love is speach.

For loe ! her eyes, the index of her minde,   145
With piercing lookes imperiowsly entreate,
And tell her lover that, too long vnkinde,
He overlookes her passionat estate.
      O heavenly Rhet'rike ! which butt words reveals
      What modesty in women still conceales.   150

But ah ! whil he is gone, and night's pale face
Day doth displace, provoking pleasant rest,
Oft she alone laments, oft doth embrace
The happy place which he of late imprest.
      Oft to her trowbled senses it appeares,   155
      That him still present she both sees and heares.

Then ȝoung Ascanius she doth entertaine,
His parents portrate perfectly presenting,
Whome in her armes she softly doth enchaine,
By sweits suppos'd, her sowres of life relenting.   160
      Thus stealing by the slowely sliding howres,
      So to subdue loves still assailing powers.

Her careles minde, slouth, meanwhile, doth supprise ;
Buildings begun ar left : ȝowth armes despise ;
No bullwarkes brave, no rampiers rare arise,   165
But all engine of warre imperfect lies.
      No martiall thought her minde doth more retaine,
      For love and slouth insep'rable remaine.

When Juno, from her azure pale, espied
With such a frensie Didoes minde infected ;   170
And when her furiows fever, such she tried,
As no reporte nor rumour she respected,
      To Venus first her cowrse she doth direct,
      And to the Goddes thus begowth to break :

" How great thy conquest, glory and renowne !   175
Thy boy and thow victoriows parte the spoile.
Have two, of heavenly issue both, throwne downe
One simple woman ?   O ! a famows foile.
 Art a beleving lady, vnadvised,
 By Cupid conquer'd, and thy slight supprised ?   180

" Oh poore weak conquest !   But to what effect
Thus keep we armes ?   Why peace and amity
Prefer we not, though earst we did suspect
Owr prowd skie-reaching wals of Carthage hie ?
 Those feares remov'd, now at thine owne desire,   185
 Thow hast what heart can wish or tongue require.

" Love-sick Eliza now thy boy doth burne.
The furiows forge Æneas feeds alone.
O ! let vs then conjoine, withowt returne,
With equall love vniting both in one.   190
 Now Dido may be tyed to Trojane mate,
 And thow receave, in tougher, Carthage great."

But Venus soone the stinging snake espied,
Hid in the grasse, quick in her guilded wordes,
And counterfeet the Siren's song she tried ;   195
To whome the Goddes answere thus affordes,
 (Perceiving that of policy she spak
 From Italy Æneas to keip back.)

" Who war so mad, with the in armes contend,
Refuse thy freindship, or thy sutes denie ?   200
If fates owr projects happily would end !
But O, I feare, when Jove owr minds doth trie,
 If he will graunt this purpose to approve,
 And if assent those partyes joine in love.

"Thow art his spowse, thow boldly may assay   205
To learne [his] will; lead thow the way I followe."
"That parte," (quoth shee), "pertaines to me to play,
That fuird, though fear'd, I hope to find but shallowe.
     But how the present purpose finish may,
     Give eare, and shortly I sall showe the way.   210

"Soone as Aurora frome her bed of roses,
Arising chearfully, beginnes to blush;
And, in the East, heavens cristall gate vncloses,
From whence big-looking Phaeton doth rush
     With flaming haire; then are those lovers two   215
     A hunting in the woddes resolv'd to goe.

"There, whil the horsemen, prancing to and fro,
Enclose abowt with hounds the trembling deir,
I, frome above, a tempest downe shall thro',
A fearfull storme, till all their troupes reteir.   220
     With thund'ring noyse both heaven and earth sall shake,
     Perforce the hunters shall the fields forsake.

"Their mates, butt more, shall all at once be gone;
None shall abide, but all in darknes stray;
With sable wings night shall envolve anone   225
The world each where: all shall in darknes stray.
     One cave shall then, (butt witnes more), containe
     The Trojane prince and Carthaginiane queene.

"Where, if thow firmely to my minde accord,
I shall be present, and with mutuall vowes   230
Mak her his wife, and him her mate and lord,
In all respects to vse her as his spouse;
     Both tying with vnseparable bands,
     In Hymen's presence joining hearts and hands."

The Goddes showing by a gracefull smile,   235
That she applauded vnto Junoes minde,
Begowth to laugh when shee perceiv'd the guile,
And gave a signe in token she enclin'd,
    And to the purpose did assent, and so,
    Whil they devise, the night away doth go.   240

Aurora blushing then at once appeares.
The gallant ʒowthes for pastime all prepare,
With nets of ev'ry sorte, with hunting speares ;
The horsemen haste with hounds, of sent most rare.
    Before the palace all the cowrt attends   245
    The Queen's aryvall, whil the morning spends.

With gold attir'd, and robes of costly worth,
Threat'ning the bitt, her palfrey stamping stayed.
With mighty traine herself then marches foorth,
With broid'red mantle, hunter-like arrayed.   250
    Of gold her quaver, gold her loks divids,
    And purple garment, tied with gold, abides.

Lo ! now, the prince Ascanius proceeds,
Accompany'd with all the Trojane peers.
Æneas last majestickly succeeds,   255
Whose brave proportion all, butt match, admires.
    With stately cariage, marching forward fast,
    Till with the Queen his troupes he joines at last.

Most like Apollo, shuneing winters stormes,
When Zanthus' floods, and Lycia's cold he flyes,   260
And to his native soile himself conformes,
To Delos, there to feast and sacrifize.
    For gladenes all th' inhabitants do shout,
    Dancing with joy the altars round about.

On Cynthus' toppes the God doth proudly space,   265
With hov'ring locks, which drest in circling rownds,
With Lawrell garlandes, and with golden lace,   ·
Are touss'd; his shafts betwix his shoulders sounds.
  So march't the stately Trojane; such his grace,
  Such was the beauty of his heavinly face.   270

    ·

How soone the' aryv'd upon the montaines hie,
And found the haunts where as the beasts had stayed;
Behold! the deir downe frome the rocks do flie,
Coursing abroad, athort the fields affrayed.
  Both heards of Hart and Hinde the hills forgoe,   275
  And in one globe with feet the dust vpthroe.

But in the vaile Ascanius doth abide,
Making his steid his ʒowthfull rider feele;
And now doth one, now others over-ride,
With dastard beasts disdaining more to deele,   280
  But earnestly wisheth for some foamie boare,
  Or that ane ramping lyon once would roare.

Heaven's ordinance with this the earth do threat,
With noyse and terrour; fire and lightnings flie;
Of raine and rageing wind a tempest great,   285
With horride darknes, dimme the worlds bright eye;
  Fire, water, air, and earth seame all anone,
  With hiddeows tumult, intermixt in one.

Not trees alone but solide rocks do shake,
Assail'd by rageing torrents tumbling downe   290
Frome toppes of steipest montaines: all forsake
The fields, affrayed in every rill to drowne.
  Their troupes, divided, search themselves to shroud
  Frome furiows heavins, with thunders roaring lowd.

One cave, whil all the tempest dark do shield,   295
The Trojane Duke and Dido both contained.
Prodigiows presages sad earth did ȝeeld,
With them when Juno in the cave convein'd.
  The guilty air gave light; the fire did glance;
  And montaine Faryes did bewaile the chance.   300

Looke! how a Comet, whose bright flamming haire
Brings tidings sad of dearth, or death of kings,
Drawes all men's eyes to gaze amidst the aire,
Conjecturing thereby of future things;
  So, whil at first, the Princes beauty shin'd,   305
  Æneas wond'ring ravish't was in minde.

Her pure vnborrowed blush, her native white,
The piercing rayes of her victoriows eyes,
Bred in his soule such singulare delight,
And did his senses suddainely supprise,   310
  In such a sort, that of all sense denude,
  He long a lifles, senseles statue stoode.

But soone her looks, of pow'r t'awaken death,
And ravish with amazement hardest hearts,
Reviv'd him frome his traunse, recal'd his breath,   315
And to his sleeping senses life empartes;
  Who instantly confines, within his armes,
  His sweetest Siren, who his fancie charmes.

Sie now how honour, love, and modesty,
With diverse colours dye her blushing cheeks!   320
When, (lay'd aside respect of majesty),
The fort to render, proud Æneas seeks.
  And whil, (desire rul'd by the blinded boy,)
  Loves sweet-stolne sport he labours to enjoy.

With faint repulses and denialls sweet,   325
Lo ! how she shrinking, strives his sutes to shune ;
But he now offers force, now doth entreate,
And still persewes, till last the prise is wonne.
    The jemme enjoy'd, which women hold so deare,
    And honour prostrate, blushing did reteare.   330

Can words, can vowes, can feeble hands resist,
With hote desire whil ȝowthfull blood doth boyle ?
Though she repine, do his assaults desist ?
Small glory is a ȝeelded foe to foyle.
    Women must still deny and vse defences,   335
    Till charming Cupid lull a sleep the senses.

This wrought to sin, anone she waxeth bold,
And mutually her mate doth entertaine ;
Loe ! how her strict embraces him enfold,
Whil as they issue frome the cave againe,   340
    Nothing asham'd to come in open sight,
    Thus vse in sinning soone maks sin seame light.

This disemall day did Didoes death begin ;
This day of all her sorrowes was the source :
Now neither fame she cares, nor shame, nor sin,   345
Nor more devises any secrete cowrse
    To cloake her love ; but mariage this she thinks,
    And at this foule offence, (effronted), winks.

Swift-flying fame those tydings quickly spreads,
And suddaine rumours soone through Africk sends.   350
Fame, which by flight and moving lives & breads,
Lurks first belowe, then straight to hevin ascends.
    With nimble wings from earth she doth arise,
    And hides her head amidst the starry skies.

Her mother earth, (whil as her brood rebelld   355
Against the gods, with blind ambition driven,
Themselves ov'rthrowne, their proud designes repell'd,
Darring to scale the batlements of heaven),
    Her brooded foorth, (they say), in great despight,
    A sister light of foot, and swift of flight.   360

A fearfull monster, horrible butt match ;
How many wav'ring plumes her carcasse beares,
Als many eyes them vnderneath do watch ;
(A wondrous thing to showe), als many eares
    Still heark both near and far, throughowt all bounds ; 365
    Als many mowthes ; als many tongues resounds.

Twixt heaven and earth, by night she nimbly flyes.
Her brazen trumpe to sownd she sleep forsakes.
Great cittyes oft by day she terrifyes.
On turrets hie she sitts, when rest she takes.   370
    And whil she showes what she hath seene by viewe,
    Things ofter fain'd she doth reporte then true.

Then diverse rumours she disperst anone,
Blazing abroad both things vndone and done.
How to Æneas, of the Trojanes one,   375
The matchles Dido dain'd her self to ioine,
    Who given to please the flesh, (a life vnjust),
    Care-les of kingdomes, live in lawles lust.

With those reportes whil she the world did fill,
To loath'd Hiarbas now she taks her flight,   380
And showes this lover even the worst of ill,—
How, he disdain'd, a stranger joyes his right.
    This king was Joves owne sone, and child most deare,
    Whome Garamanth the noble nymph did beare.

An hundreth temples in his large empire,   385
An hundreth altars are to Jove vpraised,
Where he hath consecrate a quencheles fire,
Where, night and day, th' eternall gods are praised.
    The blood of bullocks cover all the grounde ;
    Sweit smelling floures through all the flures are founde. 390

He, mad almost in minde, depriv'd of rest,
Sore griev'd and with those bitter newes displeased,
Himself in presence of the gods addrest,
And their before the altars sacrifized.
    With humble heart, and hie erected hands,   395
    Thus powring foorth his plaints to Jove he stands :

" Æternall Jove ! whom Lybianes all adore,
As heaven's most gloriows guide and judge supreme,
On carpetts ritch, to thy immortall glore
Solemnely feasting, celebrate thy name.   400
    Beholdst thow this, O father most benigne !
    Of heaven and earth the sempiternall king.

" Though, frome above, thow fire-flaughts downe dost throwe,
(Dread soveraigne !) ȝit we nothing are affrayed ;
Though by thy lightnings we thy wraith do knowe,   405
ȝit not-the-les owr wickednes is stayed ;
    As lacking force, thy fires no fear affords,
    And judgements past no mortall more records.

" A woman, wand'ring in owr coastes of late,
To whome, both towne and bounds where she remain'd   410
I gave, with lawes to governe her estate,
My mariage most vngrately hath disdain'd,
    And plac'd a stranger over her empires,
    As only Sov'raigne of her soules desires.

"And now he, Paris-like, with mates disguised,   415
Half-men, half-maids, resembling both or neither,
His curled head with Phrygian mytre guised,
With balmed haires, his spoyles enjoyes the rather.
    But we, befoire thine altares gifts do heape,
    And nothing els but fruteles fame do reape."   420

Him playning thus, with melancholiows minde,
The Thund'rer heard, and turning straight his eyes
To Carthage cowrt, (whose stately turrets shin'd
'Gainst Phœbus' rayes), where he those lovers sees,
    Drunk with delight of sin, not careing shame,   425
    Whole given to lust and misregarding fame :

"Go, Mercury, my sone, mak haste," he sayes,
"And with Æolian wings addresse thy flight
To Carthage, where the Trojane chiftane stayes,
And kingdomes given by Fate regardes so light.   430
    Go swiftly sliding through the subtle aire,
    My vncontrolled will to him declare.

"None such fair Venus promeist he shuld prove,
Nor twise for this from Graecian armes reskued ;
But one to daunt sterne Mars, not doate in love,   435
Ov'r Italy to reigne, by him subdued.
    To kythe his courage frome his noble race,
    And mak the world each where his lawes embrace.

"If no desire of glore can raise his spright,
Nor loves for praise to putt himself to paine,   440
Should he Ascanius frustrate of his right?
Amidst his foes what meanes he to remaine?
    Nor looks what justly to his ayres doth fall?
    To sea he must ! this is the summe of all !"

This said : the God hence, (swift as thought), he flew,   445
With nimble feathers to the winds displayed ;
Divides the cristall sphears and circles blew,
And cutts the clouds, with golden wings arrayed.
     The mover first, the light and shyning fire
     He leaves, descending frome great Jove's empire.   450

The Ramme, the bull, the Twinnes he passeth nixt,
With all the signes the Zodiak adorne.
Owtrunnes the cowrse of straying starres and fixt,
Of planets, which the rest in beauty scorne,
     And glist'ring bright, each in a golden robe,   455
     With gloriows lustre, grace heaven's azure globe.

Now by the Artick Pole he swiftly slides,
Owtflyes the eagle and the silver swan,
The flamming dragon, which the Beirs divides,
The Dolphin ravish't with delight of man,   460
     The croune and speare, with many many a million
     Of lamps, which light this spatiows pavillion.

This climate cold, where haill, where frost and snowe,
Where raine and thunders, heat and cold do strive,
He leaves als swift as shaft from archers bowe,   465
And in a sweitter soyle doth soone arive,
     Where as the Hydra, and the hirpling Hare,
     As mates, in the Antartick Pole repare.

A rod he bears, by which he calls againe,
And sends downe soules to Plutoes dark empires ;   470
Both giveth sleep, and sleeping doth restraine,
Lenthes and abridges life, as he desires.
     Still thus he flyes, till he discerne the tops
     Of Atlas hudge, the Pole which vnderprops,—

Of aged Atlas, whose pyn-bearing browes,   475
With sable clouds encompast all abowt,
Nor haile, nor sleet, nor wind, nor weit eschewes ;
Adowne his shoulders raging spates do spowt ;
    Whose wrinkled chin great floods do overflowe,
    And hiddeows beard maide stiff with frost and snowe. 480

Heir first his flight heaven's nimble herauld stayes ;
Hence posts with speed, his cowrse through th' ocean plying,
And as the swiftest bird, a thowsand wayes,
Now soaring hie, now low her feathers trying,
    Alongst the coast of Africk still he flyes,   485
    Till stately Carthage now at lenth he sees.

Heir whil he first with winged feet did light,
And touch't the turrets of those buildings rare,
Anone Æneas he perceaves in sight,
Raising ritch monuments amidst the aire,   490
    To building bent, begirt with sword most bright
    With jasper stones, which, starrified, gave light.

With Tyrian purpour robe arayed he shin'd,
Hung frome his shoulders, gloriows to behold,
Which gifts the noble Dido had propin'd,   495
Wov'ne by her self, and warpt with twist of gold.
    No sooner him thus busied he beholds,
    But instantly his message sad vnfolds.

"Thow most effeminatly who dost found,
And, (far from hence), heir sumptuous buildings reares,   500
Skie-reaching castells raising from the ground,
Vnmindfull of thy kingdome and effaires ;
    To the I come, to the, frome heavens above,
    The winged herauld of great thund'ring Jove.

" Hee hath given charge I should imparte his minde.   505
What meanst thow heir in Africk to remaine?
To conquere glory if thow be not inclin'd,
Nor loves for praise to put thy self to paine,
    Ascanius rising ȝit behold, and wey
    The hope of ayers from him by just degrie,   510

" To which the crowne of Italy is due,
To which the Romane empire appertaines.
To sea thow must!"   Thus said, he bids adieue,
And visible no more at all remaines
    To mortall sight : as Phœbus beames do banish   515
    A sable cloud, so did the god evanish.

But now, sad Prince, what stand'st thow thus amazed?
What passions the perplexe? why lookst thow pale?
What suddaine sorrowes on thy soule have seazed?
What froward fate hath turn'd thy blesse to baill?   520
    What woes so vive, charact'red in thy face,
    Thus overcloud the rayes of princely grace?

As one whome fearfull visions do affright,
In nature's dear embraces laid a sleep,
Whil Hydras and Chymeras mock the sight,   525
And wound the soule with apprehensions deep,
    Whil as this masse, wherein nought moves but breath,
    Oft starts, whil gastly Gorgones threatne death ;

So still he stands, nor voyce nor gesture steirs,
With armes acrosse ; his colour comes and goes ;   530
Words find no vent ; confus'd with suddaine feares,
His haires for horrour and affright vprose.
    Sad, pale, astonisht, and of sense bereft
    He seem'd ; this sight such deep impression left.

But, self-return'd, he layes aside respect 535
Of things humane to Jove's eternall will.
He must not follow what he doth affect.
What heavens command poore mortalls must fulfill.
    Now must he leave his princesse and her state.
    Who may resist inevitable Fate? 540

But ah ! (sad soule), what shall he first attempt ?
How dar he this his enterprise reveale
To furiows Dido ? how her minde relent ?
What way with her dar he begin to deale ?
    Resolving now, now changing, nought contents, 545
    In diverse partes his dowbtsome minde he rents.

At last his captaines he concludes to call,
(As only best advise to be embrac'd),
Sergestus, Mnestheus, and Cloanthus tall ;
Straight gives command their fleet to rig in haist, 550
    And by their counsell, providence, and care,
    For flight by sea doth privily prepare.

Their souldiers they do secretly conveene,
In readines remaining on the shoare,
In shining armes who suddainly ar seene 555
For feare of any following vproare,
    And cawses fain'd, to keip their plots vnkend,
    Of such novationes publickly pretend.

He meanwhile minds, whil Dido least doth knowe,
And doubts no breach of such sure founded love, 560
To try her pleasant hours most fitt to showe,
And search if he her owne consent could move.
    Their prince's pleasure they, butt more delay,
    Haste all anone with glaidnes to obey.

But watchfull Dido did the guile perceive,   565
And fand the cowrse intended for their flight,
(What slight so great a lover can deceive?
What fetch of fyne device could syle her sight?)
    Then foorthwith fame disperst for newes abroade,
    In readines their ships at anchore roade.   570

She, mov'd in minde, with looks and gesture sad,
With hiddeows clamoure railes the streets through owt,
Most like the furiows Thyas running mad,
The fearfull leader of that rageing rowt;
    Whil as the Moenads, who abhorre the light,   575
    Do sacrifize to Bacchus in the night.

With boundles rage, thus overrul'd a space,
Anger and furie in her face did flame;
Mad passions did her patience displace,
Despight and rancour reason overcame;   580
    Wraith keipt in words, sighs only passage finde,
    Whose vapours vented, ease her burden'd minde.

At last, more calme, she thus begowth to speak,
(Extremity to words a way affords:)
" Dost thow intend, deir lord," (quoth she), " to break   585
Thy solemne vowes, and violate thy words?
    Thy sad departure frome thy love to hyd,
    And frome thir shoares thus secretly to slyde?

" Whither, O cruell! whither dost thow flie?
What discontent thus change in the doth move?   590
What wrong, (alas!), or what offence in me,
Thus maks the loath and vilipend my love?
    With too much kindnes art thow overcloyed?
    Or ar my favowrs hated, 'cawse enjoyed?

"Ah ! 'twas not so, when thow did pensive sit,   595
Sigh, faine to die, look pale, protest, and sweare,
Vowing thy service at my feet, whil ʒit
For all thy oathes thy policies appear.
    By sad experience, O ! I find it true,
    That seldome lust delights in what is due.   600

"But ʒit the world in me some fault may deeme,
(For poore, weak women euer bear the blame),
Why thow my bed, as stayn'd, dost disesteeme,
Regardles of my favour, thy defame.
    But I to the appeal, if ere my ʒowth   605
    Gave proofe of ought butt vndistained trewth.

"Did my cold breast so long vnwarm't remaine
From men's deceits, and charming flatterings free,
Nor once one thought of love did intertaine,
Cruell to all, but kinde alone to the ?   610
    Keipt I so long my marble minde vnshaken,
    To be by the disdain'd, and thus forsaken ?

"Stay ʒit, O ! stay, my Deir, possesse in peace
The jewell, which of laite so dear thow prised ;
And be not author of her sad disgrace,   615
Who cannot breath and be by the despised.
    Returne, Deir Lord, leave not thy halfe behind,
    What I entreate with tears thy oathes do bind.

"Oh ! hast thow ells forgot, (when in the cave
Thy guilded words and vowes first won the field ;   620
When, to thy sutes, consent my silence gave,
And poore beleving I, myself did ʒeild.)
    How thow did swear, resolve, protest and vow,
    Still to be hers, whom thow disdainest now ?

"How can I think those sighs, so feeling, fained?   625
Those passionat regrates, but arm'd with airt?
Those looks, so sad, but for the fashion fraimed
To melt with pitty my relenting heart?
    Whil thow beneath thy passions seam'd to faint,
    And thowsand colours thy pale cheiks did paint.   630

"Those sighs, regrates, lookes, passions, colours strange,
Though faynd, in me produc't no false effects.
By those betray'd, I from myself did range,
Too prodigall of what thow now neglects;
    And headlesly to thy desires consenting;   635
    Whilk breeds in the dislike, in me lamenting.

"If thow object thy love was then entire,
What owtward virtues now in me do want?
Do not thir beautyes even the same appeare,
That did attract thine heart of adamant?   640
    No stolne vermilion blush, to charme delight
    With false allurements, did bewitch thy sight.

"That bastard beauty, and adultrate dye,
That new-found falshood, conterfoot of nature,
Shame of owr sexe, the stayne of modesty,   645
Fewell to lust, to chastity a traitoure,
    That mystery to me was still vnknowne,
    This red and white was then, as now, mine owne.

"Though loathed beauty lack perswading force,
Now overclouded with afflictions vaile;   650
Though sutes, nor sighes find pitty nor remorce;
Though passions, plaints, and prayers nought prevaile;
    And though thir eyes' bright sunne, obscur'd with
        smarte,
    Lack piercing rayes to penetrate thy heart;

"Ʒit cannot my affection nor thy faith,   655
My constant love, thy promise and right hand,
Nor thine owne Didoes miserable death ;—
Can none of those deteine the in this land?
  But ah ! whil winter's stormes thus raigeing be,
  Wilt thow endanger both thy self and me?   660

"Wilt thow, O cruell thow, to saile mak haste,
Whil boystrows Boreas threats the swelling seas?
Suppone, though Troy Ʒit vndestroy'd did last,
And to no forraine countrey now thow flyes,
  Whil furiows Neptune rageing doth remaine,   665
  Thy native Troy should thow by shipping gaine?

"Ah ! fleest thow me? Ʒit by those streaming teares,
Which leaue affliction's furrowes on my face ;
By thy right hand, by all the hopes and feares
Possesse poore lovers, by those oathes, alace !   670
  Which me betrayed, by owr espousall day,
  And by that love thow bar'st me once, I pray,

"If ever I of the did well deserve,
To the ought dear if ever Dido gave,
Showe now compassion ; firme thy faith observe ;   675
My life and croune from death and ruine save.
  O ! let my prayers Ʒit relent thy minde,
  If any place with the my sutes may finde.

"For thee, the Lybian Kings conspire my wrack ;
For thee, the hatred of mine owne I beare ;   680
For thee alone, my shamefast lyf I brack,
And Fame I lost, to me nor life more deare.
  To whom thus leavest thow me, to die with shame,
  O ghuest ? I dar no more the husband name.

"Ah! loathed Dido, must thow live to sie   685
Thy foes triumph? thy self detained a slave?
Ʒit, if at least before thy flight from me,
My luck had been succession sweet to have;
 If any small Æneas heir did play
 Within this hall, thy face who might bewray,   690

"Those sorrowes then I should not shrink to prove,
Nor vtterly forsaken should I seeme."
Thus clos'd she weeping, but no words culd move
His marble minde, he doth so much esteime
 The Thund'rer's will. With stedfast eyes he stair'd, 695
 And, obstinate, for answere thus prepar'd:

"Deir Queen! (quoth he), I never shall deny
Thy favowres far surmount my meane deserts.
Thy beauty's bountys, and thy loyaltie,
Would ravish with remorce the hardest hearts.   700
 Nor shall I euer cease, (till heavens afford
 My life's last gaspe), thy kindnes to record.

"Those dear delights which I enjoyed of the
No tract of time shall frome my minde remove.
Dear shall thy memory be still to me;   705
Dear the remembrance of Eliza's love;
 And, where so e're remov'd, thow may by right
 Esteime me still thy souldier and thy knight.

"But to the purpose briefly I replie:
As to this end I never heir arived   710
Myself in Hymen's sacred bands to tie,
To be of dearest liberty deprived.
 So, butt thy knowledge, neither did I minde
 To steale from hence, forʒetfull, and vnkinde.

"If heavens and Fortune did assent that I   715
My life, according to my minde, shuld lead,
Demolish't Troy in dust no more should lie,
And Priam's tow'rs should ȝit amazement bread.
    Those hands my native city should restore,
    And raise anone to all her former glore.   720

"To Itally, but now Apollo great,
To Itally the dest'nyes me command.
Their my delight, my countrey, mine estate.
How canst thow my departure thus withstand?
    As thow a stranger dost in Africk stay,   725
    Why may not I to Italy mak way?

"How oft dark night with shadowes overcasts
Earth's low'ring face, and glist'ring starres arise;
Anchises' ghost als oft my soule agasts
With fearfull visions to my sleeping eyes;   730
    Admonishing, with terrour and affright,
    Me to forgoe thy soyle and deirest sight.

"Ascanius als, whom I vnjustly wrong,
By dreames appeareth frustrate of his right,
Keipt from the croune of Italy so long,   735
And fatall bounds; both those steir vp my flight.
    And now wing'd Hermes, sent from Jove to me,
    Commands from hence that I in haste should flie.

"Myself the God within the walls appeare
(Whil as dayes bright beames wer shining) did perceive; 740
His heavenly voyce thir humane ears did heare.
Leaue then, (I pray), dear Queen, those things to crave,
    As may steir vp both the and me to woe.
    To Italy against my will I goe."

Him speaking thus, she, sore perplext in minde,   745
(With greiff in heart and sorrow in her face,
Rolling each where her eyes with lookes vnkinde,
As in amazement), did behold a space.
    Not able more her passion to suppresse,
    Those bitter words, at last, she doth expresse :   750

" Remorceles traitour, whom I held too deare !
Sprung from no parents, but of brutish kinde,
The Paphyen Queen such brood did never beare,
Nor the Anchises gott, O wretch vnkinde !
    But of the hoarse sea wavs, and hardest stane,   755
    Nurst by some Tigresse, thow hast essence taine.

" Why do I longer my designes disguise ?
For what things more should I myself reserve ?
Oh ! how he did my wofull plaints despise,
And stood vnmov'd, whill I for greiff did swarve.   760
    All my regrates and tears, powr'd foorth in vaine,
    From his hard breast one sigh could never straine.

" Ay me ! what shall I first lament (alace)?
Ay me ! where shall my tragoedy begin ?
Let heauens behold my sad afflicted cace,   765
The grievs and woes I am envolved in.
    Let mighty Jove, let Juno from above,
    Look on my wrongs and ill-rewarded love.

" ƺe happy maids, in fredome who enjoy
The dear delights of sacred chastity;   770
Free from the slee deceits of Venus' boy,
Secure frome danger of disloyalty ;
    Who never ƺit have knowne men's perjuries,
    Nor stand in neid of Argus' hundreth eyes ;

"O ȝe, who, (Phœnix like), do live but one;   775
Whose vertew's streame vntrubled still runnes pure;
Frie birds, whom never hand hath seaz't vpon,
From fouler's whisle and deceits secure;
    Frie from love's plague and perillows infection,
    Nor wonne by men, nor vassaills to affection;   780

"O never, never to the oaths giue eare,
Nor truste that impiows and vnfaithfull race,
Who ne're to vs do what they are appeare,
(Perniciows instruments of owr disgrace);
    And whatsomever showe they do pretend,   785
    Nought but owr shame and infamy intend.

"Their vows, their prayers, protestations, teares,
Are all but fain'd to breid in vs compassion.
None minds his oaths, nor meanes the thing he sweares,
ȝit cunningly can conterfitt a passion.   790
    Owr tender hearts with pitty which betraying,
    Works their advantage, and owr sure decaying.

"O then, how of owr favours kinde they boast,
And overcloud with black reproach owr fame!
Thus are owr fortunes mar'd, owr honours lost,   795
By those who ar delighted in owr shame.
    Let Dido's sad experience serve to prove
    Their is no trewth in men, nor trust in love.

"No trust in love, nor trewth in men remaines.
This wretch whom seas had naked cast on shoare,   800
I, (foolish I), prefer'd, who now disdaines
My self, my scepter, and will stay no more;
    Vnmindfull miser whom I did receive,
    And plac'd, as Lord, ov'r me and all I have.

"What furys thus (alace!), incense my breast?   805
Apollo now! now Oracles Divine!
Now heaven's great messenger is thus impesht!
Quhat ells?   Now thund'ring Jove doth thus encline,
        And hath his winged herauld sent to vs!
        It's like enough the gods ar busied thus!   810

"A deep invention, forg'd by fine deceit,
I neither hold it's trew, nor false repells.
Go, cruell, go! to Italy, ingrate!
Go, traitour! where thy dest'nies the compells.
        Go with such joy, such comfort, peace, and rest,   815
        As now thow leaves in my afflicted breast.

"I hope, in midst of furiows rageing seas,
(If heavens with equity behold my wrongs),
Vengeance on the, in presence of thir eyes,
For thy deserts, shall fall, the rocks amongs,   820
        Where Dido, whom thow oft by name shall call,
        With brands of fire thy conscience shall apall.

"And when death's inevitable decree
My body from my better halfe shall parte,
My angry ghost, till I avenged be,   825
Shall the persew each where with armes and airt,
        Nor earth's lowe centre, neither heaven nor hell,
        Shall shield the frome my spight and fury fell."

Ov'rcome with passion, she no more could speak,
But, preassing to eschew his hatefull sight,   830
Excesse of greiff her purpose heir did break,
(Her latest words scarce heard, nor vtt'red right).
        Her vitall powers did faill, her life did faint,
        And death his image in her face did paint.

Thus, sleeping in a traunce, his eyes she fled,   835
And left him, (wofull wight), himself alone,
Full many things prepareing to have said,
And maid reply.   With that her maids anone,
  With ruefull cryes, her frozen corps do bear,
  And her in bed they lay with duilfull chear.   840

But now Æneas, though he much enclined,
(Ov'rcome with greiff, and wounded with remorce),
T' have calm'd the tempest of her troubled minde
With chearfull words, touch't with affection's force ;
  Whil as the tears, which from his eyes did slide,   845
  If seene by her, her rage had mollifi'd ;

Afflicted soule ! what shall he now resolve ?
To heavens and her his duety how discharge ?
A labyrinth of dowbts doth him envolve ;
Pitty withstood what Jove did strictly charge ;   850
  Constraint him led at lenth, with ruefull look,
  Loe ! how of her, his last farewell he took.

Hard hearted lover to thy loyall love !
Could not the sunne-set of those lovely eyes,
(Whil death her senses stopt), to pitty move   855
Thy flinty heart?   O ! so to tyrannize
  Ov'r conquer'd beauty, to thy fame adds soyle :
  The victor seldome leaves behind his spoyle.

Now Trojanes all with earnestnes endevore
Their fleet to loose, and launch into the deepe :   860
Ships, hulks, and galleyes slide along the shore,
And frome the haven with pitched keills do creep.
  Trees ʒit vnshapen, blooming leawes for haste,
  And oakes ʒit floorishing for oares they plac't.

Them, swarming frome the portes, зow might have spyed, 865
All rushing headlongs, hasting from the towne;
As emmets, whil for winter they provide,
Disperst abroad, each running vp and downe,
  An heap of corne do spoyle, and beare away
  To those hid dennes where they intend to stay. 870

Those little troupes marche through the fields butt feare,
And through darne passages their spoyles convoy;
The greatest graine on shoulders some do beare,
With all his might each doth himself employ.
  With earnest repare the paths do seeme to sweate: 875
  So ran the Trojanes to launch foorth their fleate.

What minde, (alace!) then Dido, was to the?
What sense of sorrow? what vnkindly care?
What deep-drawne sighs? when thow, (sad soule), didst see,
(Wak't from thy traunce), such tumult every where. 880
  When all the Ocean seem'd, frome shore to shore,
  With thund'ring noyse into thine eares to rore.

O love! thow tyrant love! what humane wight
Feeles not the force of thy vnbounded ire?
What breathing creature may resist thy might? 885
Thy fierce assaults, thy bowe, thy shafts, thy fire?
  What dost thow not poor mortall's force to trie,
  Subjected once vnto thy tyranny?

Now is she forc't, who late triumph't ov'r love,
Againe to treat, againe to turne to teares; 890
A poore petitioner constrain't to prove,
An humble supplicant to closed eares;
  And least, vntried, she ought had overpast,
  Thus she resolv's to try him зit at last.

"O! Anna! Anna! siest thow now what haste 895
Those impiows traitours mak from hence to saile?
And leaue me loath'd, forsaken, and disgrac't,
Whome death and infamy alike assaile.
 Loe! where their fleet, an happy gayle to finde,
 Doth ly at anchor, waiting on the winde. 900

"If ever such an ocean of annoyes,
A waste abysse, a boundles gulf of greiff,
I could have fear'd should thus have drown'd my joyes,
Those feares afforded might haue my releiff.
 But, (sister), ʒit before my tragick fate, 905
 Go, charg't with teares, this last requeest entreate.

"For, faithles, he to the alone gaue eare,
To the alone his minde he would reveale;
Thow knows his graciows howres, O sister deare;
Thow knows his times, most fitt with him to deale. 910
 Go! I entreat, to my disdainfull foe,
 And those few words from his poore Dido shoe.

"'Gainst him with Graecians I did not conspire,
Nor vow'd at Aulis ancient Troyes disgrace;
Nor sent I navies, armed with sword and fire, 915
To sack his citty, or extirpe his race.
 Anchises' ghost, inter'd, I did not teare.
 Why, why refuses he my words to hear?

"Where hastes he headlongs? whither doth he move?
Nought ells I crave, (O! let him now obey 920
This last request of me his dying love),
Before his flight let heavens their fury lay,
 O! let him stay whil Æol's rage doth last,
 Till Thetys calme, till perill first be past.

" Rejected Hymen, now I crave no more,   925
Nor sues he should forgoe his mindes delight.
Showe him nought ells his Dido doth emplore,
But let him choose a time more fitt for flight.
     A pause to slack my fury I beseach,
     My state to mourne, till me my fortune teach.   930

" This latest fauour, this my last desire,
I humbly plead ; pitty thy sister's state,
And when thow hast obtain'd what I require,
To all my greiffs death shall afforde a date."
     Thus she entreats, thus Anna weeping goes,   935
     And thus with teares Æneas' answere sho'es.

But he, (most cruell tyger), stops his eares,
No pitty can prevale to plead remorce ;
Sighs are despised, no place is found for teares,
Her sutes vnheard, her prayers have no force.   940
     Fates do withstand, great Jove his eares hath charmed,
     And heavens him with an hard'ned heart have armed.

Most like an ancient oake or statly pine,
Which rageing winds impetuously assaile,
And threat the trembling tree to vndermine,   945
On each side striving her from earth t' vphaile,
     With hiddeows noyse which reeling to and froe,
     Now heir now their, still seames to overbloe.

Her branches beatne by the storme resound,
Her heaven-bent bewes must either bow or break,   950
Her straughtest tops are forc't the earth to wound,
But ʒit how much they do themselfs ereck
     To heavens ; als much her rootes reach downe belowe,
     And grips the rocks ; no storme can her ov'rthrowe.

Even so, Æneas, now for flight prepar'd,　　　955
With tears and prayers on each side assail'd,
Though long his minde confus'd with dowbts appear'd,
3it neither pitty, plaints, nor words avail'd ;
　　He stedfast stands, sighes can no favour gaine ;
　　Torrents of teares ar powred foorth in vaine.　　960

THE THIRD BOOKE, CONTAINING ÆNEAS DEPARTURE AND DIDOES TRAGAEDY, &c.

NOW woefull Dido, sad afflicted wight,
 Greiv'd with the Fates' vnflexible decree,
Her heavy soull abhorres the loathed light,
Charg't with affliction and anxietie.
 Heaven's cristall vaults she wearyes more to view, 5
 Resolv't at once to bid the world adiewe.

Whil as on altars she did incense burne,
It seem't she saw, (a monstrows sight to showe),
The liquours black, the wyne in blood to turne,
Presaging her approaching overthrowe. 10
 To none this fearfull vision she reveal'd,
 3ea, even from Anne, she this sight conceal'd.

Ane chappell wals as in the palace plac'd,
Where humbly heavens Sicheus earst ador'd,
Whose marble walls rare artifice had grac'd, 15
With sacred bewes, and fleeces white decor'd.—
 From thence, (whill night earth's face did overcloud),
 It seem'd Sicheus call'd her name aloud.

And als the light-envying owle, alone,
With tragick toones her smarte and sorrow shew, 20
With mourning accents seiming to bemone,
As if she knew some bad mischaunce t' ensue ;
 Then diverse things, which prophets shew of old,
 Her mangled minde with monstrows visions hold.

Her oft, by dreames, Æneas fierce doth chace, 25
Still seaming to be left herself alone,
And vagabounding in ane heavy cace
Through fields vnknowne, accompanyed by none,
    Searching her people, but she none can finde,
    A tediows journey to her wearyed minde : 30

As Pentheus mad, affray't by furyes, seam't
Two Sunnes, two Thebes, both at once to see ;
Or as Orestes in his fancy dream't
His hydra-headed mother he did flie,
    Arm'd all with snakes, and brands of burning fire, 35
    Each place seam't plenisht with revenge and ire.

In guilty conscience having now decreed,
No salue butt death could cure her inward sore,
And with her self on time and forme aggreed,
(Loathing the world, resolv't to liue no more), 40
    This fain'd device, suspicion till eschew,
    Of her designes she to her sister shew.

(Her thoughts disguising with a smiling face,
And hope appearing in her eyes to shine) :
"O Anna, now rejoyce thy sister's cace, 45
For I an way have found by rare engine,
    Which him with me to stay shall either move,
    Or teach me to reclaime from him my love.

"A land theire is, far, far remote from hence,
Which sees the sonne go downe in westerne deeps ; 50
Whose coastes abowt the Ocean doth fence ;
Of Æthiopia the name it keeps ;
    Where Atlas hudge on shoulders strong doth beare,
    And vnderprops heaven's star-embroidred spheare.

I

" A virgin preist by chance of Morish lyne,   55
Expert in magick, hath from thence repair'd,
Who keeps the garden of th' Hesperian tryne,
And feeds the dragon which the frute doth guarde ;
    Mixing with honey, and with liquours sweet,
    The purple poppy which provoketh sleep.   60

" She, by her charmes, can stop affection's source,
And whom she pleases, als can plague with love ;
Torrents ar stayed ; stars retrograde their cowrse ;
Spreits from belowe do at her word remove ;
    Dull earth doth roare, and horribly resound,   65
    And tallest trees do headlongs fall to ground.

" Let heavens and the, deir sister ! bear recorde,
And witnes to the world, against my will,
That I, constrain'd, to magick airts accorde,
And seeks redresse by such vnlawfull skill.   70
    Go thow, ereck in th' inner cowrt in haste
    A fire of wod, vpon the walls hie plac'd.

" Tak syne the sword leaft by this perjur'd wretch,
His cloaths, and als owr haples wedding-bed,
In which I perisht whil I fear'd no bretch :   75
And let those all vpon the flame be laid,
    So that no token vndestroyed may stand
    Which him pertain'd.   Thus doth the priest c̅m̅and."

Heir clois'd she, sighing sore, perplext a space
To stop the currant of her swelling teares ;   So
The crimson dy abandoning her face,
Sad, faint, and pale, she look't, confus't with feares.
    ʒit Anna doubts not that she doth intend
    Thus to disguise her death, and cloak her end.

No rage so great, no fury so extreame, 85
She dreids her sister in her thoughts conceav'd ;
Nor feares now ought more fearfull till haue seene,
Nor when Sicheus was of life bereav'd.
    Wherefore in haste, she, (simple soull), obeyes,
    And, to performe her charge, no more delayes. 90

Ane heap of wod for fire prepair'd at once,
With garlands deckt, and crownd with Cypres bewes.
The Queen her sad misfortunes first bemones,
And with her teares his portrate she bedewes.
    Syne with the bed, sword, cloathes, she layes ye
        same 95
    Vpon the heap, to perish in the flame.

In circles rownd, the altars stand abowt ;
The Priest appearing then with hov'ring haire,
With thund'ring noyse, three hundreth times doth showt
On Fiends and Pharyes thither to repare ; 100
    Conjuring by some charme or magick spell,
    The fowle three headed Hecate from hell.

Then sprinkling waters of the Stygian fount,
They search by night some sucking foale to finde,
And pull the hippom'nes from his tender front, 105
The mother's minde which to the brood doth binde.
    Collecting als, their damned work to speed,
    The milkie poyson of each ven'mowse weed.

The Queen herself before the altars stands,
With one foot bair, her garment loosse vntied, 110
With humble heart, and heaven-erected hands,
Calling to witnes, (now before she dyed),
    Her guilty starres, and all the gods above,
    Of both their partes,—his perjury, her love.

If any pow'r supreme then heavens containe,   115
Or godhead which such lovers doth regarde,
As loves sweit ʒock, and sympathie, do stayne,
And true affection with disdaine regarde,
    With fervent minde, fixing her eyes above,
    To such she prayes, mindfull and just to prove.   120

With mantle dark night now did earth ovrspreed,
Each living soull death's image pale possest.
The savage citiʒens, which life did leed
In wods and waters, all secure did rest.
    Whil as the heavenly torches, burning bright,   125
    The equall half had wasted of their light.

The skailly squadrones of the liquid lakes,
The brutish bands which in the deserts dwell,
Easing their wearyed mindes, sweet slumber takes,
Cares past entombeing in oblivion's cell.   130
    But not so Dido : neither sleep nor ease
    Vpon her self-consuming minde can sease.

Her cares increase, her sorrowes never sleep ;
No night her eyes, no rest her thoughts obtaine ;
Despight, wraith, furie,—each his place doth keip ;   135
No paussing-space her troubled spreit doth gaine.
    But now, inflamed, she burnes in furiows fire,
    Now foorth with freeʒeth in revenge and ire.

"Ah ! shall I ʒit assay, (quoth she), to speak
My scornefull victor, proud of my disgrace ?   140
Shall I with shame my former suters seeke ?
There sew for favour, there entreat for grace
    Where pitty pleaded, I so oft disdain'd ?
    Where mercy beg'd, I ruethles still remain'd ?

"Or shall I follow that ingloriows fleet,   145
Fraughted with falshood, guile, and perjuryes?
As if thy former favours now shuld meet
My discontents, and sad afflictions ease.
        O ȝes! performed pleasures, kindnes past,
        In gratefull mindes lay'd vp so long doth last.   150

"Suppone such thoughts to practise I would prove,
Should any second my desires? alace!
Who would regarde so much my loathed love,
As daigne their stips to render me a place?
        Forsaken soule, too late thow dost repent,   155
        Thow knew Laomedon's perjur'd discent.

"Shall I, alone, my bragging foes persewe,
Or raise my people to revenge and waste?
And so endanger by the seas anew,
Those, present perill who have scarce ov'rpast?   160
        Fy! Dye thyself! such is thy due desert;
        Once let this sword put period to thy smarte.

"Thow, sister, first, thow, by my teares betrayed,
Didst overloade me with this masse of care;
Thow to my foe captiv'd me vnaffrayed;   165
Thow to mine en'mie mad'st me ȝeeld butt feare.
        Ah! might I not have happy liv'd alone,
        And never more the cares of wedlock knowne?

"I needed not thus waste in teares my ȝowth,
With love's misfortunes and afflictions crost,   170
If I had keept inviolate my trueth
To my Sicheus, dear departed ghost."
        Those sad regrates, with all the wofull words
        A troubled soull could ȝeeld, she thus affords.

But, each thing now for present flight prepair'd,   175
Æneas in his schip secure did sleep,
When to his eyes the god againe appear'd,
Such as before, and thus did seame to speak,
      Lyk Mercury in all, in ӡowthfull stature,
    . In golden haires, in speach, in face, in feature :   180

" Fair Venus' issue, canst thow now tak ease,
And pond'rest not thy perillows estate ?
Hath sleep so much o'rcome thy fainting eyes,
That thow regard'st no danger nor deceate ?
      Rests thow secure, whil death doth the invade,   185
      Vnwar what plottes against thy life ar laid ?

" Hear'st thow not how the whisling winds invite the ?
Sweet-breathing Zephyr with a gentle gale
From hence to haiste seames smilingly t'entraite the ;
For death-bent Dido, full of bitter bale,   190
      Transported with a rageing spait of ire,
      'Gainst the is minded both with sword and fire.

" And flyest thow not, whil flye thow may'st in peace ?
The seas anone shall scarce for shipps be seene ;
Thy navy furiows firebrands shall deface,   195
And all the Ocean in one flame shall seeme,
      If fondly thow thy flight frome hence delay,
      Till once Aurora parte the night from day.

" Haist ! haist ! Dispatch with speed ! But more be gone !
A woman wav'ring formed is by nature ;   200
Now bent to love, to hate inclyn'd anone,
In only jnconstancie a constant creature."
      This spoken, he evanisht owt of sight
      In the ayrie essence of the sable night.

Æneas, with this vision dismay'd, 205
Rouz'd vp his sleepy senses ; loud did call :
"Awake, my mates ! too long our flight's delay'd ;
Hoase sayle in haste ! hy to the hatches all !
 The thund'rer great hath sent anone by night,
 His winged messenger into my sight. 210

"Now anchors wey ! now let's owr navy loose !
Trusse vp owr taickling ! cables cut in twaine !
Once let's set fordwart all with one applawse,
Behold, the God admonisheth againe !
 We follow the, O gloriows guide, butt stay, 215
 And thy great charge we gladly all obey.

"Be thow propitiows ! prosper owr designe !
Adjoine thy presence and thine helping might !
Grant that a prosp'rows Planet now may reigne !
Let happy starres arise to guide owr flight !" 220
 This having said, butt more the anchore roape,
 With shyning sword vnsheath't, in twaine he stroake.

One earnestnes then, one fervency to all ;
All headlongs haiste ; one ardowre all retaine ;
They rush, they reele, as heaven and earth did fall, 225
And overspread with sayles the wat'ry plaine.
 On Neptun's back all whyt with foame they ride,
 And ov'r the tumbling billows fast do slide.

Now was the time when as Aurora cleare
Over sad earth her silver mantle spread, 230
And in the Orient blushing did appeare,
Asham't to rise frome aged Tython's bed,
 When watchfull Dido from her palace spy'd
 The Trojane fleet alongst the coast to glyde.

Of shipps, hulks, galleyes, brigandines and barkes,   235
With wings owtstreatch't, all vnder equall saile,
The hudge armado, watching, she remarkes
Through Neptun's empires with ane evenly gale ;
    Whil roaring engines, throwing globes off steele,
    Did thunder foorth an horrible fareweell.   240

Beating her breast with blows, with plaints the aire,
Hope's wings cutt of, she enters in despare,
And renting foorth, (enrage't), her golden haire :
"O Jove," she cries, "who know'st alone my care,
    Thus shall he go?   And must I, in my soyle,   245
    Of such a vagabound receiue this foyle ?

"Thus is he gone?   And shall not armes availl ?
Or shall my subjects all persue the chase
With fire and sword their scornefull shipps to quail?
Fy !   People owt !   Their fleet with flames deface !   250
    Hoase sayle in haste !   Fy, now ȝowr oares employ,
    Sack, wreak, revenge, demolish and destroy !

" Complaints, farewell, which butt bewaill my wrongs,
With armes and arte I will persue to death
This traitour.   Vengeance now to me belongs.   255
In hope alone of sweet revenge I breath.
    In crwelty I will this cruell wight
    Surpas.   No sheild shall saue him frome my spight.

" But what do now prowd words availl, alace ?
Where art thow now thus frome thy self astray,   260
Afflicted Dido?   O how hard thy cace !
What suddaine change doth thus thy minde dismay ?
    Oh how accurst ! how haples is thy fate !
    These threats (alace !) thow vtters now too late.

"Such seem'd the when thy scepter thow didst render,   265
When thus the fortune of thy foe thow rays'd.
Is this his promise?   Is his faith so slender,
Whose piety each where abroad was blaz'd,
    Both to his Gods, and aged parent deare,
    Whome, worne with ʒeirs, on shoulders he did beare? 270

"Ah ! might I not long since have sent to death
This truethles tyrant and his fellowes all?
Ah ! might I not have stop't Ascanius' breath,
And torne his tender flesh in parcells small?
    Then drest him for that traitour false to eate.   275
    To fairse his belly with so kindly meate.

"O that I had their shipps once set on fire,
And ov'rlofts all with flaming firebrands fill'd !
O that thir hands at once both sonne and syre,
And all those traitours cruelly had kill'd !   280
    O, then how gladly should this hand and sword
    In that same moment als my death afford !

"Thow great Apollo, whose bright gloriows ey
With piercing rayes each work on earth doth viewe ;
Thow, Juno, guilty of my misery,   285
Sacred Diana, with thy silver hew,
    Whose triple-horned forhead doth controule
    Skies, earth and hell,—the night's swift moving soule ;

"ʒee heavenly pow'rs, just, bountyfull, divine !
ʒe, in whose safegarde wretch't Eliza lived !   290
And ʒe, O furyes ! O vindictive tryne !
Who venge their wrongs who are vnjustly grieved,
    Pitty my plaints !   O ʒeeld to my desire !
    Vpon those traitours exercise ʒowr ire !

"If so must be this exsecrable wight   295
At heaven's dispose must passe the Stygian tide,
And after death enjoy that wished sight,
Ferry'd by Charon to the farther side,
    Зit grant! O grant, whil flesh his ghost doth wrap,
    Plague, sword and famine, be his surest hap!   300

"Of awfull natiounes let him feele the force,
Frome place to place persu'd, in saifty never.
Exil'd, in neid, butt any man's remorce,
Dissev'red from his only child for ever.
    Imploring pitty, let him none obtaine;   305
    But see his people with dishonour slaine.

"And if he ever peace on earth enjoy,
Short be his reigne; soone may his dayes be spent.
And, whill he breathes, be never butt annoy;
But by vntimely death his powr prevent;   310
    Syne rott on ground butt honour of a grave :
    This I emplore, this with my blood I crave.

"Last, to his linage showe despight and ire,
Deir people whose true love a life I fand!
This latest favoᵣ onely I require,   315
Let never love nor league betwixt зow stand!
    O let mine ashes, after death, afford
    One to destroy those clownes with fire and sword!

"As time and place permitts, both now and ay,
Let discord alwise, and debate domine!   320
Let shoare to shoare, let streame 'gainst streime, I pray,
And let owr ofspring ever armes reteine!"
    Heir closing, deeply she doth now revolve,
    What way she soonest may her life dissolve.

Then calling on Sicheus' aged nurse, 325
(Of purpose only to be left alone),
" Go, Barce ! carefull nurse, direct thy cowrse
To Anna, pray her heir arive anone,
 With waters purg't from each polluted thing,
 Expiatory offrings caws her bring. 330

" And thow, enfold with sacred cloithes thine head ;
The rites intended now I minde to finish
To Stygian Jove, which must afford remead,
Whereby my cares may peice and piece diminish."
 With aged pase, this said, to haste enclin'd, 335
 She stagg'ring foorth did show her fordward minde.

Now deathbent Dido, (trembling fast for feare
Her horrible attemptings to persue,
Rolling her eyes, which bloody did appeare,
And flaming sparkles of her fury showe, 340
 With sorrow-tainted cheiks, and deadly hew),
 Look't pale for horrour of the fact t'ensue.

But quickly ent'ring where the flame was fram'd,
The wodden heap she doth amount anone ;
The haples sword she in her hand retain'd 345
Vnsheath'd, which once pertain'd to him was gone ;
 That cursed blaide, that instrument of death,
 Ordained never to abridge her breath.

Thair whil her eyes, which still butt motion stair'd,
Th' acquainted cowtch and remnant weids did viewe, 350
Paussing, (now vtterly of life despair'd),
With gushing teares her breath a litle d[r]ew ;
 Syne tumbling on the bed, withowt moe words,
 Thir latest speaches she, poore soull, affords :

"O thow sweet vesture! and O happy bed!   355
Whil heavens above and dest'nyes did permitt,
That once, ah! once with ȝow my life I led,
Receive this soull, frome 'me which hence doth flitt,
    This fleshly preson ready now to leave,
    And of all earthly toyles ane end to have.   360

"My glasse is spent; my time I have owt-lived;
The race is runne, which Dest'nyes did designe;
And as the heavens my terme of life contrived,
Swa have I lived, accomplisht in my reigne.
    So now this earthly shaddow goeth to grave;   365
    So now at once this loathed lyf I leave.

"Skie-matching Carthage from the ground I rais'd;
Her staitly walls 1 floorishing did viewe;
My wrath vpon the prowd Pigmalion seas'd,
My lord Sicheus trait'rously who slewe.   370
    Happy, (alace)! too happy had I beene,
    If never Trojane ship my shoare had seene."

With drowping gesture and dejected eye,
"Die shall I," sayes she, "and no vengeance finde?
Butt die thow must, faint Dido, boldly die: 375
Thus, thus my breath I render in the winde.
    Now let the traitour viewe, though not regrate,
    This flame, the presage of my present Fate.

"But oh! ȝit art thow, (feeble flesh), affray'd?
Why trembles thow to be depriv'd of breath?   380
Oh coward hand! and art thow als dismay'd
To be the executioner of Death?
    Though hands, though flesh doth faint, O fearles knife,
    End thow my cares, and cut my threed of life!"

With gushing teares, those words whil as she spak,   385
The cursed blaide but more her purpose brak,
Which in her breast vnto the hilts she strak,
Withowt remorse : O exsecrable fact !
    The wepon, foaming in her luk-warme blood,
    Maide open passage to the gushing flood.   390

Her Dams attending see their mistris fall
On piercing sword, with armes abroad owthrow'ne,
Sprauling in paine, with blood begoared all,
Which freshly from her wonded breast was gone :
    The skreigh is rais'd, with many rewfull cries,   395
    The clamours great reverberat the skies.

Fame through the citty blaz'd her fall anone ;
Anone the streets with those sad newes ar fill'd ;
The women wailing ʒeeld a pitteows mone,
Viewing their Princes and their lady kill'd.   400
    Showts, sighs, smarte, sorow, all each where abound ;
    With hiddeows noyse the hallow hevens resownd.

Most lyk, as by some vnexpected plott,
The rageing en'my ent'red had the citty ;
The bulwarks brave downe batt'red all with shott ;   405
With dint of sword destroying all butt pitty.
    Whate'ere occur'd made objects of their rage,
    Regairdles both of sexe, of ʒowth, of age.

Whil rageing flames of furiows spreiding fire,
The buildings both of gods and men devore :   410
Whil rewfull cries of those who life require,
With dying groanes for pitty who emplore,
    For rewth would rent a flinty heart a sunder :
    Such were the clamoures through the air did thunder.

But Anna, wofull nymph, ran trembling there,   415
Confus'd and speachles, where the noyse was heard.
Faint, breathles, pale, astonisht, full of feare,
To see this rewfull object she appear'd ;
    Then, preissing through the throng, her call'd by name,
    And oft, "Dear Dido! Dido!" did exclame.   420

" Ah sister! wast for this thow sought by slight
To syle my sight, thy curs't designes to cloake?
Ah! wast for this the flame I built on hight?
To this intent or did the altars smoake?
    Ah wretched wight, left now thyself alone !   425
    Forsaken soull ! what shall I first bemone?

" Did ever I demerite such disdaine,
That thow thine Anna hast at death debarr'd
To be thy convoy? to partake thy paine?
And reape with the the fruits of thy reward?   430
    Hast thow despis'd thine only sister thus?
    Such guerdon never was deserv'd of vs.

"O ! since one sword, dy'd in a crimson streame,
Had in one moment both bereft of breath.
But ah! and have thir hands, (O lasting shame !)   435
Prepair'd the flame, as guilty of thy death?
    Call'd I my Gods at altars, prostrate lowe,
    Alace ! ʒit absent at thy last ov'rthrowe.

" Thy self, thy sister, and thy subjects all,
Thy citty, senate, kingdome and estate,   440
Each by one stroak destroy'd, with the do fall,
And perish all by thy abortive Fate."
    This said : her bleeding wounds she bath'd in haist,
    And kyndly her in dying armes embract.

Then seazing on her death-seal'd lipps to knowe 445
If any sponk of breath as 3it remain'd,
The streaming teares her face did overflowe,
Whil as she, clasping in her armes, retain'd
    Her half-dead sister, faintly drawing breath
    In dead-throwe ent'ring at the gates of death. 450

She, feeling in this agony of minde,
(With soft though sad embraces oft bestowd),
Herself in such frequented bounds confin'd,
As mindefull of the favo^r Anna show'd,
    To lift her eyes assay'd, but streight did faill : 455
    Her heart fix't wounds presage a sad farewell.

Then leining on her elbowe, preis'd in vaine,
Thrie times her body from the bed to rayse ;
Three times she fainting tumbles downe againe,
Death on her senses ready now to seaze. 460
    Three times she strove to see the cristall skies,
    And three times clos'd again her gazing eyes.

Then heaven's Arch-empresse from her azure tent,
Viewing this dead-lyve lover's toylsome end,
Her stormy breast compassion did relent, 465
And Iris quickly from the clouds did send
    To calme the combat, and compoise the sight
    Betwix her drossie flesh and ayrie spright.

For sith no dest'ny did abridge her breath,
Nor due deserved death her day prevent ; 470
Both spightfull rage did antidate her death,
And turn'd the Glasse befor her howr was spent.
    Her haires as 3it Proserpine had not touch't,
    Nor by such gift th' Elysian groaves enrich't.

On saffroun pincouns soaring then anone,   475
The winged Iris cutts the cristall skies,
In thowsand colours shining 'gainst the Sunne,
Doth light at lenth where this poore patient lyes :
    Syne off'ring vp her haires at Pluto's shryne,
    "Leave, leave," (quoth she), "this corps, O soule
       divine !"   480

Thus whil she said, with fingers heavenly white
The golden fleece clip't frome her head in haist.
The native heit her limmes abandon'd quite,
Then in ane instant, by cold death displac't,
    Her breath expiring, ane eternall sleep   485
    Did piece and piece vpon her senses creep.

                         Finis.

A

Spirituall Hymne.

or

The Sacrifice of a Sinner
To be offred upon the Altar of a humbled
Heart to Christ our Redeemer.
Inverted in English Sapphicks from the
Latine of that Reverend, Religious,
and Learned Divine, Mr Robert
Boyd of Trochorege

By

SIR · WILLIAM · MVRE.

Y^{o.} of Rowallane, Knight

By whom is also annexed a Poeme entituled

Doomes-Day

Containing Hells horrour
and Heavens happinesse.

Edinburgh
Printed by John Wreittoun, and are to be sold
at his shop a little beneath the Salt Trone
Anno Dom : 1628

K

THE
SACRIFICE
OF A SINNER
TO
CHRIST OUR REDEEMER.

—————◆—————

a Eph. 4. 15.
b Luk. 1. 33.

c Ioh. 1. 16.

CHRIST, of thy Saints the aHead, the bKing,
    Whose bountie's vn-exhausted spring
Doth to thy meanest c members bring
    Eternall streames of grace,
Give mee, (sweet Saviour,) Thee to sing   5
In holy hymnes, with heart condigne,
Which eating age, nor envyes sting
    Shall in no time deface.

d Ioh. 1. 9.

Thou Lord, with glorious beams d all bright,
Blazing around thy Throne of light,   10

e Exod. 33. 20.
1 Tim. 6. 16.

e Outreaching farre my feeble sight,
    Heere, in death's shade exylde,
Sin's clouds dispell, guilt's loade make light,
Which doth surcharge my fainting spright,
That I may spreade thy praise, thy might,   15
    With heart pure, vndefyl'de.

ª Ioh. 4. 24.
"With worship chast, in soule sincere,
  Thou shouldst bee celebrate in feare.

ᵇ Mat. 7. 6.
Hence, yee ᵇ vncleane, that darre appeare
  With hands, with hearts prophaine.   20

ᶜ Esay. 6. 7.
O ! let a ᶜSeraphim draw neare,
  A flamming Coale whose hand doth beare,
  My lips, my heart, from Heauen's high spheare
      to purge from double staine.

Then shall these documents divine,   25
  By which thy crosses fruits do shyne,
  To happie Life conducting Thyne,
      my Thoughts by day, by night,
  With meditation deepe consyne :
  At morne, midday, my weake engyne,   30
  While Heaven's clear Torch his course decline
      shall in thy praise delight.

ᵈ Ioh. 1. 12.
Sonne, with thy Syre in ᵈ yeares, in might,
ᵉ Phil. 26. 15.
ᶠ Ro. 11. 33.
ᵍ Heb. 1. 3.
   Col. 1. 6-67.
In all ᵉ co-equall : ᶠman's dimme sight
  Transcending : ᵍ like thy paterne bright   35
      An Other, and the Same :
ʰ Matt. 1. 16. 1.
   Gen. 28. 11.
True God of God, mild ʰMaid-borne wight,
  Blest ⁱLadder, reaching earth aright,
  Co-apting things of greatest hight
      with lowe : Light's glorious beame.   40

Safetie of Soules, Sight of the blinde,
  Haven, where the shipwrakt shelter finde,
  End of all toyles, Ease of the minde,
      press'd downe with sinfull loade ;
  Reward of works due in no kinde   45
  To conflict past, the Palme assignde,
  Soules' cure, with sin's sore sicknesse pynde,
      the banisht man's aboade.

a Gen. 9. 14.

Blest ^abow, bepaynting azure aire,
Thy pledge who did the World repaire;   50

b Gen. 6. 14.

^bArke, rendring Thine secure from care
     of ouerflowing floods;
Their Crowne that sight, their pryze most rare
That sum: earth's peace, heauen's joy, hell's feare;

c 1 Cor. 10. 4.
d 1 Cor. 12. 3.

A saving ^cRock to thine, a ^dsnare   55
     to such as sinne secludes.

e Luc. 2. 32.
f Luc. 10.

^eIsrael's glory, ^fGentiles' light,
Summe of the father's wisht-for sight,
Of Paradise the deare delight,
     eternall Tree of life;   60
On source which watering day and night,
In foure cleare streames divided right,
Preserues, from yeares, from dayes despight,
     but arte, or gardner's knife.

g Rom. 10. 4.
h Act. 10. 40.
i 2 Cor. 3. 14.
k Col. 2. 17.
l Io. 1. 36.
m Heb. 13. 10.
n Heb. 2. 17.
o Rev. 13. 8.

The ^gLawes, the ^hProphet's scope, who shew   65
Thy face when Thou the ⁱvaile withdrew;
Of Types, of ^kShads, the body true;
     ^lLambe, ^mAltar, ⁿPriest at ones;
^oLambe, kild before the World's first view;
Altar, which sinne inherent slew;   70
Priest, who in man did grace renew,

p Heb. 9. 24.

     mounting alone ^pheauen's Thrones.

q Heb. 9. 15.

I sing my ^qMediator's praise,
Whose hand o're all the scepter swayes;

r Col. 1. 20.

Who ^rAngel's fall did stint, yet stayes;   75

s 1 Cor. 1. 30.

     ^sman falne did raise againe.
Who filde the breach by wondrous wayes
Of Heauen's proud Apostats, hell's preyes,
Earthlings adornde with Angells' rayes,
     'mongst the immortall traine: 80

But say, (sweet Iesu,) what procurde
ᵃ Phil. 2. 7. Thee, in a ᵃservant's shape immurde,
To pittie man in sinne obdurde,
　　God's rebell to beefriend?
To pleade for him who thee abjurde,   85
Suffring thy Godhead lurke obscurde,
ᵇ Phil. 2. 8. Last, on the ᵇTree, (O Tears!) indurde
　　an ignominious end?

ᶜ Tim. 1. 15. ᶜ Else perisht had the World for aye,
ᵈ Col. 1. 20. ᵈ No other Meanes God's wrath could lay,   90
ᵉ Rom. 6. 4. ᵉ None else, could, (working death's decay,)
　　Man's Image first, infuse.
ᶠ Gal. 3. 13. ᶠ None else, Law's paine severe could pay;
Heauen's walls to scale no other way;
ᵍ Rom. 8. 11. ᵍ To vernish fresh graues rotten prey,   95
　　Means Thou alone couldst vse.

Without thee Lord, supremely blest,
ʰ Phil. 2. 9, 10, 11. ʰ Whom highest honour doth invest,
ⁱ Esay 53. 7, 10. ⁱ For Man with paines extremly prest
　　by spoyles of conquer'd Hell,   100
Heaven's glorious courts had neere encrest:
Nor should our fleshes loade, to rest
Aboue the Spheares, its selfe addrest,
　　'midst heauen's blest hosts to dwell.

Hence sprang Man's ease exyling toyle,   105
His hopelesse groanes, which so did boyle
Thy breast, that Thou pourd'st in the oyle
　　of Mercie in his wounds.
ᵏ Esay. 53. ᵏ His Plaints procur'd thy soules turmoyle,
That Thou his lot didst take, to foyle   110
Sinne, Death and Hell, O Glorious spoyle!
　　which reason's ray confounds.

Our guilt's foule shame shame did deface,
Empurp'ring thy vnstained face ;
Thy clouds, thy care, our light, our peace,   115
    Our Victorie thy listes ;
Thy hels in heauen procurde vs place,
Our honour grew by thy disgrace ;
O Wisedome ! if not found by grace,
    Man's wit involves in mists.   120

O Sauing Knowledge ! which of right
[a] The deepest Polititan's sight
Oresyles, drownde in eternall night,
    Jn clowdes of self-conceate !
O contrares ! which by nature fight,   125
Thus reconcil'de, mix'd by thy might,
Things weightie ballancing with light,
    O change ! O wonders great !

Thy dumpes our doolefull hearts did cheare ;
Our teare-blind sights thy teares did cleare ;   130
Thy deepe afflictions calmde our feare ;
    Thy bands vs fred from paine.
[b] Thy wants our wealth procur'de ; we weare
Roabs by thy rags ; grieves thou didst beare,
Our greifes, our languishings en-deare,   135
    thy blood did ours restraine.

[c] That crimson sweat, these drops which drownd
Thy blessed face, with rayes ours crownde ;
[d] Sin's leprous spots, which soules confound,
    from Parents' seede they purgde.   140
Thou, shak'd by death's approaching wound,
'gainst death mad'st vs secure be found,
Thou of our innocence the ground,
    for vs, with guilt was vrgde.

[a] 1 Cor. 1. 21.

[b] 2 Cor. 8. 9.

[c] Luc. 2. 44.

[d] Rev. 5.

a Mat. 27. 46.
^aAnd when thou seemde some space to bee   145
Depriv'de from heauen of all supplie,
Yet banisht Man, still deare to Thee,
        Thou neuer didst forsake.
Man's state was still before thine Eye,
Till entring Hell, Thou sett him free,   150

b Deut. 23.
O ^bCrosse once curst, now happie Tree,
        Source whence all good wee take !

When Thou thy selfe triumphde o're sho's,
Nailde to the Crosse, exposde to blo's,
Chargde by thy proud insulting foes   155
        with infamie, with shame ;
Torne, naked, pale, a mappe of woes,
Whilst floods of wrath thou vndergoes,
Thy syde trans-fixde, from which forth floes

c Ioh. 19. 34.
        a ^cdouble gushing streame ;   160

d Luk. 23. 46.
^dThy soule commending to thy Syre,
e Luk. 23. 39.
While twixt two ^eTheeues Thou didst expire ;
f Col. 2. 15.
^fLoe ! then enlarging thine Jmpire,
        Thy foes Thou Captiues led ;
Triumphing on the Tree, hell's ire,   165
g Hos. 13. 14.
^gDeath's sting, Earth's Kings that did conspire,
Bound, hand and foote, thy wrath's hote fyre
        their shame before Thee bred.

Thou ledst, (great Victor,) foylde in fight,
h Hab. 2. 14.
Those ^hbands, in darknesse that delight ;   170
Roots of man's ruine, foes to right,
i Rom. 8. 2.
        ⁱSin, bound Thou didst detaine ;
To Heauen's high courtes, a glorious sight,
God's Rebells vanquishde by thy might,
Condemnde in chains of horride night,   175
        for euer to remaine.

a 1 Cor. 15. 26. Loe ! heere, death's ªdouble-poynted sting,
b 1 Cor. 15. 56. ᵇLaw's hand-writ there traverst, (death's spring,)
Trode vnderfoote, in triumph, bring
c Col. 2. 14.   Thou didst, ᶜnail'd to thy crosse.   180
Thee, swallowing vp, (death conqu'ring King,)
d 1 Cor. 15. 55. ᵈDeath to it selfe the graue did bring ;
On rav'ning Wolfe preyde ravishde thing,
    Victorious by losse.

By death insulting held as dead,   185
Death's death Thou was, and death's remeed.
e Iohn 1. 18. ᵉO ! Thou who dost God's secreets spread,
    Author, revealer wise,
Heauen's pure delight, the woman's seede,
f Gen. 3. 15. Who, ᶠtreading downe the Serpent's head,   190
To wretched Man didst pittie plead,
    Way, leading to the Skyes !

Oh, what had beene our fearefull fate,
Deare soules Redeemer? what our state?
Of ire what hudge, inunding spaite,   195
    had quenchde our of-spring weake?
Without thee, Lord, hell's preys of late,
g Col. 1. 1. ᵍWho mongst thy saints didst vs relate,
And mounting heauens with glorie great,
    deathes brazen barres didst breake?   200

Who saues vs in the day of ire,
When all shall be refinde with fire?
Who with thy Sp'rit dost vs inspire,
h 2 Cor. 5. 5.   ʰ Arls of eternall Life?
Eph. 1. 13, 14. Thy Sᴘ'ʀɪᴛ of peace, our pledge, our hyre,   205
Who, all vnites of thy empire
To Thee, our Head, our soules desire,
    for ever shunning strife.

His seuen-fold grace doth vs defend
From snares; the World, the flesh forth send;   210
From Fiends infernall, which doe bend
 theirs pow'rs 'gainst Thine, by night;
Which flie like ^apestes by day; in end
On winges, with faith and hope empen'd,
Heauen's starrie circuits wee transcend,   215
 by vertue of his might.

Hee, who eternallie foorth came,
With Father and with Sonne, the Same
Third ^bbranch, joynd with that twofold stream,
 ^cwitnesse on earth to beare :   220
By him confirmde, wee ^daccesse claime
To God's hie Throne : with feare and shame
Brought low, by him wee doe proclaime,
 ^e*Abba*, O Father deare !

^fHe, sending vp a secreet grone,   225
Doth penetrat God's eares anone ;
No wordes, no cryes can reach his throne,
 nor speedier pierce the skies :
He doth vnsyle the eyes alone
Of soules sincere, to them is showne   230
The lawes hid sense : Hee doth enthrone
 the lowe ; the proud despise.

Soules languishing his grace revives ;
To wandring steps hee regresse gives ;
The falne liftes vp, deathes throe's relieues,   235
 by warme light of his flame.
The hardest heart of flint he reaues ;
For subjects, Rebells home receiues ;
Subdues the stubburne, that believes
 no hardnesse breedes him shame.   240

^a Psal. 91. 5, 6.
1 Ioh. 5. 8.
c Rom. 8. 16.
d Eph. 2. 18.
e Rom. 8. 15.
f Rom. 8. 26.

Ev'n as perfumes, which most excell,
Worke on weake sents, and doe dispell
All former loathings : So befell
    Thy Saints, the Virgines deare :

ᵃ How soone thy Name's sweet fragrant smell   245
Was powred foorth, all prostrate fell,
Who gainst Thee did before rebell,
    Thy yoke now gladly beare.

ᵃ Cant. 1. 23.

O ! let this dewy showre descend,
Of thy sweet Oyle, that We in end   250
That Rocke of safetie may ascend
    admitting no retreat.
Conduct vs who on thee depend,
(ᵇLife-giuing essence,) vs defend,
Who here our days in dangers spend,   255
    which vs each moment meete.

ᵇ Col. 3. 4.

Lead vs, poore Pilgrims vnexpert,
Our Compasse, Pilote, Pole, who art,
Through this inhospitall desert,
    this vaile of bitter teares,   260
Where perill lurkes in euerie part,
Where Asps their poys'nous stings forth dart,
Whose plaines no pleasures else impart,
    but scrotching drought and feares.

ᶜ Lead vs, those rivers to frequent,   265
Where milke and honey yeelds content.
O ! euer blesse, with good event,
    the wrestlings of thine owne,
Till, comming in the firmament,
Unlookt for by earth's trembling tent,   270
When time's last ᵈPeriod shall bee spent,
    Thy glory thou make knowne.

Esay. 55. 1.

ᵈ Rev. 10. 16.

ᵃ Rev. 6. 14.
That Day shall rest ᵃ Heauen's rolling spheares,
Earth's refluous tumults, deathes pale feares,
ᵇ Rev. 22. 5.
ᵇO day, which neuer night outweares,   275
  Night, by no day displac't !
Then, to the source flood's course reteires,
Time lurking then, no more appears,
Hid in the vast abysse of yeares,
  from whence it first did haste.   280

ᶜ Rev. 21. 4.
ᶜO day, which doth all blesse impart
To all, who vpright are in heart !
ᵈ Rev. 21. 8.
ᵈO day of horrour, full of smart,
  to all of sprite impure !
ᵉ Rev. 21. 4.
ᵉDay, which shall sobs of saints convert   285
In songes of Joy !   Day which shall dart
Wrath on the wretcht, who then shall start
  wak'd from their sleepe secure !

ᶠ Mat. 24. 31.
ᶠThat Trumpet's terrifying sound,
That day, their ears, their souls, shall wound,   290
In sin's deepe Lethargie long drownde,
  to heare a fearefull doome ;
Whose noise, whose murmurings profound
Shall call, whate're earth's limits bound,
ᵍ Rev. 20. 13.
ᵍOr who in floods o'rewhelmde are found,   295
  hid in the Ocean's wombe.

ʰ Thess. 4. 16. 17. ʰWho cheard are with the World's bright Eye,
Jnvest'd yet with mortalitie,
Or whose dead ashes scattered flie,
  dispersde through earth or aire ;   300
This dayes sharpe tryall all must see,
If entered once lifes miserie,
Yea, babes, which scarce yet breathing bee,
  must at this sound appeare.

a 2 Thes. 1. 8.
aWhen flammes shall furiously confound,   305
Lightning thy glorious Throne around,
Whate're shall bee their object found,
   in this inferiour Frame,
Shaking the World, ev'n to the ground,
Razde from its center, laid profound,   310
Dissolving what earth's fabricke crownde
   with greatest Arte, or fame ;

b Mark 13. 24.
bThe Sun's cleare beames clouds shall enfold,
c Rev. 6. 13.
cStarres losse their light, (earth's pride controld,)
What Earthlings did most precious hold,   315
d 2 Pet. 3. 10.
drecords of wit, of strength,
e 2 Pet. 3. 10.
eShall with this monument's rare mold
More quicklie melt than can bee told,
All this great All shall, (as of old,)
   a Chaos turne at length.   320

f Esay. 19. 20.
fThen when the screiches, and frightfull cryes
Or such, God's wrath as vnderlyes,
Encrease the noise of rushing skies,
   of earthes disjoynted frame,
g Mat. 25. 22.
gHee makes divorce that's only wise ;   325
The damned goates hee doth despise ;
h Rev. 7. 14.
Poynts out his lambes, hwhose sinfull dyes
   hee purgde with bloody streame.

i Rev. 7. 9.
iWhen blessed soules shall, fred of feare,
Thy Throne encircling, Thee draw neare,   330
As dayes comforting Beame, the spheare,
   the Orbe of purest heauen ;
k Rev. 11. 12.
The clouds transcending, kshining cleare,
l Rev. 14. 14.
lThy footsteps streatched foorth to beare,
Those trembling bands shall streight reteare,   335
   downe to the Center driven.

Trembling to heare the thundring noise
Of thy three-forked fearefull voyce,
Which streight their soules with sad annoyes,
    with terrours strange shall pierce :   340
ᵃMat. 25. 41.   ᵃHence, hence yee cursed ! hell's convoyes,
Who of this Portion earst made choyse,
In chaines of darknesse end your Joyes,
    amidst hell's furyes fierce.

Goe curst for aye, exylde from light,   345
ᵇRev. 14. 12. From hope, from ᵇrest, from all delight,
Where wormes ne're dying, wrath and spight,
ᶜMatt. 25. 20.   ᶜgnashing of teeth, and teares.
O ! then, what horrour, what affright
Shall on those hopelesse prisners light,   350
Debarrde eternally his sight
    who on the Throne appeares.

ᵈRev. 5. 9. ᵈDeare World's Redeemer ! let thy bloode,
Mee, from this multitude seclude,
Affraide to see the raging flood,   355
    of thy vnbounded ire :
ᵉMatt. 5. 8. Grant J may 'mongst thy ᵉblessed broode
Surfet vpon that heauenly foode
Of thy sweet face ; the chiefest goode
    Thyne haue, or can desire.   360

That life which did thy bandes releiue,
ᶠRom. 8. 11. When laide in graue, ᶠmay mee revive,
Raisde from deathes Jayle with thee to liue,
    eternally above,
Joyes more than mortalls can belieue,   365
Contents, which thou alone canst giue,
Hid treasures, which no wrong can reave,
    enjoying of thy loue.

Cloyde with delights, with dainties rare
With which heauen's tables charged are, 370
1 Cor. 2. 9.   ^aWhich man's weake Eye, amazed Eare
    nor Heart, can right conceaue,
Things hid by his eternall care,
Who doth them for his Saintes prepare,
Who, gaining him, the fairest faire, 375
    they All in all things have.

^b 1 Cor. 15. 24.   ^bWhen conquring life hath death subdued,
^c Rev. 21. 1.   This World's false ^cshew our sight eschued,
Whose face and countenance renewde
    shall more delightfull seeme, 380
Thou, who with grace thy Saintes indued,
Whose shield them from this wrath rescued,
Transport mee thither, all bedewed
    with blood did mee redeeme.

^d Rev. 22. 16.   ^dBright Starre—illightning darkest night, 385
Attractive loadstone, full of might,
Jnflamt by thy transpeircing sight,
    there draw my heatlesse heart;
Winge my desires, that raisde on hight,
^e Rev. 21. 4.   ^eI may arriue by heauenly flight 390
There, where's no feare of ill, no spight,
    but blesse, without desart.

Where J, thy praises may make knowne,
Three vndivided Trinall One!
Joynde with thy Saynts about thy Throne, 395
    in hymnes not made by Men.
Grant this sweet Sauiour, Thou alone
Crowne these desires, here to Thee showne,
As to its end this raptur's flowne,
    Sweet Jesu, say Amen. 400

Μȣνῶ δοξα θεῶ.

Finis.

Doomesday

containing

Hells horrour and Heavens happinesse

By

S^{R.} WILLIAM MVRE

Yo: of Rowallane Knight.

1628

DOOMESDAY

CONTAINING

HELLS HORROUR AND HEAVENS HAPPINESSE

BY

Sᴿ· WILLIAM MVRE
Yo: of Rowallane Knight.

———•———

B UT now, my Sprite refresht a space,
  Forbearing pressed steppes to trace,
Aspires aboue the vulgar prease,
  to raise a second flight.
I feele my bosome, peece and peece,   5
Warmde with vnusuall flammes : Giue place
Eare-charming fancies, Artes disgrace,
  affoording false delight.

Thoughts, which aboue the spheares inclyne,
Wings, furnish to my weake engine,   10
ᵃ 2 Sam. 22. If Thou, O Lord, the ᵃHorne of Thine
3.   in mee, this Rapture wrought.
Bee present by thy power divine,
Grant in my lines thy might may shyne,
From drosse of sinne my sprite refine,   15
  raise from the earth my thought.

But why thus pants thou in my breast
Affrighted soule, deprivde of rest ?
What sudden feares thy joyes molest ?
    what jarres disturbe thy peace ?   20
Why tremblest thou, with terrours prest,
To heare that fearefull doome exprest
By that great Judge, who euer blest,
    is just, as full of grace ?

Heere pause a space, (My Soule,) acquent   25
Thy selfe this judgement to prevent :
No moment of our time is spent,
    which thither doth not lead.
The dangers seene which doe torment
Thy troubled mind with discontent,   30
Gainst them let fervent sutes be sent,
    Immunitie to plead.

Haste, haste my Soule, shake off delay,
Which too much of thy time makes prey.
Lay vp provision for that Day   35
    there boldlie to arriue,
Where Reprobats, accurst for aye,
Shall wish in vaine their lifes decay,
That earth would to their soules make way,
    them swallowing vp aliue.   40

Oh ! what encounter sad shall bee
Twixt soules from darknesse chaines set free,
And bodies, mates in miserie,
    calde foorth to bee combynd,
Not for reciprocall supplie,   45
As friends new joynde in amitie,
But neuer dying, aye to die,
    in quenchlesse flammes confynde.

Death's loathsome den, detested Jayle,
Scout, following sin with stretched sayle,   50
Which fleeting froaths, which pleasures fraile,
    on Rocke of shipwrack led.
Maske of mischiefe, sin's slender vaile,
Good Motions euer bent to quaile,
Which in the birth thou didst assaile,   55
    them burying as they bred.

Wretch, who to pamper dust didst doate,
Whom Hell attends with open throate,
Readie to retribute the lote
    to thy deservings due.   60
Oh ! what hath violate death's knot,
That still in graue thou didst not rot,
Masse overspred with sin's foule spot,
    raisde anguish to renue.

Thus, (too, too late,) the Soule shall rayle ;   65
Re-entring this abhorred Iayle,
Which recombyned, while both bevaile
    Life's misgoverned raines.
Then Angels shall to Judgement haile,
There, whence no party can appeale,   70
To heare deathe's sentence countervaile,
    Lyfe's Ioyes, with endlesse paines.

O wretch ! who Judgement heere delayes,
Whom false securitie betrayes,
Who ne're thy Sins' blacke summe surveyes,   75
    which future anguish breedes.
Then shall the Auncient of dayes,
Who all men's works in ballance layes,
Examine all thy wordes, thy wayes,
    thy thoughts, thy foule misdeeds.   80

None shall this search seuere eschew,
From bookes laide open to the view
A summar processe shall ensew,
    conforme to thy trespasse.
Thy sins all summond, Thee which slew,   85
Approving thy damnation due,
When all the blest cœlestiall crew
    shall on thee verdict passe.

Thou, who to lewdnesse now art prone,
What shame, what smart, (lif's pleasures gone,)   90
Shall on thee seaze, when gazde vpon
    By earth, by angrie heauen?
When naked, comfortlesse, alone,
Thou trembling stands before the Throne,
Under God's wrath, guilt's loade doth grone,   95
    Feares with thy faults made eauen.

When thy tormenting conscience torne,
Thou guiltie stands that Iudge beforne,
Whose Image did thy soule adorne,
    who did infuse thy breath.   100
Who, pittying thee to sin forlorne,
Left heauens, was of an earthling borne,
Liude loth'd, dyde with contempt and scorne,
    Emptyed the Cup of wrath.

Witnesse earth trembling at his paines,   105
Dayes beame, which all in clouds detaines,
The silver Moone, which pale remaines,
    For horrour of the sight.
Witnesse his hands, with bleeding veines,
Of this great All which holds the raines,   110
His side pierc't through to purge thy staines,
    Polluted sinfull wight.

Where shall thou then safe shelter finde
Soule, than the sightlesse Mole more blinde,
When with those straits extreame confynd,   115
    Faint, pale, confusde thou stands?
By doome which cannot bee declinde,
Adjugde for euer to be pinde,
Where day nere dawnde, Sunne neuer shinde,
    Mongst the infernall bands.   120

Where tears no truce, playnts find no place,
On either hand in desp'rate cace,
Behinde thee, who thy pathes did trace,
    Attend thy woefull lote.
Before thee, flamms Earth's frame deface,   125
Aboue, an angrie Judge's face,
Below, Thee gaping to embrace,
    Hell's sulphure-smoking throat.

Thy feares shall be with cryes encrest
Of damned Soules, with anguish prest,   130
With greife, with horrour vnexprest,
    Of due deserved ire.
The fyre-brands of a conscious brest,
Shall of thy terrours not be least,
While worms, which on thy conscience feast,   135
    Thy ceaselesse paine conspire.

But when, (most like a thunder dart,)
[a] Mat. 25.   That separating doome, [a]*Depart*,
41.   Pronounc'd, shall pierce thy panting heart,
    With a most fearefull knell,   140
Which shall thee from God's presence part,
Exposde to torments that impart
Nor end of time, nor ease of smart,
    While headlongs hurld in hell.

Their shalt thou dive in depthes profound,   145
Still sinke but never meete a ground,
In waves still wrestling to bee drownd,
    Deluded still by death ;
Crying, where comfort none is found,
Pynde, where no pittie rage doth bound,   150
Thy Cup with floods of vengeance crownde,
    Of the Almightie's wrath ;

Bathde in a bottomlesse abisse,
Paine still encressing, ne're remisse,
Where scorpion's sting, where serpent's hisse,   155
    Wormes, neuer satiate, gnaw ;
Rackt, thinking what thou was, now is,
Deprivde for aye from hope of blisse,
For toyes, eternall joy didst misse,
    Nor crub't by love, nor aw,   160

Paine of
Sense. No torments doth it selfe extend
Heere all the members to offend,
Which Vniversall griefe doth send,
    Doth every part entrinch :
These paines, which reason's reach transcend,   165
On Soule and body doth descend,
No joynt, nerve, muscle, without end
    But sev'rall plagues doe pinch.

Lascivious Eye, with objects light
Which earst did entertaine thy sight,   170
Weepe, there exylde in endlesse night,
    Lockt vp in horride shads.
Nyce Eare, whose Organ earst did spight
All sounds, whence flowde no fals delight,
There, horrour ever and affright,   175
    Thy curious sense vpbraids.

Smell, earst with rare perfumes acquent,
Still interchangde to please thy sent,
For incense, sulphure, (there) doth vent,
    Smoake for thy odoures sweet.   180
Taste, vnto which to breed content,
Rob't were the Earth, Sea, Firmament,
'Mongst soules which penurie torment,
    There, famine Thee doth meete.

Vile wormeling, Thou whose tender pride,   185
The weakest sunshine scarce couldst byde,
There, plungde in this impetuous tyde,
    Must feele the force of fire.
Where damned soules on every syde,
Howling and roaring still abyde,   190
Which finde no shelter them to hyde
    From this eternall ire.

There, the Ambitious, who in skies
Did, (late,) on wax-joynde winges arise,
Of base contempt is made the pryse,   195
    The Proudling pestred downe.
There *Dives*, who did earst despise
Of famisht soules the piercing cries,
Shall one cold drop of water pryse
    Aboue a Monarche's crowne.   200

Loe! there the vile, licentious goate,
Whom lawlesse lust did earst besotte,
Enchainde in the embracements hotte
    Of furious raging flames.
There, to the drunkard's parched throate,   205
Justice doth scrotching drought allote,
In floods of fire, which judgde to floate,
    Still vaine refreshment claimes.

On covetous, on cruell wight,
Shall equall weight of vengeance light   210
With byting vsurie, with spight,
    The poore ones who did presse.
So, to the remnant that did fight
'Gainst heauen's decrees, their conscience light,
God's wrath shall bee proportionde right,   215
    By measure more or lesse.

Soule, which vnpittied euer playnes,
Heere, suff'ring for thy sins' foule staynes,
Flammes, lashing whips, rackes, fyrie chaynes,
    Tormenting outward sense.   220

Paine of
Losse.

Of all, most terrible remaines,
Losse of God's face while thou sustaines,
O hell of hell! O paine of paines!
    Still to be banisht thence.

But when thou hast as many yeares   225
Those tortures felt, as shyne in sphears
Lights, fixed and straying, eyes haue teares,
    Or waves the azure plaine,
No nearer are their end those feares,
Ever beginning which thou beares,   230
No change abates, no date outweares
    Thy euer pinching paine.

O dying life! O living death!
O stinging fyre, blowne by God's breath!
O boyling lake no ground which hath,   235
    Destroying nought it burnes!
O overflowing flood of wrath,
Which damned soules are drencht beneath!
O pit profound! O woefull path
    Whence Entrer ne're returnes!   240

a Rom. 5. 10. Sweet ^aReconciler, Prince of peace,
Who pittying man's most wretched cace,
Didst hellish agonies embrace
    In soule, in bodie shame,
Let mee in those extreames finde grace,   245
Illightned by thy glorious face,
Rank't 'mongst thy Saints, the elect race,
    Whose wayes Thou didst proclaime!

O ! Let me safe protection plead
Unto my soule, which full of dread,   250
Hanges ouer Hell by life's fraile threed,
    Conservde but by thy might ;
That when heauens, whence it did proceed,
Its separation haue decreed,
b Gen. 8. 8. With ^b*Noah's* Doue, Thou mayst it lead   255
    There, whence it first tooke flight.

Oh, how it longes on winges to rise,
(Secure from sin's contagious dyes,)
Endenizde citizen of skies
    With Thee for aye to rest !   260
O, how it doth the Jayle despise,
In fleshes fetters it which tyes,
And lets it to enjoy the pryse,
    With which thy Saints are blest !

For Thee I thirst, O living spring !   265
Pure source of life, who guides faith's wing.
By flight to reach the hyest thing,
    To compasse things most hard.
When shalt Thou mee from danger bring
To Port of peace ? my God ! my King !   270
Blest giver, and the gifted thing ?
    Rewarder, and reward ?

When shall I, from exile set free,
My native home, my country see?
When one immortal pineons flie?   275
    That holy Citie reach,
Whose streets pure gold, gold buildings bee,
Apoc. 19. 21. Walls, stones most precious beautifie,
Ports, solide Pearles, Guests neuer die,
    Whose peace no paines empeach?   280

Eternall spring, (shrill Winter gone,)
This climate constant makes alone,
Nor flamming heate, nor frozen Zone
    Distemper heere doe breed.
From Lambe's sweet breath, on glorie's throne   285
Enstalde, are balmie odours throwne,
Time hath no turnes, heere change is none,
    No seasons doe succeed.

Pale envy, emulation, spight,
Nor death, nor danger heere affright,   290
Heere hopes, nor feares, nor false delight,
Apoc. 21. 23.   In sublunarie toyes.
No Lampe dartes foorth alternat light,
The Lambe's sweet face here shines ay bright,
Which of the Saints doth blesse the sight,   295
    Who doe in him rejoyse.

Heere simple beautie scorneth Arte,
Rose-cheeked youth, old age's dart,
Joye's perpetuitie impart,
    No warre disturbs this peace.   300
O! this God's Palace royall arte,
1 Pet. 1. 20. Preparde in these, with all desart,
For all that vpright are in heart,
    Ere light did paynt heaven's face.

Thou, by whose pow're the spheares are rold,   305
Earth's hanging orbe who dost vphold,
Great Architect, King vncontrold,
    Lord of this Universe,
Enstalde heere on a Throne of gold,
Dost diamantine scepter hold,   310
Givest Lawes to earth, hence dost behold
    How wights below converse !

If heere, such eye-enchaunting sights,
Amazing beauties, choise delights,
This Mansion low, of dying wights,   315
    Earth's brittle orbe adorne,
What wonders then, what glorious lights,
Must beautifie those reachlesse hights,
Thy blest aboade, which daye's, which night's
    Vicissitude doth scorne?   320

If these such admiration breed,
What Thou, who did'st heauen's Curtain spread,
Earth stayde midst aire, that it doth neede
    Its weight nought to sustaine,
Who full of Majestie and dread,   325
Of intellectuall pow'rs dost plead
Attendance, on thy face which feede?
    O ever blessed traine !

Archangels, Angels, clothde with might,
Thrones, Cherubs, Seraphins of light,   330
Princes and Powers all shining bright,
    Dominions, vertues pure,
With beames that sparkle from the sight,
Inflamde, which flie no other flight,
But satiat rest, rapt with delight,   335
    Which doth for aye endure !

O sweet societie ! how blest
They, who these orders haue encreast,
From labour free, in peace who rest,
    Surpassing humane sense ?   340
Where blesse, where glory doth invest
Apostles, Martyres and the rest
Of holy Saints, with tortures prest
    To death, in Trueth's defence.

The Patriarchs, Prophets, Lights divine,   345
(Cleare starres on earth,) bright suns here shine.
Heere all the elect hoast, deathe's line
    Which yet haue ouerpast.
Jncorp'rat in their Head, incline
One way, Joyes common all combine,   350
This band no discord can vntwine,
    Loue doth eternall last.

1 Cor. 4. 6. Of glorie 'mongst these bands elect
Degrees there are, but no defect,
Full vessells all, none can expect   355
Dan. 12. 3.   More than the lest containes.
Man's heart no pleasure can project,
But greater doth from hence reflect,
One cause in all workes one effect,
    Of measure none complaines.   360

O Joyes ! my drossie sprite which wing
Upwards, aboue the spheares to spring,
(Time's Father) where thy praises ring,
    Which Saints, which Angels raise :
Apoc. 9. 1. Where all around Thee in a ring,   365
Heau'ns hoasts high Allelujahs sing,
O heavenly consort ! Blessed King !
    Blest people, Thee who praise !

No woefull earth-confined wight,
With owlish eyes can view this light, 370
The meake horizon of Man's sight,
    Farre, farre which doth outreach.
This vnexpressible delight,
Doth reason's dazelde eye benight,
What I cannot conceiue aright, 375
    Lord, let experience teach !

Give mee, that in some measure small
(While fleshe's bands my sprite enthrall)
J may, a farre, a glance let fall,
    At these contentments poynt, 380
These termlesse Joyes which, (one day,) shall
In honny turne Saints' bitter gall,
From guilt, when flamms shall purge this Ball,
    This Engine hudge disjoynt.

1 Cor. 15. 52. When the Arch-angel's voice shall raise 385
The graues pale guests, the World amaze,
1 Thes. 4. 16. Around all burning in a blaze,
    Suffring for man's offence,
What Joyes, then, sleeping Saints shall seaze,
How much this long-longde sight them please, 390
This sight, death's fetters which shall ease,
    All passed cares compense ?

O what a happie houre ! how deare,
How glorious shall this day appeare
To thee my Soule, when fred from feare, 395
    Grimme death thou darst outface ?
Luke 21. 28. When, (thy redemption drawing neare,)
Life's toyles shall trophees to Thee reare,
Which cank'ring Tyme shall ne'er outweare,
    Nor foes' despight deface. 400

Though tyrants haue, by doome vnjust,
In furious flammes thy carcase thrust,
Not daigning It to earth to trust
    With honour of a graue.
No Atome of thy scattered dust   405
But see this solemne Meeting must,
Purgde from corruption, from rust
    Of sinne did It depraue ;

Thy shape renewde, more glorious made
Than when it entred deathes darke shade,   410
Raisde by his viuifying aide,
    Death's powres who did controule ;
With flesh adornde, which ne're shall fade,
Nor rotte, in earthe's cold bosome laide,
But liue for aye, the Mansion glade   415
    Of a Triumphing soule.

No beautie nature brought to light
Did ravish most amazed sight,
Which, as farre short from day as night
    From This, shall not be found,   420
Which shall adorne each new-borne wight,
Co-partner of this hid delight,
The lame shall leape, proportionde right,
Esay 35. 6.   The dumbe God's praises sound,

1 Thes. 14. Caught vp, when on immortall wings,   425
17.
1 Cor. 6. 2. To aire this stage which ouerhings,
To meete thy Head, the Saints who brings
    To judge the damned traine.
(Saints, earst accounted abject things,
Objects of scorne, weake underlings,   430
On thrones enstalde, now sceptred kings
Apoc. 10.   Eternally who reigne.)

What bands enclustred thee around,
Shall make the Heauens with hymnes rebound,
That Thou, a straggling sheepe, art found,   435
     Their numbers to encrease?
If they did such applauses sound
At thy conversion, how profound
Shall be their Joyes to see thee crownd,
     With them to acquiesse?   440

Luk. 15. 7¹.

As pansiue Pilgrime, sore distrest,
Wearie and weake, with famine prest,
Whom feare of Robbers doth infest,
     Straying alone, in need,
If Hee, while dreaming least of rest,   445
Should in an instant bee addrest,
Where hee might live for ever blest,
     How should his Joyes exceed?

Even so my Soule, (now on the way,)
Too easily seduc't astray,   450
When Thou shalt find this solide stay,
     This Center of repose,
How shall the pleasures of this day,
Adorning Thee with rich array,
Thy suffred labours all delay,   455
     Afflictions all compose?

What boundlesse Ocean of delight
Shall quench all paines, all passed plight,
Endured wrongs, digested spight
     Of tyrannizing pride,   460
By Angels, Messengers of light,
When brought in thy Redeemer's sight,
Set free from deathe's eternall night,
     Adjudg't, in blesse to byde?

Mat. 14. 3.

M

Mat. 25. 34.
35. 36.
When large Memorials shall record   465
The meanest good thou didst afford,
To poore, to sicke : when deed, nor word,
    Shall want the owne rewarde ?
1 Ioh. 2. 1
The Judge, thy Advocate, thy Lord,
Who now absolues, Thee, first restorde :   470
O bond ! O double-twisted cord !
    O vndeserved regard !

But O ! when Thou casts back thine eyes,
Thy voyage dangerous espyes,
Foes and ambushments, laide to surprise   475
    Thy wayes, when thou dost vieu ;
The traines set foorth Thee to entise,
Base pleasures, which Thou didst despise,
What boundlesse joyes shall thence arise,
    What Solace sweet ensue ?   480

What strange applauses thence shall spring,
When Saints doe shout, when Angels sing,
When Heauen's hie vaults loud Ecchos ring,
    Of that *Absoluing* voyce ?
Come yee, whose faith did vpwards spring,   485
Contempt who on the World did fling,
Blest of that great Sky-ruling King,
    Enter in endlesse Ioyes.

O Joyes, with these as farre vn-even,
To Man which to conceiue are given,   490
As loftiest of the Planets seven
Gen. 3. 24.
    Earth's Center doth transcend !
(By wit, who prease to pry in heauen,
Backe by a Cherubin is driven,)
Man's Reason is a vessell riven,   495
    Can litle comprehend.

O Joyes, as much bedazling sight,
As day's bright Beam the weakest light,
Aboue small Gnats as Eagles' flight
    Amidst the Clouds ensphearde !   500
Ioyes, as farre passing all delight
Yet euer heard by humane wight,
As ghastly screiches of Owles which fright,
    With Larks' sweet layes comparde !

1 Cor. 13. 12. These boundlesse Joyes, this endlese peace, 505
In this claims principally place,
To see God clearely, face to face,
1 Joh. 3. 2.   Him, as He is, to view.
(Not heere, as doth fraile *Adam's* race,
Who through a glasse this sight embrace, 510
And steps of things created trace,
    To reach these pleasures trew.)

With Judgement pure, to know, as knowne,
These Persons three, in essence One,
God varying in names alone, 515
    Father, Sonne, holy Ghost.
To know why Man, to lewdnesse prone,
(Angels o'repast) God did repone
In state of grace, why mercy showne
    To some while damnde are Most. 520

Which Joyes, on all the Saints elect,
On Soules and bodies both reflect,
By ravishing the *Intellect*,
    The *Memory* and *Will ;*
Which all the *Senses* doe affect, 525
With pleasures farre aboue defect,
Who can the rich contents detect,
    Those blessed Bands which fill ?

How more perspectiue, pure and free,
(Sequestred from mortalitie,)   530
The Understanding facultie,
    How prompter it perceiues !
How more sublime the Object bee,
The Union inward and more nie :
Joyes of a more supreme degrie   535
    The Intellect conceaues !

Here charg'd with chains of flesh and bloode,
We apprehend by Organs roode,
The drossie mindes of Earth's weake broode
    Imaginde knowledge swells :   540
There, bathing in a boundlesse floode
Of blesse, we shall, (as sprites which stoode)
Know, (vnpuft vp) our Soueraigne goode,
    In him, all creatures els.

What object can, in greatnesse, hight,   545
In glorie, majestie, in might,
This paralell, whence all delight,
    All pleasure only springs ?
With rayes of vncreated light
Which cherish, not offend the sight,   550
Who shines most blest, for euer bright,
    Eternall King of Kings.

What Union can so strict bee found,
So firme, successionlesse, profound ?
Man's deepest speculation drown'd   555
    Is in this vast abisse.
This gulfe, this Ocean without ground,
The ravisht minde doth wholly bound,
It drencht heerein, with glorie crownd,
    Bathes in a Sea of blesse.   560

If charming sounds, ensnaring sights,
In mindes of wonder-strucken wights,
Doe moue such violent delights
    As passe the bounds of speach,
The Joyes then midst these reachlesse hights,   565
Ay bright with euer-burning lights,
Must farre transcend the loftiest flights,
    Wits most profound can reach.

The fluide Joyes which here entise,
From things corruptible arise,   570
No Union, but externall, ties
    The sense and object fraile.
How should wee then these pleasures prise,
Which euer laste aboue the skies?
This Union strict all change defies,   575
    This bonde can neuer faile.

What superexcellent degrees
Of Ioy, the Intellect shall seaze,
When It, with cleare, vnsyled eyes,
    The speces, natures, strength,   580
Of beastes, of birds, of stones, of trees,
Of hearbes, the hid proprieties,
Th' essentiall differences sees
    Of Creatures all at length?

Of Ioy, what ouerflowing spaite,   585
Inunding this Theater great,
Drench with delight shall euery state
    Here marshalled aboue?
Till now, euen from the World's first date,
When Saints secure from sin's deceate,   590
2 Tim. 4. 8. Their Palmes, their Crownes receiue, who late
    Earth's vtmost spight did prove.

Nor shall the knowledge of the paine,
The torments which the damn'd sustain,
The cryms which earst their soules did staine,   595
    Impare these joyes divine !
These blacke Characters show most plaine
God's justice, their deserved bane,
The brightnesse of the blessed traine
    Opposde, now cleare doth shine.   600

Their Vengeance shall the Just rejoyse,
(Heaven's blesse comparde with hel's annoyes,)
As earst by regal Prophet's voice,
    Divinely was fore-told.
Psalm 58. 10. Saintes should, incompassed with Joys,   605
Bathe in their blood, whom death destroyes,
Happie, who so his life employes
    'Mongst Saints to bee enrold.

Heere oft, (with wonder rapt) wee find,
The punishment with vertuous minde,   610
The fault with the rewarde combinde,
    At which the Just repines.
There, fault with punishment confinde,
Rewarde, to vertuously inclinde,
Eternall justice vndeclinde,   615
    Impartially assignes.

As these and more joyes vnexprest,
The Understanding doe invest,
As in the Center of its rest,
    So heere, the *Will* doth pause   620
In peace, which cannot bee encrest,
Not wrestling passions to digest ;
O calme tranquillitie ! how blest
    They whom this loadstone drawes.

Hence spring such ardent flammes of loue   625
To God, to all the Saints aboue,
That not one ioy these hoasts do proue
    Which It doe not delight.
Hence It no fewer joyes doe moue,
Then God, Co-partners doth approue,   630
Joyes infinite, which ne're remoue,
    Nor weakned are by slight.

As soules, which horride shads enchaine,
This doe not feele their meanest paine,
With mates most hated to remaine   635
    For ay, by just decreite :
How happie then, this glorious traine,
With these eternally to raigne,
Who mutuall loue doe entertaine,
    Insep'rable vnite !   640

From thence a quiet, calme *Content*,
A sympathizing sweet concent,
Satietie, which vnacquent
    With loathing, doth arise.
Man heere in earth's ignoble tent,   645
Desires vnbounded still torment,
The more hee hath, the more is bent,
    Things fading to comprise.

O soule ! which life doth heere expose
To inward feares, to outward foes,   650
Deluded by deceaving shows,
    With shads of seeming blesse,
When with content thy Cup oreflows,
When hopes nor vast desires thou knowes,
How deare shall bee this sweet repose   655
    Which aye beginning is !

O Peace! on which all hap depends,
Man's vnderstanding which transcends,
To Thee alone our labour tends,
    Our Pilgrimage aspires.   660
Happie in Thee his life who spends,
In Joy, in peace which never ends,
To present Toyles which solace sends,
    Encentring our desires.

By perfect *Justice*, what excesse   665
Of Joy shall to the *Will* accresse,
Out-shining *Adam's* righteousnesse
    In innocent estate?
(But O! this Joy who can expresse?
Not tongues of angels, Man's much lesse,   670
O ravisht Soule! heere acquiesse,
    Drencht in this Ocean great.)

His Reason, *Adam's* sense and will
Did serve this God; but changeable
Was this submission; now, but still   675
    All doe themselves subject
To God; by bonde most durable,
Fearing no fall, secure from ill,
Rendring the soule most am'able
    To God, selfe, Saints elect.   680

O soule dejected, plungde in feare,
Which stinging thoughts, mind's horrors teare,
Thy wounded sprite who canst not beare,
    With inward terrours torne!
O how invaluable, how deare,   685
Would this integritie sincere
To Thee, (in conscience rackt) appeare,
    Which doth the saints adorne!

This innocence which doth exclude
All spots, polluting earth's fraile broode,   690
Pure, vndistainde, perfectly good,
    Free from least sinfull thought :
Saintes aye refreshing with that food
Of God's wingde messengers, which stood
Confirmde in grace by purple floode,   695
    Which Man's redemption wrought.

Nor shall lesse measure of content
To *Memory* of Saints present,
How life's small period heere was spent,
    Encompassed with cares.   700
From warres most pittifull event
If settled, sweetest peace is spent,
The Soule, which earst did most lament,
    Joyes most, now fred of teares.

Of passed fight the doubtsome [fate]   705
The souldier doth with joye relate.
The sea-tosde wight, in dangers great,
    If gone, most pleasure finds.
Past miseries inunding spaite
Most sweetens Saint's triumphing state,   710
Foes spoyles, which no invasion threat,
    Lesse ravish noble Minds.

From passions fred, for happiest lote
Their purest parts which did bespotte,
Strugling, as exhalations hote   715
    In humide clouds inclosde ;
From flight of dartes, the World foorth shot,
(Entisements which the best besotte,)
While these in their remembrance float,
    How much are they rejoysde?   720

Revoluing in this calmest peace,
How God, by his preventing grace,
Our steps restrainde, whilst we did trace
        The tempting paths of death ;
Of monstruous Sinnes in hottest chace,   725
How Hee in loue did us embrace ;
In this to joye, Saints ne'ere shall cease,
        While they in blesse doe breath.

The long vicissitude of years,
Of Times, the Memory endeares,   730
Since World's first Age, aboue the spheares,
        Of blest celestiall bands.
Which, while this Companie admires,
Cause of these changes, cleare appeares
In *Prouidence* large book, which beares   735
        Records of Seas, of Lands.

In this great Volumne read they shall
Why Angels first, first Man did fall,
Why God did this, nor These recall,
        Of his eternall grace.   740
Why Hee did *Abram's* seede enstall,
Peculiar most of nations all,
And why to, Gentiles, these made thrall,
        Were planted in their place.

In these great Archives scrold is found   745
Why dearest Saints are trode to ground
By Tyrant's pryde, to which no bound
        Oft is below assignde.
To wit, more glorious to bee crown'd,
As their affection did abound,   750
Joyes may proportionall redound,
        As crosses them confinde.

Mat. 12. 43. Nor shall the *Bodie*, now all bright,
The fellow souldier of the spright,
Bee frustrat of these Joyes, by right   755
    Of its redemption due.
Of all, the noblest sense, the *sight*
Impassible, not harmde by light,
Aboue all measure shall delight,
    Amazde with wonders new.   760

Mat. 13. 43. How shall the ravisht Eye admire
When Suns past number doe appeare?
Dark'ning that sparke, our hemispheare,
    Which cleeres with chearefull rayes?
On all hands, Nought, when farre and neare,   765
Encounters sight but objects cleare,
Blest Empyrean bands, which weare
    Crowns, Palmes, immortall bayes?

How shall this Beautie vs amaze?
How on this glorie shall wee gaze?   770
How on our bodies, which doe blaze
    With brightest beames of light?
Our bodies, which ere death did seaze,
(Death, which no prayers can appease)
Most loathsome burthens were to these   775
    Whom most they now delight.

What breast can bound this joye's full spaite,
To see falne Angels' chayrs of state
Filde with our friends, familiars late,
    Love long dissolvde, renewde?   780
To see, to know, (O wonder great!)
Saints all, all times did heere relate,
Since *Abel's* blood, (a long long date,)
Gen. 4. 8.   His brother's hands imbrued?

By force of flammes which all subdue,   785
When broght to nought this world's false shew,

2 Pet. 3. 13. Of Heauen, of earth, the fabricke new
    What wonders shall afford?

Rev. 19. 2. Things which before wee never knew,
Charming our euer-gazing view,   790
With pleasures endlesse, perfect, true,
    Which tongue cannot record.

But none of all these objects rare,
Can with thy sight, O Christ, compare.
Fulnesse of Joy reflecteth there   795
    On these at thy right hand.

Psal. 17. 15. In Righteousnesse thy face preclare
Who viewing satisfied are,
For which a place Thou didst prepare
    Before Thy throne to stand.   800

If that great Herauld of Heaun's King,
Record of Thee sent foorth to bring,
For Joy, did in thy presence spring,
    An Embrion yet vnborne.
If yet a babe, thy sight benigne   805
So *Simeon's* soule with joy did sting,
That hee his Obsequies did sing,
    With age and weaknesse worne.

If Easterne *Sages* spar'de no paine,
By Pilgrims' toyles, thy sight to gaine,   810
An infant, borne but to bee slaine,
    In manger meanlie laide;
What soule then can these joyes containe
Which shall arise to see Thy raigne,
The glory of thy heauenlie traine,   815
    Whose pompe shall never fade?

But O ! (Mee thinkes) of heavenly layes
A consort sweet my sense betrayes,
By organs of mine Eare, allayes
    All mind-remording cares.   820
Aboue time, motion, place, which raise
My ravisht thoughts, to heare his praise
Proclaimde which heauen's blest hosts amaze.
    By notes of Angels' ayres.

O harmony transcending Arte !   825
Of which the hopes ease present smart :
Thrise happie they who beare a part
    In this cœlestiall Quire.
O blest Musitians most expert,
Whose Ditties all delight impart,   830
Whose hymnes exhilarate the heart,
    And entertaine the Eare !

Of Ambrosie, of Nectar, streames,
(Heaven's dainties hid in heathnish names,)
An endlesse feast the Lambe proclaimes,   835
    To all the Saints above.
The Saints refresht more with his beames
Then worldlings with vaine pleasures dreams,
O how desiderable seemes
    To Thine, this feast of Love !   840

If beggars vile themselves hold grac't,
At tables of great Kings to feast,
With curious cates to please their taste,
    With choise of rarest things :
O ! what a heavenly sweet repast   845
Doe Saints enjoy, which aye shall last,
Who at immortall Tables plac't,
    Feast with the King of Kings.

Of all these Millions which frequent
This Paradise of sweet content,   850
Perfumes most rare refresh the sent,   .
    From a perpetuall spring.
Comforting oynments odours vent,
Sweet'ning the heauens' transparent tent,
Which flow from him his blood who spent   855
    His to blesse to bring.

Which, (as in smell, taste, hearing, sight,)
In feeling als enjoy delight,
The Body changde, spirituall light,
    Apt euery way to moue;   860
Nimble, as thought, to reach by flight,
(Unwearied,) heauen's supremest hight,
The Center low, from Zenith bright,
    As It the Minde doth move.

By Motion swift, heere, Bodies tost,   865
If thus endangered to bee lost,
The feeling sense, affected most
    Participats most paine :
What Joyes (to view this numbrous host)
The Elementar regions crost,   870
When both vnharm'd throgh heauen's way post,
    Shall then this sense sustaine?

If Spasmes, if Palsies pincing throes,
If Colick paines invade, (health's foes,)
These torments Feeling vndergoes,   875
    Most sensible of griefe,
Now when sequestred from those woes,
Which marre lifes vnsecure repose,
How shall this sense, set free, rejoyse,
    Exult at its reliefe?   880

But euen as one, (more bold than wise,)
A Pilgrimage doth enterpryse,
O're *Atlas'* tops, which hid in skies,
    Crownde are with Winter glasse :
Hudge Mountains past while hee espyes, 885
Impenetrable Rockes arise,
Forc't to retire, his course applyes
    By smoother paths to passe.

So, while aboue the Spheares I prease,
Steps not by Nature reacht, to trace, 890
The clowds to climbe with halting pace
    Lets infinite impeach.
Those reachlesse Ioyes, this boundlesse peace,
In number, measure, weight, encrease :
That scarce begunne, my song must cease, 895
    These hights transcend my reach.

Μ𝔤νω δοξα θεω.

FANCIES FAREWELL

SON. 1.

Too long, my Muse, (ah) thou too long didst toile,
An Æthiopian striving to make white ;
Lost seede on furrowes of a fruitlesse soile,
Which doth thy trauells but with Tares acquite.
Hence-foorth fare-well all counterfeit delyte,   5
Blinde Dwarfling, I disclaime thy deitie,
My Pen thy Trophees neuer more shall write :
Nor after shall thine arts enveigle mee.
With sacred straines, reaching a higher key,
My Thoughts aboue thy fictions farre aspire :   10
Mounted on wings of immortalitie,
I feele my brest warmde with a wountless fire.
    My Muse a strange enthusiasme inspires,
    And peece and peece thy flamme in smoake expires.

SON. 2.

Houres mis-employed, evanisht as a dreame,
My lapse from Vertue and recourse to Ill,
I should, I would, I dare not say I will,
By due repentance and remorse redeeme.
Love's false delight and beautees blazing beame   5
Too long benighted haue my dazled eyes.
By Youth misled, I too too much did prise
Deceaving shads, toyes worthy no esteame.
Plungde in the tyde of that impetuous streame,
Where fynest wits haue frequent naufrage made.   10
O heavenly Pilote, I implore thine aide !
Rescue my Soule, in danger most extreame :
    Conduct mee to thy Mercyes Port, I pray,
    Save Lord ; oh let mee not bee cast away !

SONNET 3.

Looke home my Soule, deferre not to repent,
Time euer runnes : in sloath great dangers ly :
Impostumde soares the patient most torment,
While wounds are greene the salve with speed apply,
Workes once adjourn'd good successe seldome try,
Delay's attended still with discontent :
Thrise happie hee takes time ere time slyde by
And doth by fore-sight after-wit prevent.
Look on thy labours : timouslie lament :
Trees are hewde down vnwholesome fruits bring foorth.
Thy younger yeares, youthes sweet Aprile mispent,
Strive to redeeme with works of greater worth.
     Looke home, I say, make haste : O shunne delay :
     Hoyse sayle while tyde doth last : Time posts away.

Finis.

THE
Trve Crvcifixe

for

True Catholickes

or

The way for true Catholickes
to haue the true Crucifixe

By

S^{R.} WILLIAM MOORE, Y^{O.}
of Rovvallane, *Knight*

IOHN 4. 24

God is a Spirit and they that worship
Him must worshippe Him in
Spirit & in truth.

Edinburgh
Printed by John Wreittoun, and are
to bee sold at his Shop, a little beneath
the Salt-Trone. 1629

TO THE READER.

CHRISTIAN READER,—

Looke rather to what is intended, than what I have attained. My principall aime and purpose is to show that who soever doth love to see the true purtrate of IESUS CHRIST our LORD, must verse Himselfe in holy Scripture except Hee will chuise to ly open to delusion. If it please Thee to read and seriously perpend what is said to this purpose, I have eneugh for my paines. I haue contriv'd it in a measured stile, that thou mayst read with lesser wearying. Looke not for elaborat words, for not only the weightinesse of the subject made mee shunne whatsoever might breed obscuritie, but I ever held the whorish ornaments of affected eloquence an vnsutable ornament to garnish pure Truth. If it seeme to Thee I haue extended the worke to more than a competent length, some few moments shall serue Thee to runne thorow the margents, Howrs thou mayst reserue to what further it shall please [Thee] to make search for in the work. If my stile seeme any where sharpe against the abuise and abuisers of the Artificiall Crucifixe, weigh my reasons without prejudice, and I hope I shall not neede, to stand in feare of thy condemning censure. If the maner of handling of this Subject seeme to thee more proper for a Preacher than a Gentleman of my place, refuse it not for this, for a worthy Preacher, of my neere and deare acquaintance, out of His loue to CHRIST and thy Salvation, did not only stirre mee vp to build this peece of work, but both by Conference and Counsell, (as my weaknesse stood in neede of advise) did fordwardly concurre to furnish helpe

to the materials. Thou shall doe well therefore to passe by the
insufficiencie of the Instrument ; that, likeing the purpose neither
the better nor the worse for this respect, but looking (chiefly) to the
Truth of that which is spoken, by occasion thereof Thou mayst
bee stirred vp to a further study of the
knowledge of I ESUS C HRIST, and
Riches of grace and truth in Him,
and so to a greater love of
Him, and communion with
Him, for which end I
pray the Spirit of
I ESUS be with
Thee.

THE TRVE CRVCIFIXE

FOR TRVE CATHOLIQVES.

———————

a 2 Thes. ii. 12.

I F sacred ^aTruth did not conciliate trust,
　My doubt remoue by satisfaction just,
But muse I could not, how from time to time,

b Gen. 2.

Man, (^bbut a masse of animated slime,
A cloud of dust, tos'd by vncertaine breath,　　　5
A wormeling weake, soone to stoupe downe to death,)
Durst bee so bold, his pow'r as to enlarge ;

c 2 Command,
Levit. 26. 2.
Psal. 97. 7.

And ^c(proudly vilipending God's discharge)
A frantick freedome to himselfe durst take,
An Image for religious vse to make.　　　　　10

It is strange that
mā should call the
worke of their owne
hands.
d Levit. 10. 1.
Agnus Dei and Cru-
cifixus, Christ his
proper stiles, and
ascribe such virtue
as flows fromCHRIST
his person to them,
and trust and leave
and giue religious
worship to thē, and
yet plead to passe
free of Idolatrie.
Agnus Dei, is as
much as the lambe
of God.
Crucifixus, as
Christ nailed on
the Crosse.

And now I can not halfe enough admire,
How fondlings (^ddaring offer vncouth fire)
The naughtie issue of a noysome seed.
Like errour yet should to lyke madnesse lead,
CHRIST of his honour due induc't to reaue　　15
Vnto their owne inventions, it to giue
A peece of abject waxe, clos'd in a clout,
For GOD's *lamb*, blushing not to beare about :
Nor (sense distracted) CHRIST's owne proper stile,
The *Crucifixe*, forbearing to defile,　　　　　20
It attributing to their Christs of drosse,
(A man's faind shape, fix'd on a fancied crosse)

With honours, stiles, and titles, not a few,
To crucified CHRIST JESUS, only due.

To ^a*Paule* no Crucifixe besids was knowne,   25
Saue CHRIST.   ^bSonne of the living GOD alone :
This crucifixe of His, our ^cGod, our ^dLord,
By all should be obey'd, serv'd, lov'd, ador'd.
Our harts for Him, whose heart for vs did bleed,
A rowme should bee to rest in, and reside.   30

Hee should our glorie, ^eour rejoycing bee,
Wee ^fliue to Him, who chusd for vs to die.
His image in our lyfe we all should beare,
Walking as Hee, ^gpure, innocent, sincere,
Our ^hflesh, our soule affections mortifying   35
Heere, to be His for ay, ⁱour selues denying.

As ^kto the world, as crucified to sinne
Readie ^lfor Him, with each thing els to twinne
Wee labour should, while heere wee borrow breath,
In bleeding hearts ^mto beare about his death.   40

To this intent, in pure Truth's sacred booke,
Our dayly task should bee on Him to looke ;
To ⁿsearch the Scripturs, which of Him record,
And crucified before our eyes afford.

We should those holy ordinances haunt,   45
His Sacraments, means which Himselfe did grant,
And Registred left in His latter will,
His death to keepe in fresh remembrance still :
And with a longing soule and listening eare,
The Gospell's joyfull tidings bent to heare,   50
Such wee should bee, ^oas knowledge all hold vaine
Saue CHRIST to know, and for our sinnes Him slaine.

Thus ^pPaul him suffering to all eyes exposd,
Which ^qmisbeliefe and ignorance not clos'd,
Thus may wee all Him by faith's piercing eye   55
In Glasse of his owne institutions see ;
Thus bee preseru'd from following Christ-lings vaine
Shewd in the juggling trickes of wits prophane,

Marginal notes (left column):

^a 1 Cor. 2. 2.
God's Spirit calleth Christ himselfe the crucifixe, and nothing else.
^b Mat. 16. 16.
^c Isa. 40. 9.
^d Iohn 20. 28.
Isa. 43. 11.

^e Gal. 6. 14.
2 Cor. 10. 17.
^f 2 Cor. 4. 11.
Ibid. 5. 16.

^g Philip 2. 15.

^h Gal. 5. 14.

ⁱ Mat. 16. 24.

^k Gal. 6. 14.

^l Mat. 19. 27.
Mark 10. 28.
Luke 18. 28.

^m 2 Cor. 4. 10.

No right nor lawfull resemblance of Christ crucified but such as Himselfe hath made.
ⁿ Iohn 5. 39.
Isa. 8. 20.

^o 1 Cor. 2. 2.

^p Gal. 3. 1.

^q 2 Cor. 4. 3. 4.
In God's Word and ordinances CHRIST may be seene as in a mirrour.

Which Numbers lead astray; amongst which crew
No doubt but chosen soules are not a few;   60
To whom cleare eyes GOD once to see will giue,
As others, who did in like error liue,
That meanes none els, CHRIST'S knowledge can
      afford,
But such, himselfe hath stablisht in his word.

    Thou knowst (sweete CHRIST) the pitifull respect,
Those simple soules I beare which thee affect,   66
And faine would find thee, but astray are ledde,
With vaine inventions in man's fancie bredde,
Who searching thee, cast in a curious mold
Of baser mettle, or of purest gold,   70
Worship to thee, vnwarranted allow,
And basely to a lying idole bow,
Intending thus to impetrat thy peace
Doe loade themselues with sin, thee with disgrace

    With pittie mov'd, with indignation just,   75
To such, a better pourtrate wish I must;
Which to draw foorth, LORD furnish me with airt,
Bee thou my Patrone, who my patterne art;
My hand, my pinsell, let thy Spirit guide,
That (all humane respects farre laide aside)   80
Free from presumption curiously to trace
Each subtile line of thy Immortall face.
Thee shaddowing foorth, my draughts may not
      debord
From sacred mirror of thy sauing word.

    Teach Thou my straines to flie no other flight, 85
Still leade mee with the Lanterne of thy light,
That with thy loue enflam'd, I may with feare,
Thee in that Glorious mirror still admire :
Where, to our measure, Thee abridg't we haue,
Of Thee at least sufficient truth to saue.   90
Yet so that what thou to reueale hast dain'd,
A part can bee but of that part attain'd

Which as Man's Soule thy Spirit doth empire,
Some more, some lesse, none fully can acquire :
The soberest measure, euen the least of all   95
If thou vouchsafe, LORD serue my purpose shall.

M AN'S prime felicitie and soveraigne blisse,
His onely chiefest good, which most doe
misse,
By combination of eternall bands,
In his Communion with his Maker stands.

This Vnion first spirituall must bee found :   5
The Soule our better halfe to GOD bee bound,
To him conjoynd, before our Bodie's loade
Can bee admitted to his blest aboade.

This band to make, of GOD the knowledge true
So needfull is, to man ere sinne hee knewe,   10
That life it was his GOD to know aright :

Now life eternall is, since put to flight
By disobedience, truly GOD to knowe,
And CHRIST his Sonne, the source whence life doth
flowe.

GOD's Rebell aSathan, man's malicious foe,   15
Debard from grace, since first by pride brought low ;
Depriud of happinesse, bexild from Heaven,
Hopelesse to be restor'd, to darkenesse driven,
In malice set, by subtiltie and slight
Man's happinesse to marre with all his might,   20
Him from his GOD, and Soveraigne good to part,
Striues, of his GOD the knowledge to pervert.

In man (his cMaker's image) GOD infus'd
A light too glorious to haue beene abus'd,
A dHeavenly knowledge (forefault by his fall)   25
Both of himselfe and things created all ;
In which faire volume Man might dayly looke,
And exercise his witts, as in a Booke,

Which him to reade, to studie did invite,
God's boundlesse pow'r, his wisdome infinite.   30

The ᵃSerpent offring to augment this light,
By greater knowledge to vnsile His sight ;
(For yet his eyes had still beene closde to ill,
No wicked thoughts perverted had his will) ;
Did vnawarres thus worke his ouerthrow,   35
Sinne making him at once commit and know.

Thus not alone by treason did seclude
Himselfe from grace, lost God, his chiefest good,

ᵇ But guiltie made his offspring by his fall,
Which puld in him the fruit which poysond all :   40
Thus (Errour ruling Reason's sacred raigne)
False Gods, Imaginarie Good did faine
Iustly of skill, of will, of strength denude,
To know, loue, follow, what was truely good.

But O the bountie ! O the boundles loue   45
Of God, whom mercie no desert did move,
Hee of his goodnesse willing to reclaime
Those Rebells, objects vile of wrath and shame,
Did with himselfe determine to bringe backe,
And His, wretcht Man, by double title, make,   50
Restoring him to more since his offence,
Than he enjoyd in state of innocence :

So bound himselfe by promise to this end
A *Woman's Sonne* vnto the world to send,
A *Man* in Wisdome, Majestie and Might,   55
Equall with God, to frustrate Sathan's slight :
The Serpent's heade to breake, his works destroy,

Lost happynesse that man might re-enjoy.
The father of deceitt, That lyar bold,

Now blinded Man in darknesse striues to hold,   60

And, with his owne prevailing did pervert,
And harden cursed *Cain's* cruell heart,
And such as hee, his misbeliving seede,
God's faithfull word and promise to disside.

God appointed sac-
rifices and obla-
tions as spectacles
to helpe man's
dimme sight to see
Christ the Lambe
slaine from the
beginning of the
world.
But Sathan stroue
to make men gaze
on the spectacles
only, and not looke
through them to
CHRIST.

To help man's weaknesse, GOD in offerings shew   65
His holy Lambe set foorth to publicke viewe,
Him outward figures shadowing beneath :
To manifest the vertue of his death.

The Devill of all their types the trueths did hide :
Man made vpon the outward worke abide :   70
To set all labor'd (whom his sugred hooke,
To swallow over he could moue to looke),
Beyond the signes to their appointments end,
That so for trueths men might on shads depend.

After the flood God
made it yet more
manifest that his
Sonne should be a
man incarnat by
apparitions, and
personall types.

a Gen. 19. and 32.
24.

GOD yet this mysterie to make more plaine,   75
His Sonne for Man's redemption to bee slaine
More clearly in the flesh to manifest,
Good hopes to Man did giue, on which to rest,
To ªmortall eyes presenting now and than,
The *World's Redeemer* in the shape of man.   80

Iosh. 5. 13.
But Sathan stroue
to destroy this light
by inuention of
images in *Sem's* pos-
steritie where the
visible kirk was.

Now Sathan seeing hee did moyen lacke,
CHRIST'S comming in man's Nature to keepe backe,
New slights assayde, and so his purpose wrought,
That he, in *Heber's* house, (*Sem's* offspring) brought

b Compare Gen.
31. 30. with the
34 & 53 verses of
that cap.   Nixt
Iosh. 24. 2. and
14. 15.   Last
Ezek. 20 from
the 5th to the
10th, and cap. 23.
3, 14, 19, 21, 27.
c Gen. 12. 4.
GOD called foorth
Abraham frō the
societie of Image
worshipers.
d Rom. 4. 11.

ᵇ Imagerie of mettell, wood, and stone,   85
Perswading those the safest means alone
God's knowledge both to haue and keepe acquird,
Man's ouerthrow thus craftily conspir'd ;
Wonne to giue way thus to inventions vaine
Abraham's stocke idolatrie did staine.   90
From ᶜthis contagious crew which thus did fall,
The ᵈ*father of the faithfull* GOD did call,
And (separat from their societie,)
His Church did stablish in his familie.

e Ezek. 20. 7. 8.
But Sathan so farre
preuailed with the
world by this be-
wiching deuice that
everie age almost
he ensnared by
imagerie the people
of God, Abrahās
offspring, till the
captiuitie of Baby-
lon.

By ᵉSathan's arts, by Egypt's foule infection,   95
Here yet ensued anone a new defection,
Till God brought foorth his people, did his law
By his owne finger on two tables drawe,
Midst flames promulgate ; that no liuing soule
His will presume should after to controule ;   100

Yet base imagerie, in such a sort,
Corrupted man's conceat did so transport,

a Iudg. 8. 33.
Ibid. 3. 7. and 10.
13.
Deut. 32. 15.
Ier. 2. 13. &ct.

That ªeuerie age almost, afresh they fell,
Though plagued for this sinne did thus rebell,
And on this fancie never ceasde to dotte,   105
Till GOD made even with their deserts their lotte.
Them (after heauy stroakes of his disdaine,)
Delyuering to proud Tyrants to detaine
In fearefull bondage, slauerie worse than death,

b 2 King 24. 15.
2 Chron. 36. 17.
Ester 2. 6.

In ᵇBabell 'mongst idolaters to breath.   110
Hence Iewes (wee reade) did neuer image make,
Loue, beare about, their God for such forsake,
But as they did of the *Messiah* heare,
Did to the ancient Prophecies giue eare.

When GOD had ban-
ished images out of
his church, Sathan
labored still to
make man miscon-
ceiue the promised
Messias so to mar
the true knowledge
of Him.

Yet Sathan's thoughts on evill ever fixd,   115
Not ceassing his intent to follow, mixd
With GOD's pure Truth traditions, not a few,
Which lasted till our LORD did all make new ;
And 'mongst GOD's people, and peculiar race,
For outward idols finding now no place,   120
Wholly his slight extending, did neglect
No meanes in minds an idole to erect :
Of many, whom his subtiltie did make
GOD's oracles, the Prophecies mistake,
To dreame that CHRIST should bee an earthly king,
To earthlings earthly dignities to bring,   126

c Mat. 13. 15.
Isa. 6. 10.
d 2 Cor. 4. 3. 4.

Their Eyes ᶜlockt vp, giuen ov'r to Vanitie,
GOD's true spirituall meaning ᵈblynd to see,
That Saducees secure, who nought did care,
But things for present life, which vsefull were,   130
Soules Immortalitie, the general doome,

e Acts 23. 8.
Mat. 22. 23.

The ᵉbodies rising fables durst presume
Of cheieffe accompt, of speciall respect,
Became with men, tho Atheists in effect.

f Act. 23. 6. 7.

Thus ᶠSuperstitious Pharysies Prophane   135
And Godlesse Saducees, (Religion's staine)

Did almost all the Iewish Church devide,

(The Blinde giuen ouer to the Blinde to guide,)

At last Christ came himselfe that all might gett the right knowledge of Himselfe. Till GOD in end, Man pittying thus misled,

Sent in the flesh his CHRIST the plea to redde,   140

His mourning Saints to cheare these broils among,

Which did for *Israel's* consolation long.

Thus Man to GOD, earth to conceale to Heauen,

ª Eph. 1. 10. Gal. 4. 4. In ªtime's full terme, by Him the SONNE was giuen,

Hee to the world, did to this onely end,   145

b Gal. 1. 15. The *expresse* bImage of his Person send,

c Heb. 1. 3. In whom the cbrightnesse of His Glory shind,

Immortall GOD in mortall shape enshrind,

d Isa. 9. 6; Act. 20. 28. e Io. 1-14; Heb. 2. 14. f 1 Tim. 2. 5; Heb. 9. 15. g Phil. 2. 7. h Io. 1. 14. i 1 Io. 4. 9. k 1 Tim. 2. 5. dTrue GOD, etrue MAN, a fMediator meet

To GOD his Soueraine good, Man to vnite   150

In gman's base shape, GOD thus made manifest,

The hWord made flesh, to grace man repossest,

GOD's wisdome infinit, His iLoue sincere,

Thus in the kMan CHRIST IESVS did appeare.

His Trueth vncomprehensible was than   155

In Him made sensible to shallow man,

Who saw in Him the Rays of Heauenly light,

χαρακτὴρ τῆς ὑποστάσεως ϲαυτοῦ. The viue character of His paterne bright,

Which did not in His outward featurs shine,

Heb. 1. 3. But in his doctrine, life and works divine :   160

Which did all eyes in admiration draw,

Ioh. 14. 9. That *who the Sonne, the Father* also saw.

But Sathan stroue that man should looke onely on his bodily shap and not looke through the Vaile to his godhead dwelling in the man Christ. Gainst this restoring of GOD's knowledge true,

Man to his GOD, in malice Sathan flew,

And boldly dares renew the auncient warre,   165

With envy swolne, this glorious worke to marre ;

He streight did stoppe Man's vnattentiue eare,

That man should not His heauenly doctrine heare.

2 Cor. 4. 4. Mat. 13. 55. Mark 6. 3. With foggie mists, with sinne's thick clouds He blinds,

The mirror darke of world-distracted minds,   170

That they no further than his outside pierce,

The glorious beames His Godhead did disperse,

O

In all his actions dazling so their sight,
That with weake eyes they might no view this light;
But Him disvaluing, Them who dearely lov'd,   175

Iohn 10. 38.
Nor with His life, not works, nor wonders mov'd ;
They onely pore vpon His outward frame,

Philip. 2. 7.
Who in a seruant's shape most meanly came,
Cladde with our Nature's imperfections fraile,

Rom. 8. 3.
Inwrapt (as seem'd) in sinfull fleshe's vaile,   180
Whom viewing with the cloudie eyes of sense,
No wonder that the world conceiud offence,
That Hee who came the world to saue alone,

Rom. 9. 33.
Isa. 8. 14.
Thus to the world did proue a *Stumbling Stone*.

Thus did the *Iews*, thus *Turks*, thus *Heathens* fall.
Thus *Saracens*, thus *Machometans* all,   186
Rejecting CHRIST cause man's basse shape He bare,
Ly taken in the craftie hunter's snaire.

But CHRIST who came, lost mankind to reclame,
Least this humilitie should marre his ayme,   190
GOD in himselfe invisible to show,
And manifest to Earthlings heere below,
That Essence Infinit, Omnipotent,
Most Good, most Glorious, most Excellent,
Did wonderfully in His Heavenly brest,   195
(Tho never but in motion) ever rest,

To remed this error,
Christ remoueth his
bodily presence &
causeth write His
Natures,   Offices,
Wordes,   Workes,
life, death, and all
that serued to sal-
vation.
Hee, his Apostles, Messingers divine,
Pen-men, in whom pure Trueth vnstain'd did shine,
Inspyrd, as Hee did by His Spreit endite,
His birth, lyfe, death and testament to write,   200
So that (tho Atheists this wovne coate would rend,
GOD's WORD by heavenly inspiration pend,)
What These, what His Evangelists record,
Sweet straines, in sweetest harmony accord ;
Which *holy ditements* as a mirrour meete,   205
Ioynd with the Prophesies in Him compleet,
Might serue His Glorious Image to present,
To such as sought Him with a pure intent,

To make Him truely to salvation knowne,
To all that loue Him, ev'n to all His owne.   210

Onely the outward
shape & lineaments
of His face and
bodie. He will haue
conceilld and not
written in scriptur.

In These His Pen-men whose skild pencill drew,
Not His adulterat, but his pourtrait true,
In mirror of the Scriptures He imprents,
Vntouched to leave His outward Lineaments,
His bodies frame, the features of His face   215
To Him but common with fraile *Adam's* race,
Giues charge his person, properties to paint
The world with His life, doctrine, death, acquaint,
His Nature's offices, His wonders wrought,
His suffrings, sayings ; not omitting ought   220
That to His praise, Man's profite might redound
In all whats needefull to Saluation found,
Which might our Faith confirme, our Loue inflame,
Or paterne proue to which our Life to frame.

And this our LORD did wiselie : for the sight,   225
Of man's base shape, in Him, but dim'd the light
Of GOD's perfection, and did onely show,
The fraile infirmities from flesh that flow.

The bodily sight of
the lineaments of
our Lord his face
and bodie was a
stumbling block to
many that saw
him: the rehearsall
whereof in Scrip-
ture hee thought
not expedient.

And what of These, could the record haue wrought ?
What good His bodie's just proportion brought,   230
Since, face to face injoyd, His living sight,
As heere he did present an earthly wight,
So little helpt the world in Him to view,
Of GOD Invisible The Image true ?

At These the world did stumble : These espyde
With nature's twilight, millions made to slide.   236
These were the barke, through which (with pleasing
    strife,)
Illightned eyes did view the Tree of life :
These were the Caske, which peirc'd, sweet balme
    did yeeld
That to an angrie GOD wretcht man conceild.   240
These were the vaile the Godhead's beames did hide,

Coloss. 2. 9.

In Him did dwell and bodily abide,

Which cloud to peirce, this Sunne which did withhold,
Did all behooue, who view His Godhead would.

These but the superfice, which cover did   245
The richer substance of the Treasures hidde
Of knowledge deepe, of wisedome most profound,
Of vnseene graces, which in Him were found.

Christ's bodily shape did not show what a one Hee was, much lesse is the faind shaddow of that shape, fitt to show to vs what a one he either was or is. Thus what of CHRIST was set to outward sight
(While seene on Earth of Heaven to make vs right)
His bodie's shape, His lineaments of face,   251
The featurs choice, which Him did chieflie grace,
Him to point foorth were equall in no sort,
And what a one Hee was, to show came short :

Againe, of what the Eye a-lyfe espyde,   255
A lifelesse picture can no be denyed
Yet short to come : for Painters doe not ayme
The soule of Him, whose shape the hand doth frame
To set in sight : They striue alone to leaue
His Bodie's figure, whom they paint or graue,   260
And that but for the present day or houre
They did the Paterne see, but having pow'r,
Time, wrinkled age still hastning by degrees,
Their arte to mock, which mock mistaken Eyes.

The Scripture onely is a fitt mirror wherein we may gett a right sight of Iesus, and of whatsoever is to bee knowne of him for confort and salvation. But these viue draughts whose Heavenly luster shine,
By arte most exquisite, in write divine   266
Not superficially his shape doe show,
But solidly make vs our Saviour know ;
Not as our Image, but as GOD'S He bare,
In our fraile Nature, Man as men wee are ;   270
Not in one Nature, but in both vnite,
God-man conjoynd, a Sauiour compleet,
Not in one act, one case, or one estate,
But from his birth, even to His life's last date,
From his descending to Earth's lower parts,   275
The Virgin's wombe, this mirror bright imparts
Him fully, till He suffering did ascend,
At GOD'S right hand to raigne, world without end.

He must therefore
verse himselfe in
Scripture who de-
sires to see Christ
and not to be de-
luded with conceats
of a false CHRIST.

If CHRIST's true pourtrait truely then to see,
Thou longst, the Scripture must thy mirror bee, 280
The Spirit (heere) thy LORD, then yeeres more
    old,
What one He should bee, ere Hee came, foretold,
And, ere humanitie did Him invest,
His purtrait wonderfully (heere) exprest,
For vs not onely serving on the stage, 285
But all the Elect, since the world's first age.
The auncient Church did all in substance see,
Know, loue, beleeve, enjoy, of Him what wee.
    Heere, as the Spirit in this mirror cleare,
Him singled foorth, His sight, by faith sinceere, 290

Iohn 8. 56.

Did patriarchs all and Prophets so enflame,
That in His day they joyd before Hee came.

In the old Testamẽt
you shall see Christ
described as the
Faithfull before His
comeing saw him.

    Loe ! heere the Iewish Church by *Moses'* Law
Conveend, His suffrings in some measure saw,
Him slaine for sinne, though dimly to their view 295
The torchlight of their Sacrifices shew :
On Him they weakly, yet with pleasure deepe,
Through lattices of Typs, and figures, peepe,
And (as they may) behold, from this dark cloud,

a Mal. 4. 2.

The [a]Sonne of righteousnesse Himselfe vnshrowd,

b Ioh. 1. 29.
Apocal. 13. 8.

That [b]Lambe of GOD, that taks away sinne's
    staine, 301
Ere world was made, who for the world was slaine,
Feeding on Him their souls, as wee, by faith
Thus to bee fred with vs, from endlesse wrath ;

c 1 Cor. 10. 3.

Both [c]by one cuppe, by one spirituall foode 305
Refresh'd, both sav'd by vertue of His blood.

d Gen. 28. 12.

    To see this ladder was to [d]*Iacob* given,
From Earth's low centre, reaching highest Heaven,

e Gen. 49. 10.

Till [e]*Shilo* came who cleerly did impart,
The Scepter should from *Iudah* neuer part, 310

f Iob 19. 25.

[f]*Iob* liu'd perswaded, while most deeply grieu'd,
That for his safetie his *Redeemer* liu'd.

Isa. 9. 6.

    This Prince of peace, this counseller most wise,
The Father euerlasting, Blessed thrise,
A Child of wounder, euen the GOD of might,   315

Luke 2. 32.

Israel's Glorie, and the Gentile's light,

ᵃ ӡach. 3. 8.
Isa. 11. 1.

Esay foretold (a ᵃbranch of peerelesse worth,)
From *Iesses* stemme, shall in the Flesh sprout forth,
A King on whom the gouernement shall stay,
Of all the world who shall the Scepter sway,   320
A pow'rfull Prophet, by the LORD anointed,
Good tydinges to the meeke to preach appointed,

Ibid. 42. 3.

Who shall bind vp, not breake the bruised reed,

See the 53 cap.which
is full of cleare Pro-
phesies of CHRIST.

The weakely smoaking flaxe not quenche, but feed.

Isra'ls Sweete singer did his straines accord,   325
All to set forth the Glorie of this LORD,

Psal. 110. 4.

Whom Hee a *Priest* for euer doth detect,
After the order of *Melchisedecke*,

Psal. 22. 7.

Him doth point forth, now as expos'd to scorne,

Psal. 22. 16.

His hands and feet most pitifully torne,   330

Ibid. 18.

By lot his vestures parted, in his neede

Psal. 69. 21.

Made vinegar to drinke, on gall to feede,
Constraind to crye, with sense of horror shaken,

Psal. 22. 1.

My GOD, *My* GOD, *why hast thou Me forsaken?*

Psal. 68. 18.

Now as victoriously on high ascending,   335
Him twentie thousand thousand Angels tending,
A captiue making of captivitie,
To His proclaiming peace, and libertie,
The swelling pride of proude insulters laid,

ᵇ Psal. 2.
ᶜ Psal. 110 ; Ier.
23. 5.
1 Chr. 11. 17.

His ᵇfoes crusht downe, His ᶜfoot-stoole being made.
    Of this Eternall, ever budding *Braunche*   341
To be raisd vp to *David* (who to quench,
His burning thirst with *Bethlem's* streams did long)
The Spirit spoke by *Ieremia's* tonge,
Him setting forth a King, whose prosperous raigne
Iustice and judgement should on Earth maintaine, 346
Who *Iudath* save, who *Israel* should reclame,
The Lord our Righteousnesse designd by name.

In short, no age did revelatioun lacke,
CHRIST the *Messiah* manifest to make   350
From time to time, who by degrees of light,
By Types or Prophecies was set in sight,
Till from the Arke, the outward covering drawne,
This glorious Day-starre in the flesh did dawne.

Looke yet a little in this mirror rare,   355
Predictions with accomplishments compare,
With wonder ravisht, heere thou shalt behold
All done, what earst was to bee done, foretold,
Of Typs the clowdie Mysteries explaind,
Shadows sequestred, reall Truths attaind,   360
The legall rites, the ceremoniall lawe,
By Him abolisht, who the vaile did draw,
Of CHRIST affording a more liuely sight,
A clearer knowledge, and a nearer light,
So that the tenderest sight, the weakest eye,   365
Him now vnmasked in this glasse may see.

For now the Spirit (*Moses*' face vnvaild,)
A ᵃ*Babe* presents Him, ᵇdeath and hell who quaild,
The ᶜ*Ancient of dayes* a suckling weake,
Who ᵈfrom His daughter's bowells birth did take,
An Infant, ᵉcoeternall with his Sire,   371
Whose ᶠIncarnation Angels did admire,
Prizd by the foolish with contempt and scorne,
Because a weakling of a weakling borne,
In humble state, layd in a homelie stall,   375
To narrow bounds confind, who boundeth all,
The comfort crauing of Her Virgine brest
Who gaue Him birth (his wants by cryes exprest,)
Borne and exposd at once to Tyrant's spight,
Constraind His lyfe to saue by secret flight,   380
The stormie flood of bloodie *Herod*'s rage
Let loose on all the equals of his age,
Who, to assure Himselfe of Him alone,
Cruell to all, prou'd pitifull to none.

In the new Testament you shall see more clearely Christ revealed than the Prophets sawe Him vnder the Law.

ᵃ Luke 2. 7.
ᵇ 1 Cor. 15. 54.
ᶜ Dan. 7. 9.
ᵈ Rom. 1. 3.
ᵉ Iohn 1. 1.
ᶠ 1 Pet. 1. 12.

Luke 2. 7.

Mat. 2. 14.
Mat. 2. 16.

Heere shalt thou see Him even while thus despisd,

By Princes of the East, a *Saviour* prizd,   386

His God-head who no sooner doe behold,

But offering gifts of Incense, Myrrhe, and gold,

Mat. 2. 11. Fall downe, adore, and to their LORD approue,

Pictures cannot de-
scribe that which
the   Scriptures
speake of Christ
his infancie. Their faith, their hope, their loyaltie and loue.   390

Since costliest Crucifixes, Picturs none,

Since craftsman's skill on mettall, wood, nor stone,

This can so liuely to the Eye present,

As doth His written Word and Testament,

Why fondly then prefer phantastick men   395

The Graver's toole to the *Apostle's* penne?

Luke 2. 46. Hold on, thine eye fixe on His Youth's sweet
spring,

Which doth faire buds of Pietie forth bring,

Inciting tymouslie our tender yeeres

To true devotion (since no act appeares,   400

In which he provd to vs a President,

The which was not for our instruction ment.)

Luke 2. 46. 47. Heere thou shalt find Him in the Temple sett

And Heavenly knowledge from His child-hood gett,

Israel's doctours hearing Him demand,   405

Who at His doctrine all astonishd stand,

Ravisht to see, yeeres so vnripe admitt

Such full perfection of a hoarie witt.

But now, the Spirit doth invite thine eye

Thy Saviour drencht in *Iordan's* streams to see : 410

ᵃ Luke 2. 21. Loe, ᵃHee who formerly was circumcis'd,

ᵇ Mat. 3. 13.
Mark 1. 8. By His great ᵇHarbinger must be baptiz'd :

Thus sanctifying by those *scales* divine,

The auncient Church, the Church that was to shine :

Those actions His pure bodie must endure,   415

Which should have force to clense our soules impure ;

ᶜ Col. 2. 9. Tho Him, ᶜin whom (vnseene) the Godhead raignd,

ᵈ Heb. 4. 15. Nor ᵈfilth, nor fore-skinne of corruption staind,

So that, except for vs, the LORD of life,
Did need nor streams, nor circumcising knife : 420

2 Cor. 5. 21. Yet sinne for vs himselfe hee made, that wee,
In Him the righteousnesse of GOD might bee.

Mat. 4. Hence by the *Spirit* led, hold on thy pace,
Mark 2. 12.
Luk. 4. 1. Thy SAVIOVR's footsteps to the deserts trace.

There shalt thou view in single combat foyld, 425
By proper armes, troad vnder foote and spoyld,

1 Pet. 5. 8. That pow'rfull Aduersare, the dragon old,
Apoc. 20. 2. Who to assaile the SONNE of GOD was bold.

Fullnesse of grace when thou in him dost see,
Truth, mercie, pittie, loue, humilitie, 430
All wisdome, meeknesse, patience, prudence, peace,

Nothing can ex- Which in perfection but in him found place,
presse Christ his
growing age, & No wonder then this Mirror thee amaze,
variety of vertues
except the holie Since in no corner Thou heereof canst gaze
Scripture.
Which doth no liuely set before thy sight 435
A lanterne to thy lyfe, the LORD of light.

Deluded soule, these who forsak'st to view,
Of *living waters* in the fountaine true
The Scripture, digging to thy selfe in vaine

Ier. 2. 13. Such cisternes as no water can containe, 440
What can the Pencil's most industrious art,
By pictures dumbe to Thee of these impart ?

But you, (poore soules) beare not alone the blame,
In others chiefly lyes the fault, the shame,
Dumbe Doctors ceassing when for ease to preach,
Or would not, or els could no people teach, 446
Least men by vse should loath, at length despise
Their often-mumbled matins did devise,
Guyses to gaze on, showes men's soules to feed,
An vncouth language for their dayly bread ; 450
To charme the Eare did mix a sweete concent
Of Melodie, by voice, by instrument,
With choise divisions of an hundreth kinds,
About to moue, and melt the hardest minds ;

If pictura did decipher the corruption of the doctrine and life of Churchmen als clearelie as the Scriptures do, they should bee in lesse request among the Roman Clergie.

Books turnd in blocks, blind dotards to delyte ;　455
These, they were sure, would neither bark nor bite,
For did they teach the Trueth, their faults expose,
As Scripturs, which their lewdnesse doe disclose,
They surelie should such intertainment lake,
And (thrust to doores) the Scripturs' bonds partake,
Which ly in fetters of an vncouth leid,　461
Keept vp from sillie soules, which faine would read.
Claspt by authoritie, that on this booke
Saue privileged persons none may looke,
Because in this engrav'd *Christ's* portrait true　465
Is by the Spirit set to publike view,
Plainely proclaiming, what doth them displease,
Crying a WOE to Scribes and Pharisees,

Called blind guids.
Faind Church-men, who pretend the saint to feed,

Mat. 23. 6.
Luke 11. 52.
Mat. 23. 13.
Mat. 23. 2.
Ibid. 4. &ct.
Luke 11. 46.
By lanterne of GOD's Word, weake soules to lead,
Of knowledge key, them meantyme doe debarre,　471
So both their owne, and others' entrie marre.
　　Who set in *Moses'* chaire, doe over-charge
With grievous burdens, impositions large
The People's backs, denying ev'n the aide　475
That by their little finger may be made.

Luke 11. 42.
In lifelesse ceremonies most precise
To seeme who studie, to obseruing eyes,
Yet soules committed to their cure neglect,
And truth and mercie hold in small respect.　480
　　Who cloaking by Religious pretence
The grossest sinne, the grievousest offence,

Mat. 23. 14.
Mark 12. 40.
Luke 20. 47.
Mat. 23. 27.
Devouring widowes houses, doe betray
The innocent, poore Orphans make their prey.
　　Like painted Tombs who clense the vtter side,　485
Where nought within but rotten bon's abide,
To satisfie GOD'S Iustice daring stand,

Ibid. 28.
Mat. 23. 3.
Ibid. 24.
Ibid. 15.
For works of Righteousnesse of Men's owne hand.
　　To doe who care no, much delight to prat,
Hudge Camels swallow, straining at a gnat,　490

A Proselite to make who spare no paine,
Whom, with themselues they adde to Sathan's traine.
   Whom so Ambition blinds, so pride transports,
That life and beeing them no more imports,

Marke 20. 38.
Luke 11. 43.

Then tumide Titles, Greetings, caps and knees,   495
Prioritie of place of all degrees.
   Harke how in all sorts Christ doth sinne rebuke,
In These but chieflie, set to ouerlooke
His flockes, *lights* in the chayre of truth to shine,
Call'd to dispense his mysteries divine,   500
O with what care their sacred charge to tend,

Luke 22. 24.

Doth hee vnto his *watch-men* recommend,

Mat. 20. 25.

Warning least they should by ambition slyde,
By worldlie grandour, statelinesse or pride.
Lordly dominion, Raines of Sov'raignetie,   505

Mat. 15. 23.

Prohibiting by them vsurp't should bee.

Mark 7. 7, 8, 9.

   Him thou mayst heare establishing His word,
A rule from which vnlawfull to debord,
In matter of Religion, worship true
Of God in doctrine to Salvation due ;   510
Traditions all rejecting, to this square
(How old soever) which repugnant are.

Psal. 69. 19.

   Lo ! now He comes in flames of firie zeale ;

Mat. 21. 12.

Flie, flie, O yee, who of His house make sale,

Isa. 2. 13, 14.

Base *Simonists* beware, the Lord of Lords   515
Hasts with a whip, a lashing scourge of Cords,
All mercenarie misers to expell
Buyers and *sellers* from His house to Hell.
   With frequent warnings (now) He armes His owne,
By future errors least they bee o'rethrowne,   520
Of Hypocrits doth (now) vnmaske the face,
How ere their outsids shine with showes of grace,
Cowsning the world with a pretence of goode,
(Their fruits neere comming further than the bud,)
Who, tho they Vice can deck in Vertue's dye,   525
Yet sile they can not His all-seeing Eye.

Such doctrins as be these, not motiues least
Haue beene, to bring dumb Idols in request,
CHRIST's speaking purtrait such haue put to peace,
(This stocks and stones admitted to outface,)   530
But hearken thou, to his sweet voice giue eare,
From His owne mouth, thou by the Sprit shalt heare
The word of Trueth, Him powring foorth sweet
    streams
Of *living waters*, to the soule that cleams
Refreshment, feeling want, in feare to sterue,   535
Such (heere) shall find, what may to saue them serue.

Math. 14. 25. O ! view Him walking on the raging waues,

Mat. 8. 26. The winds rebuking, sinne's possessed slaues

Mark 5. 9. From Legions of foule Spirits setting free,

Mat. 9. 25. The dead recalling to mortalitie :   540
Yea ; raising vp thy selfe from sinne's dark cave,

Iohn 5. 21, 25. A Lazare, stinking in corruption's grave

Iohn 11. 44. To see the danger, the deserved wrath,
The guilt, thy trembling soule lyes drencht beneath,
By which if humbled, Hee shall comfort speake, 545
Thy wounds bind vp, vnloade thy conscience
    weake,
Invite thee with thy burden to draw neere,
Offring for thee the *Father's* wrath to beare ;
Whom, that thou may'st from filth of sinne bee purg'd,
Thou shalt behold arraign't, condemned, scourg'd,

Onely the scriptures Sighing and groaning, with thy burden prest,   551
expresse CHRIST
his miracles and Expos'd to paines which can not be exprest,
passion.
Weeping, and bleeding, suffering death for thee.
O Love ! O Pittie, in a strange degree !
Now in this combat entring Him behold   555
Of his sad *passion*, tryed as purest gold
By fire dissolv'd, in which no drosse is found,

Mat. 26. 37. Deeplie afflicted, prostrat on the ground,
The Garden watering with a Crimson flood,

Luke 22. 44. From all his pores distilling streams of blood,   560

His Glorye's beames obscurd, His Might allayed,
His Courage seeming quaild, His Strength decayed ;
Crusht downe with weight of GOD's incumbing wrath,

Mat. 26. 38.   His guiltlesse soule made heavy to the death,
Thy Crimes the cause, thy sinnes inunding speate,
The meanes from Him which drew this bloudie
    sweate,   ·   566
Whom (notwithstanding) Hee did (so) esteeme,
That all His suffrings did most pleasant seeme
Thee, wretched wormeling, to redeeme from death,
Perdition's heyre, sinne's slaue, the child of wrath ;
To thee the Father's favour to acquire,   571
Not shrinking to drinke off the dregs of ire.

The Popish cruci-   These bee the suffrings, counterfits which scorne,
fixe doth but mocke
& not expresse the   Which lyfelesse draughts deface, but not adorne.
sufferings of Christ.   These be the suffrings which perplexed soules   575
Most sensibly conceiue, sunk deep in scrouls
Of tender bleeding hearts, The only way,
Most liuelie felt which make his Torments may ;
Who (heere) the dolors of his death engrosse,
Best feele the fruicts and comforts of his crosse.   580
     O wounderfull respect ! O loue vnheard !
O deare affection matcht with misregard !
Loe, Hee who bought Man at so deare a rate,

a Mat. 26. 14, 15.   By Man is a sold, betrayd by Man vngrate,
Mark 14. 10.
Luk. 22. 3.   The traitor's mouth, which flowd with fraud, with
Luk. 22. 47.   hate,   585

b Isa. 53. 9.   His lips dare touch where found was b no deceit:
1 Pet. 2. 21.
Mat. 26. 50.   Friend whether comst thou ? (Christ his friend yet is :)
The SONE OF MAN betrayst thou with a kisse?

Iohn 18. 6.   Hee who those armed bands did cast to ground,
Them, with his breath, all able to confound,   590
With this soft speech, this gratious checke alone,
Doth wound, not wonne, the traytor's heart of stone.

Mat. 26. 52.   See how Hee doth *His* forwardnesse represse,
Who preasd, by arms, this offred wrong redreesse,

And healing instantlie the harme receav'd,   595
Yet did not mease the causelesse spight, conceau'd
In hardned hearts so farre from grace, from loue,
That miracle, nor favour them can move.

O see Him in a most opprobrious forme

Mat. 26. 56.   Led hence, transported with this raging storme,   600
Ibid. 27. 2.   Left by His owne, yeelding His conqur'ing hands,
Thee to set free, to ignominious bands.

Mat. 26. 47.   With lamps, with lanterns led, they apprehend
Iohn 18. 3.   The Sonne of *truth*, incarnate to this end.
Iohn 18. 37.

That glorious *Beame* of vncreated light,   605
By flesh and bloode invaild, hid from their sight,
Thus all foretold gainst actors of this *Ill*,
Against themselves do perfitly fullfill.

O Earth! O ashes who thyselfe turmoylst,
And with vindictiue flams of furie boylst,   610
Tormenting others, darst revenge avouch,
Vpon thy reputation's slendrest touch,
See, with what patience, with what silence deepe,
While *Iews* disgrace vpon disgrace doe heape,

Esa. 50. 6.   Thy Sauiour to the *Smiters* giues his backe,   615
Mat. 26. 67.   Doth from the *Nippers* not his cheeks keepe backe.
To shame, to spitting, doth expose his face,
The path not only pointing thou shouldst trace,
But treading euerie steppe, hath taught the way,
From which t'is shame, yea dangerous to stray.   620

Isa. 53. 7.   Loe in this hight of scorne, depth of disgrace,
Act. 8. 32.   With cheare vnchang'de he dares his foes outface,
If 10000 pictures Yet from his lips not one intemperat word,
were forged, they
shuld all come His mercilesse tormenters doth remord.
short in showing
that which the new
Testament declares   CHRIST's *Testament* which these and all contains,
of Christ crucified.
Yet Christ's Testa- That Hee did suffer, shame or outward paines,   626
ment is in small
estem with many Needfull for Thee to know in one small *Booke*
in comparison of a
fond & fals picture. Is found, on this in steade of pictures looke:
The BIBLE sets not
so well as the cru- This beare, this weare, this reverentlie reade,
cifixe doth where
poperie prevailes. When read, at least attentiuelie take heede,   630

This doth make known the Will, the legacie,
Which thy deare LORD a-dying left to thee.
    With this *love-token* Hee remembred hath,
Each loue-sicke soule to Him betroathd by fayth,
His loue thus showne, to kindle loue againe,   635
That mutually love wee might intertaine;
    If *Christ* thy loue be, then what hee hath left
Nor let by wrong nor violence be reft,
But striue to know what written for thy well,
With's owne deare blood thy louing LORD did seale.

Iudg. 16. 16. See our true *Samson* yeelding now at length,   641
Spoild of the hayres of his vnmatched strength,
A bloodie butchrie suffering for thy sake,

*Mat. 27. 28. Stript naked, torne with whips, faint, pale and weake,
The Souldiours mocking His enfeebled might,   645
Combining, in His torment, sport with spight,
His offices all branding with reproch,

Luk. 25. 32, 37. With blasphemie Him charging, they encroch
Vpon his Priest-hood with a bitter blow,

Luke 22. 64. Now, siling vp his eyes, Hee streight must show 650
Who him did most with causelesse strips infest,
As Prophet this by him must bee exprest :

Mat. 27. 29. Then, cloathd in purple, crownd with pricking thorne
As King, is made the object of their scorne.
    But ah ! behold He comes : O heavie sight,   655
Bright *Eye of Heaven*, O now shut vp thy light ;
Salt fountains all of tears be now enlarg't,

Gen. 22. 6. Weake *Isaak's* tender shoulders (loe) are charg't,
With wood, Himselfe to sacrifice prepar'd ;

Iohn 19. 17. Lo ! neither is from shame Thy Saviour spar'd, 660
From pressing loade of that disgracefull Tree,
The means appointed of his death to bee ;
See, faintlie staggring, how He grones beneath
The pondrous weight of GOD's incumbent wrath.
    O see the bloodie banner now display'd,   665
The SONNE of GOD by Souldiours disarayed,

Cladde only with our sinnes, in Garments red,

Esa. 63. 2, 3. The vine-presse of the Father's Ire doth treade,

Fixt to the crosse, his hands, his feete transpierced,

Exposd to paine, to horrors vnrehearsed,   670

His gratious armes foorth streatching all the day,

Rome 10. 21.
Es. 65. 2.
Phil. 2. 6. To rebells walking in an evill way.

Who (GOD not robde) equalitie did plead,

Deut. 21. 23.
Gal. 3. 13. With robbers matcht, for thee a *curse* is made

And even to death, endures vpon the Crosse,   675

Mat. 27. 46. In soule, in bodie, pains of sense, of losse.

Heavens suted to their Makers mournefull state,

Mat. 27. 51. Mask't vp with clouds, in their owne kinde regrait,

Ibid. 51. Loe, Earth doth tremble, flintie Rocks doe rend,

Ibid. 52. Graves backe to light their sleeping guasts doe send,

And loe, while ev'n his life's last spunke is spent, 681

The Temple's vaile is to the bottome rent.

Col. 2. 14. See, now through tears, how He himselfe presents

Nailling vnto his Crosse Thy oblishments,

Cancelling those Inditements which did tye   685

GOD'S wrath in iustice Thee to vnderly,

Heb. 6. 6. Resoluing more by sinning, to abstaine

To crucifie The LORD of life againe ;

Rom. 3. 23. On his owne death, who freelie of his grace,

Did ground thy life and euerlasting peace.   690

In short their is no-
thing thou needst
to know of Christ
but all is in His
testament. THIS, and what more to search for, thou aspires,

What faith can wish or what thy soule desires,

The *Spirit* in this mirrour shall disclose,

And to thy sight of Him as much expose,

As may thy soule heereafter serue to saue,   695

And guide thee (heere) with comfort to the graue,

Except His inward vertues thou neglect,

And but his outside carnally affect.

This, GOD hath thought vnnecessare to show,

This farre vnnecessare for thee to knowe ;   700

Sufficient that, which These who knew Him best,

And best did know to make him knowne, exprest

Haue left, enregistred in holy write,

Which They did penne, GOD's Spirite did endite.

Luke 16. 29.   Thus hath the Lord his will most clearelie showne,

These who saw
Christ with their
bodilie eyes knew
him not to be that
Christ till hee
opned their eyes
to behold him in
the scriptures.
By other means refusing to bee knowne   706

Then by his word alone, where faith's bright eye,

His hidden graces may most liuelie see,

So that (except this way) no knowledge true,

Accrest of Him, vnto the outward viewe   710

Of These, admitted in his humane state,

To touch Him, ev'n with Him to drinke, to eate.

THIS being then the course by God prescriv'd

To Man, of other means of grace depriv'd,

To know the Sonne, and in the Sonne the Sire,   715

Col. 1. 19, 26.   The Sonne, concealler of the Father's Ire,

Christ to make men
know him hath set
foorth the Scrip-
tures and hidden
his bodilie shape.
But Sathan strives
by meās of the
Roman Clergie to
expresse his bodilie
shape which can
not show Him and
suppresse the scrip-
tures which might
make Him knowne.
O judge what *Spirit* this great worke to marre,

This course to crosse, the Scriptures would debarre

And hide this Mirror from the longing sight

Of Soules, which faine would see this Sunne of
          light,   720

Enjoyning such, this knowledge to attaine,

By pictures false, or some resemblance vaine

Of that externall shape, which GOD did hide,

Least any in this fruitlesse search should slide?

No *Spirit* doubtlesse els, but Hee, whose slight

Seeks GOD and Man, to seuer day and night,   726

With envy boyling, at man's good who griev'd,

Hath ay a lyer and a Murtherer liv'd;

Gen. 3. 6.   His point for once who gayning, seeks yet still,

To disconforme man to his Maker's will;   730

Even Hee, who since his fall, with wondrous art,

From GOD'S true worship man did still divert,

2 King 23. 5.   By whom to such prophanenesse mortals driv'ne,

Haue worshipt Sunne, Moone, Starrs, the host of
          Heaven;

1 King 11.
Iudg. 6. 25.
Ibid. 3. 7.
2 King 23. 5.
For *Moloch, Milcom, Baal, Ashtaroth,*   735

Who made the nations God's true worship loath;

P

Who Images of GOD, hath oft devysd,
And Men's deluded fantasies entysd
A furtherance in GOD'S seruice to conceat,
By means engendring his eternall hate ;   740

Exod. 32.   Thus *Aaron* did the *golden calf* erect ;
Iudg. 27.   These vain surmises *Micah* did infect.
A house of GODS, a *Levite* to his *Priest*
Who having This of blessings held no least ;
The error of Christ his earthly King- dome was so com- monlie receiued that the Apostles were possessed with it & not de- livered of it till after the Resurec- tioun. Act. 1.   Of the *Messias* who possest Man's braine   745
With fond conceats, Imaginations vaine
Before Hee came, that when in humble state,
Not seconding their expectation great,
Hee did a servant's shape assume, whom they
Conceiv'd, the scepter of the world should sway, 750
An earthly *Monarch*, a triumphing King,
Who by resistlesse force should freedome bring
To their subjected state, Himselfe oppose
To tyranizing pride of conqu'ring foes,
Whom finding Other then they did surmise,   755
2 Thes. 2. 11.   With strong delusions led, the world agrees,
The true *Messias* cruellie to kill,
Expecting their fore-fancied Saviour still :
Although our LORD, inviting oft there view,
In Scriptures to behold his paterne true,   760
Which, holy Prophets livelie had exprest,
Ere fleshe's vaile His God-head did invest,
Yet He, this Glasse who hid, their eyes did sile :
His guiltlesse blood must needs their hands defile.

The same is Hee who trauells in excesse,   765
Yet from the world the Scriptures to suppresse,
And from the knowledge true of CHRIST, therein,
The world debarring keeps the world in sinne :
Cous'ning poore people by deceitfull slight,
Of paynters arte, affording false delight,   770
Filling their hands, robt of GOD's sacred word,
With pictures, from their paterns which debord,

Which bold blasphemers, destitute of shame,
Now CHRIST, the holy *Crucifixe* now name.

What *Spirit* els, except GOD'S auncient Foe,   775
Would striue to hide what God hath meant to show?
Or who, except alone that *Spirit* bold,
That dare raike vp, which GOD ly buried would?
What *Spirit* els the world to looke would let
In that pure Mirror, whence faint soules might get
Refreshment, by the sight of Him alone,   781
Who in His word is seene, is rightlie knowne?
Who els would sweate the multitude to leade,
By lying Images, GOD'S peace to pleade,
By which the world is rather led astray   785
After dumb Idols in damnation's way?
Iudge then whom These, who willfull Agents bee,

Patrons prophane of this impietie
Doe serue, who superstitiouslie maintaine
This forg'rie, Man in darknesse to detaine,   790
The *Romane* Clergie, who of pow're too weake,
The *words* pure light to make the world forsake
By craft doe cast about another way
To dimme the luster of this *Lamps* cleare Raye,
The holy Scripture branding with disgrace,   795
Which to traditions they but second place,
Making the world It, with a just neglect,
Corrupt and poysond in the source suspect,
Imperfyte, and in vulgare tongues to bee
Translated, needlesse, not from danger free.   800
Thus from foule mouths maliciouslie they spew,
Aginst the Scriptures not aspersions few,
Furthering the world (so farre as in them lyes),
GOD'S *word* as hard, yea hurtfull, to despyse,
  Yet CHRIST'S pretended Image on the Crosse,
Their leaden braines with superstition grosse   806
Doth so distract, that This, they madly seeme,
To honour more than Him did them redeeme,

To which they teach, as CHRIST's Resemblance true,
Religious worship, yea divyne is due,   810
Yea that same worship, which to CHRIST they owe,
If Hee Himselfe did personally showe.

The Scripture thus defended from the *Lay*,
Traditions vncontrold fynd patent way,
Their *canons, constitutions, Popes' decrees*,   815
False *definitions, legends* stuft with lyes,
Doctrines deboarding from the *written Word*
With *Scripture* equall credite thus afford,
Yea of the *Scripture* thou mayst nought beleeue,
But in what sense the *Pope* is pleasd to giue :   820
Thus, to the blinded world's astonishment,
Their *Lying wonders* with beleife they went,
Thus from the *People* they their *Errors* hyde,
Which, by the sharper sighted if espyd,
The *word* withdrawne, their labour lighter is,   825
To make them thinke they did decerne a-misse.
Thus must the *People* found their *fayth* on trust,
For as their *Church-men*, so belieue they must.

This fyner threed doth to their arts-men giue,
A net of *merits*, of *good works* to weave,   830
By which they fish, (from such as may be brought,
To apprehend that Heaven may thus bee bought,
With excesse to maintayne Those who have charge,
Of convents, cloisters) Rents, dotations large,
And if this fully doth no worke their end,   835
A larger Net of *Pennance* they extend,
From which to bee exem'd, they waird, they watch,
The *Rich-ones* by *Indulgences* to catch,
Who by their purse chuise rather to bee purgt,
Then fast from flesh, then suffer to bee scourgt.   840
But if some *Fish*, free from the danger leape,
And both the one and other doe escape,
To bee assur'de then both of poore and rich,
A *Hose-nett* they of Purgatorie pitch,

The suppressing of the common reading of the Scripture makes such way to all errors, that the Romane clergie rules secure-lie and rainges over all kingdoms, coū-tries, and com-mounwealths, while they get place over King's crowns, men's consciences, their soules, bodies, lands, rents, and movables, and all at their pleasure.

By which they seaze a-like on each degree ;   845
Heere *Great ones* stick, yea not the *Frie* go free ;
All, by the doctrine which these Clerks do found,
Vngratious, yea vnnat'rall must be found,
(At death at least) except with minds devote,
Allowance, in some measure, they allote,   850
Some kynd remembrance, *Masses* to maintaine,
Soules to set free, from *purgatorie's* paine.
    Thus do those *Glow-wormes* which but shine by
      night,
The substance of the world suck vp by slight,
By shows of holynesse, by secreet stealth,   855
Congesting mountaines of entysing wealth,
To which, as *Ravens* which doe a Carion see,
Trowps of *Church-orders*, swarms of *Shavelings* flie,
Of which none idle, all on worke are set :
By Cous'ning miracles, some doe credite get,   860
To Cristen bels, tosse beads they some appoint,
Some crosse, some creepe, some sprinkle, some
    anoynt,
Some hallow candles, palmes, crisme, ashes, wax,
Some penitents admitt to Kisse the Pax ;
And while this crew in these imployment wants, 865
They multiply both male and female *Saints;*
A severall Church they to each Saint allote ;
By raysing Altars they must seme devote,
In one Church diverse, to a diverse end,
Which men enabled with new meanes must tend. 870
    No wonder then they vrge a strict restraynt,
Of Scripture, Seene, which would the World acquynt
With these Imposturs, damnable deceats,
Indang'ring vnder trust, so great Estates,
Which if they licenc't were GOD's Word to view, 875
Should doubtlesse bide those *forg'ries* all adiew.

Act. 19. 24.   For *Images* looke what did set on fire
What earst did kindle the Ignoble Ire

Popish crucifixes bring more gaines to the Popish craftesmen and Clargie, than the Images of Diana, or any idoll to the craftsmen of Ephesus.

Of that EPHESIAN confused crew,

All in a Mutinous concurse which flew,   880

While of this *Monster* the seditious *Head*,

Demetrius for *Diana's* shrines did plead.

What motives then did these incense, the same,

Place now for their *Imagery* doe clayme,

Them stirring vp more turbulent, how much   885

Their trade doth breed them greater gayne, then such.

For but the mettel's worth and craftsmen's paynes,

Did breed *Ephesians* answerable gaynes,

But of their Picturs what the eye espyes,   889

'Tis nought ; their worth in forme nor matter lyes,

These valued are, on these the world doth doate,

As Church-men *holinesse* to them alloate,

As sacred *vertue Men* in them conceave,

Which *Pope* or *Prelate*, at their pleasure gave,

Thus by conceit, the Simple to entyse,   895

These by opinion, not by worth who prise.

Thus doe they farre those *Silver-smiths* out-flee,

In witty traffiquing, in policy,

Masking their avarice with greater slight,

Than these who sold but what they set in sight, 900

Their consecrated *Crucifixes* be

Most prisd for their supposed sanctitie.

It is strange that their being so many pretended Crucifixes, and sensible differences betuixt everie one of them, yet men will beare it out that every one of them ar purtraits of Christ.

But this in mee moves greatest admiration,

Tho every day bring foorth a new creation

Of these false pictures, an adulterat brood,   905

So that in number, number they exclude,

Yet all of them, though of a diverse frame,

Each diffring from another, boldly clame,

CHRIST vively to exhibite to the eye,

Stretcht foorth to death vpon an abject tree ;   910

So that, it seems more CHRISTS they either make,

Or CHRIST doe for the damned thiefe mistake,

Sith neither Graver's toole, nor Paynter's arte,

Doe other difference, saue in thoght impair,

Yet howsoeuer, whether This or that   915
They doe resemble, all of them they rate,
And doe in as high estimation hold,
(Though infinite in number) as of old,
Ephesians did their One *Palladium* prise,   919
Which they did fancie *Ioue* sent downe from skyes.

The Bible serues
not for Poperie as
fained Crucifixes
doe and theirfore
sell the worse, yea
are thrust out of
the Market.

CHRIST'S purtrate thus in Scripture is supprest,
Lest their abuses It should manifest,
And lying Pictures in its place are thrust,
Yet vnder colour of a reason just,
Since *Images* (say they) by silent speach,   925
As bookes, the rude, the ignorant doe teach,
Since *Scripture* to the vse of all, least free,
Oft misconceiud doth lead to *heresie*.

The pretense of
Images serving for
books to the Laicks
answered.

But who but poore deluded soules can trust,
That Images, inventions but of dust,   930
In teaching *truth* GOD'S sacred word doe match,
That Scriptures serue but heresies to hatch?
    Shall *Idols* dumbe, be speaking Teachers prisd?
Shall speaking scriptures be *dumbe rules* despisd?
By Craftsman's arte on mettle, woode, or stone,   935
Shall CHRIST more lively to the world bee showne,
Then by Their dytments who did him behold,
And left His words, deeds, life, & death enrold?
    If holy write some impiously abuse,
This to maintaine lewd heresies who chuse,   940
Must guiltlesse soules, must people innocent,
Of their offence endure the punishment?
Thus should wee shunne the Sunne's conforting light,
Which (happily) hath hurt some stairing sight,
Thus losse the comfort of GOD'S creatures goode,
Since some that poysons which is others' foode.   946
If *heresies* (by which are most misled)
In learned, but vnhallowed brayns are bred,
Since hatcht, nor nurst by the simplicitie,
Of vulgar braynes these deepe delusions bee,   950

Why then doe holy harmelesse people smart,

For heady *Churchmen's* fault, without desart?

The 4 answere.   If *Error* (which wee should as death despyse),

Mat. 21. 16 & 42.
Mat. 22. 29. Doth from not reading of the word aryse,

As CHRIST doth teach, why then (in Christ's de-

    spight),   955

To keepe from erring smother they this light?

    But all that to their minds doth disagree,

Is repute Error, held for heresie ;

Though *Peter*, *Paul*, or *Prophet* did perswade,

Though CHRIST Himself affirmd the contrare

    hade,

Their words must either not bee hard at all,   961

Or vnder Popish dispensation fall

To passe for Scripture, so a sense receave,

In other meaning than the Spirit gave,

A glosse the Text confounding quyte ; because   965

For *Error* all they hold that hurts their *cause*.

The Scripture such a mirror to shew Christ that it changes the student into the liknesse of Christ while there he beholdeth him by fayth.   The Mirror pure, in which *Christ's* face doth shine

The Scripture is, that register divyne

Of holy write, that sacred, saving *Booke*,

In which our LORD hath licenct vs to looke,   970

Where, if wee labour earn'stly for His sight,

The skailes of darknesse which our eyes be-night,

He doth remove, and maks vs clearly see

With *open face*, the beames of Majestie,

2 Cor. 3. 18. And true Beholders by a manner strange,   975

Doth peece and peece in His owne likenesse change,

And in this study as wee progresse make,

Wee of the *Glory* which wee see partake,

Exod. 34. 29. Changt in our soules by CHRIST's renuing grace,

As on the mount was changed *Moses'* face.   980

The impietie of suppressing the scripture.   Why doe they syle poore mocked peoples' sight,

CHRIST's face from viewing in this *mirror* bright?

Why hinder they faynt sin-chargt soules to see,
CHRIST whom they search for, where hee found may
    bee?
The Spirit's working which doth men renew,   985
By means of this true sight, this inward view,
The change of soules from sinne why do they marre,
Why saving knowledge from the world debarre?

    What helpe can all their pow'rlesse purtraits make,
From forger's fancie which doe fashion take,   990
Truely to teach CHRIST's *Naturs, Essence, Will,*
Or in CHRIST's Image men to change from ill?

Shall Their false picturs, *Crucifixes* faynd,
CHRIST's Mirror bee (that sacred fountaine staind),
In these or shall the Spirit men make see,   995
Or what CHRIST is, or what themselves should bee.

    O three times impious! O blasphemous speach!
These nought to lookers on but lyes do teach,
And like themselves, their favourits they make,

As *heads* they have, but *vnderstanding* lake,   1000
As *mouths* which speike no, *feete* which never
    move,
As *eyes* that see no, yet doe set on love,
And justly doe of wit, of sense bereave,
Disciples all, such *Teachers* as beleave,
Suffering themselues to bee debard the sight,   1005
Of holy write, which truely teach them might.

    Great is the *miserie* of man by Sinne,

The *Ignorance* of GOD Man binds therin.

The way to freedome from these heavy bands,
In GOD's true knowledge principally stands;   1010
GOD truely's knowne but in his Christ to none,
And GOD in CHRIST who know fynd life alone.
Now CHRIST, who onely GOD Himselfe who so,
That man may GOD, Man must Himselfe make kno.
The fittest meanes Himselfe to manifest,   1015
To His owne searchelesse *Wisdome* knowne are best.

Hee knows what neede wee of this knowledge
    have,
And how without it nothing vs can save,
And how the losse of Mankynd he doth beare,
Doth by His Death, to bring vs life appeare.   1020
His loue to saue vs, Him who did despise,
Did set on worke His *wisdome* to devise,
All *Meanes* which of Himselfe the knowledge pure
And so of GOD, might to our soules procure,
And so in him bee reconceild, so fred   1025
From wrath, so to eternall life bee led :
And what His *Wisedome* for our well devisd,
His constant care, in holy write comprisd
Hath left, the *Meanes* thus setting in our sight,
Which of Himselfe the saving knowledge might   1030
Sufficiently disclose ; *Meanes* onely meet
To make Him knowne, *Meanes* in themselues com-
    pleet,
Without the forg'ry hatcht in humane braine
Of lying pictures, *Crucifixes* vaine,   1034
Which for His knowledge Hee hath thought vnfit,
Since mongst His *Meanes* these He doth not admit.
    Thus hath Hee not the *Means* alone prescriv'd,
Which point Him foorth (*Means* in His Word
    contriv'd).
But All doth charge, who warm'd are with His loue,
And *Means* to make Him rightly knowne would
    proue,   1040
To search the Scriptures, if for life they looke ;
In all men's hand CHRIST puts this saving *Booke :*
This, Hee doth warrant, to eternitie,
A constant witnesse of Himselfe to bee.
    But *Picture-mongers,* mad *Demetrius'* heires,   1045
Vnlawfull gayne to make of worthles wares,
By other *Means* then CHRIST, to lead to Heaven,
New bookes haue fayned, new directions given.

Therefore the skarring of people from the Scripture, and putting in their hands Images & pictures vnder whatsoever pretence, is a chalenging of Christ, either as witlesse or lovelesse or cairelesse who did not recommend in his testament such a meane as they aledge the artificiall crucifixe to be.

Poor simple *Laikes* (they in substance say),

By searching of the Scriptures erre yee may,   1050

Pictures are plaine, these harmelesse bookes doe show

What needfull is for you of Christ to know,

In Scripture darke 'tis dangerous to prye,

Such curious search concernes not you to trye.

    Thus impudently teach the world they dare,   1055

That both vnfit and vnsufficient are

CHRIST'S *Means;* their owne devices more import

The well and safety of the weaker sort.

    Thus argue they of *Ignorance* our LORD,

The *Means* most fitting, who could not afford;   1060

    Of *Envie,* means who would not recommend,

Which choysen, most might to our safetie tend;

    Of *Carelesnesse,* sith He forgot to give

Charge, in his *Latter-Will* these meanes to leave.

    For peoples *Well* thus will they seame to be   1065

More *Wise,* more *Loving, Carefuller* than Hee.

What else is this, by a pretence to teach

CHRIST'S knowledge, but *Christ's* knowledge to empeach,

By faining a false *Christ,* to barre the way

By which the *True* attayne wee only may,   1070

Who, not attaind, GOD neither can wee know,

Since GOD in Him alone Himselfe doth show?

Thus are the bonds of Man's most wretcht estate

By Nature, straitned by the Devil's deceate.

Albeit civile Images for civile vse bee lawfull, yet no religious Images of man's device for religious vse are lawfull.

    Let civile *Images,* for civile vse   1075

Haue place, we challenge only the abuse.

That paynter's Pencil pleasure doe impart

Wee hinder no, let craftsmen vse their arte:

But howsoever humane wit debord,

Exod. 19. 18.

GOD in *Religion* must alone bee LORD.   1080

The 2 commãd of the first Table which is the Law for

    While from Mount *Sinai* Hee the Moral Law

Promulgate did, (where Him no mortall saw)

religion expresly
forbids religious
Images of man's
device.

Incompast all about with flames of fire,

As Royall Roabs which *Majestie* attire,

Hee, onely as His owne *Prerogatiue*,   1085

Did, of Religion, plead the *Rule* to giue,

And Man, (with vaine presumption swolne), at large

Madly with *This* to meddle doth discharge,

Deut. 4. 15.
Exod. 20. 22.
We may make a
Image which re-
semblesSomething,
but not an Idole
which resembles
Nothing sayes the
Papist: No says the
Lord, you shall not
make the liknesse
of any thing in
Heaven &c. Deut.
4. 23.

Binding His hands, by words expresse and plaine,

Of Him, no foolish *Counterfit* to faine,   1090

No Image, for Religious vse, to make,

Of ought, in Heaven or earth did being take;

Nor made, to honour, with the least respect,

Save They with Him their *Covenant* would breake,

Kindling gainst them His iealousie most just,   1095

Rankt as *Adult'rers*, (from His service thrust)

Who, worship with Him, or besyde Him, gave,

To others, due for Him alone to have.

Exod. 23. 24, &
34. 13.

Thus GOD hath banisht, from Religion's bounds

This worship vaine, His worship which confounds,

All vse of Images, by Man devysd,   1101

To GOD Man hatefull rendring and despysd.

2 Thes. 2. 3. 4.

But Hee who doth exalt Himselfe to raigne,

Why may not the
people and the
Church apoint
Images sayes the
papist. I am the
Lord says God, that
is it is God's Royall
prerogatiue to
apoint the meanes
of his owne Honour.

Of Princes all *Monarchick Soveraigne*,

That Man of Sinne, perdition's Sonne, the slave

Of Sathan, yet pretends CHRIST's place to have, 1106

Dare gainst this Law most impudently stand,

And GOD's great VETO boldly counter-mand.

Of GOD, of Man, he images dare make,

Why may wee not
give some Religious
worship & honour
to Images sayeth
the papist. I am a
Ielous God sayes
the Lord, that is,
Religious worship
is due only to God
the husband of the
Church,whatsoever
is given to another
is adulterie, that is
Idolatrie & provoks
God's Ielousie.

Thus Mocketh CHRIST, even suffring for our sake:

To these, Religious worship Hee allowes,   1111

And *This* their *Due* most shamelessly avowes.

Whyle of this Rav'ry wee a reason crave,

O how themselves they willfully deceave!

The *custome of their Fathers* They pretend,   1115

The love of GOD, *of* CHRIST, this is the end

Why they Their purtraits reverently respect,

Whose persons They so dearely did affect,

Our forefathers vsed Images sayes the papist. I will visit the sinnes of the fathers vpon the children sayes the LORD.

But O weake shifts! pretences worthy tears!
Evasions serving more to mocke the eares,   1120
Of simple Hearers, than this Error vaine
With meanest show of reason to maintaine.

We make and hon-our Images out of loue to God, sayes the papist. They hate mee that keepes not my com-mandemēt sayes the Lord.

God's Law most clearely these detects : the same
Excuses for this foolishnesse they frame
Which clearely are condemnd (shifts farre amisse),
In that *Command* which Rankt the *Second* is :   1126

When the Church of Rome scraipt out the 2 command out of the vulgare books & made two of the 10 command, they saw that their Images could not abyd the assise of God's law.

Which, GOD of purpose, gainst this Sinne did place,
This wickednesse so staring in the face,
That when heereof, they can not stand in sight,
Accusd, convict by their owne conscience light,
To burie it from vulgare eyes they striue,   1131
And this of place amongst the Ten depriue,
Braunching the Tent in twaine ; to hide the thift,
Vsing a shamelesse sacrilegious shift,
Least seene the people should these *snares* forsake,
Layde (doubtlesse by the devill) their soules to take.

To elude God's Law Image lovers haue vsed as (they yet vse) many pre-tences, but notwith-standing of them all, God reiects this invention, refuts it, condemnes and curses both it and the maintainers of it.

Thus, though our LORD, as a religious *Meane*,   1137
Condemned hath to *Images* to leane,
Yet still doe *Image-doatars* GOD's decreit
Striue to make Irrite, as vnjust, vnmeet,   1140
Thus pleading profite to the Simpler sort,
Who come of knowledge by the Scripture short
But by the Eye inform'd, are brought in mynd,
Of what by These they represented fynd.

Ierem. 10. 3.

But harke O *fondling*, who thy GOD dost faine,
GOD by his *Spirit* cals this custome vaine.   1146
Those *creatures* of thine owne, nor care, nor feare
Thou needst, which Thee can neither see nor heare.

Ier. 10. 8.

How foolish they who doe on such depend,

v. 5.

Which neither *Friend* can help nor *Foe* offend? 1150

v. 8.

The *Stocke* which GOD they to resemble frame,
Doth doctrines but of vanity proclame.

v. 11.

These perish shall from Earth, from vnder Heaven,
Their *Founders* to confusion shall bee driuen,

v. 14. Whose arte but *Error* serves to vnderproppe,   1155
Whose worke is falshoode, forgt in Sathan's shoppe.
    This foolish Toy, this hell-devised slight,
    Men charming with a naturall delight,
    Loe, GOD doth scorne, the workman's fruitlesse
        paynes,   1159
    The zeale poore people which hood-winkt detaynes,
    Him seeking whose pure worship they professe,
Is. 40. 18, 19, 20. By some *Resemblance* fondly to expresse.
Isa. 4. 20.   GOD to a dispute challengeth in end,
    Such as dare graven Images defend,
    Deluded soules and blinded by deceate   1165
    GOD proves them, who transported with this
        spaite
    Of madnesse, basely doe crouch downe before
    The crafts-man's worke ; which ought to have no more
    Respect, then as much mettell, timber, stone,
Is. 44. 9, 10. Appointed for the basest vse, or none.   1170
    Hee laughs to heading their conceats, to see,
    What lavish chairges spent in *Making* bee,
    In *Consecrating*, what obsequious care,
    What *Superstition*, straitning Sathan's snaire,
    What base *Devotion* madly they bequeath   1175
    Vnto their *Idoles*, which (tho voyde of breath),
    On shoulders mounted they on high doe reare,
Isa. 46. 5, 6, 7. And in ridiculous *Procession* beare.
    Let blind *Idolaters* with errors streame
    Transported headlong, vse and profite dreame,   1180
Isa. 44. 9. By these devices ; GOD professeth plaine,
    Hee knows no profite by these *Meanes* profaine,
    Meanes to bee made vnworthy, *Meanes* to trust
    Intolerable ; teaching lyes to *Dust*,
    Whence beeing they did take.   The *Curse of Woe*,
    Of Vengeance, thundred foorth they vndergoe,   1186
Hab. 2. 18, 19, 20. Who *Prayer's* sweete perfume to such present,
    Whom words nor vows can with or wants acquent.

Deut. 27. 15. *Cursd* by the Law, is Hee, who toole doth take

Or grav'ne, or molten *Image* for to make,   1190

GOD thus abhominably to disgrace.

Cursd, for devotion, who in secret place,

The *Crafts-man's* worke, GOD'S worship to confound

Set vp, the People all *Amen* resound.

Psal. 97. 7. Harke, how the *Prophet* doth confusion threat,

A *Curse* denunceth both to Meane and Great,   1196

That boast of Idols, Images doe serue.

The reason why *Such* do this curse deserue,

Rom. 1. 23. Saint *Paule* expresseth.   For, from GOD estraingt

His Glory Incorruptible, transchangt   1200

By them into an Image, made in all,

Like Man corruptible, proclive to fall,

Rom. 1. 25. They even GOD'S Trueth, have turned in a *Lie*,

Ascribing worship, in more high degrie,

Vnto the *Creature* subject to decay,   1205

Than the CREATOR, who is blest for ay.

Obiection. Yet notwithstanding all, *Some* dare avouch,

But O sayeth the papist I find my affection stirred & my devotion helped by Images & namelie the artificiall Crucifixe. This pretence answered. That while before a *Crucifixe* they crouch,

Or on a well done *Image* fixe their eye,

Their frozen *Zeale* they fynd enflamt to bee,   1210

Their half-dead *Faith* reviv'd, their faynting Loue

To CHRIST, incitements wonderfull to prove,

Passions of joy, of feare, of griefe increst,

Fitting to further their devotion best,

So, though the world, (they openly avow),   1215

Though all authoritie these disallow,

Which in their brests such strange effects doe bread,

And whence such motions of the *Sp'rit*, procead,

They can not bee induc't, so much as doubt,

But GOD aproves, even to be borne about,   1220

Sollicitously keept, devoutely kist,

To bee falne downe before, these *Means* most blest,

Means, of that worship worthy held to bee

Even due to CHRIST ; though not in like degree.

Affections and motions accompanying Image worshiping are but the whorish allurments of the spirit of idolatrie.

But O *Blind soules* these folyes which frequent,
If with GOD'S will yee truely were acquent,   1226
In holy write reveald, and did believe,
These *Means* suspition should not faile to give;
Thus narrowly yee should that Serpent's slight

Cor. 15. 14.

Examine, in an *Angel* changt of light,   1230
GOD's *Spirit* counterfitting, whose deceat,
Vnder pretence of peace procuring hate,
By bastard *Motions* of the minde doth make,
Deluded soules grosse *Lyes* for *Truths* mistake.

'Tis most absurd, even in the least degree,   1235
To thinke GOD's *Word* and *Spirit* disagree,
This, striving to restraine and stop the way,
That, grounds to this impiety to lay.
GOD's holy *Spirit* by no other *Meanes*
Doth worke, but such as GOD Himselfe ordaines,
Whatever superstitious potards dreame,   1241
Forbidden *Meanes* He hates; and these by name.

A contrair *Spirit* then *This* hold wee must,
Insinuating Himselfe to settell trust
In the deluded soules of such, as find   1245
Such seeming-sacred-*Motions* of the mind,
Warming with woontlesse flames their frozen hearts,
Enveigling man's conceit with wondrous arts.

These (doubtlesse) must the whoorish *Motions* bee,
Even of the *Spirite* of Idolatrie;   1250
The fire of worship false; entysing traines
Layd by that crafty *Foe*, who spairs no paines
Wretcht Man to make vnlawfully delite
In what GOD most condemns, in *sacred write*.

Exod. 32. 19.

Deut. 9. 21:
Exod. 32. 20.
1 King 13.

Such were the *Motions Jewes* made *daunce* for joy
Before the *Calfe*, which *Moses* did destroy.   1256
Such, made the *Prophet* by those *Tribs* contemnd,
In *Dan* and *Bethell*, who their *calues* condemnd.
Such earst (wee reade) was the deluding dreame,

Iudg. 17. 13.

Made *Micah happy* in his owne esteeme.   1260

Such vncouth *flames* made men the Temple leaue

a Deut. 7. 5; &
12. 3.

Worship to ^a*Images* in groaues to giue.

Such zeale made *Israelits* of sense denude,

b Isa. 57. 5;
Deut. 12. 31;
Levit. 20. 1, &
18. 21.

Bathe ^b*Molech's* Image with their children's blood.

The *Devill*, who Them did to this madnesse driue

As subtile now as earst, is yet a-liue :   1266

And still goth on, by all the craft hee can,

From service of the *Living* GOD, fond man

To tempt, *Spirituall Whordome* to *commit*

With *Idols* dombe : who, destitute of wit   1270

With the inchaunting *Motions* of the minde

Is charmd, in Scripture which no warrant finde.

Though *Motions* follow not *Means* vsd in *Faith*

Which for His service GOD appointed hath

As men would haue, or in their hearts project,   1275

Yet such (wee find) haue ever good effect.

But *Motions* which without GOD'S *Meanes* doe worke

Are still to be suspect : the *Snaike* doth lurk

Beneath the blooming flowre : the deadliest blow

Is to bee fear'd from a disguised foe.   1280

Who so, come by such *Motions*, can not flee

By Sathan's snaires but must entangled be.

Isa. 53. 2.

By GOD'S *Prophetick Spirit* when inspird

Before Christ came
Isaiah prophesied
that Christ should
neither have forme
uor comlines for
which we should
loue him.   There-
fore the lying re-
semblance of our
Lord's form in the
artificiall Crucifixe
must haue lesser
force.

Isaiah CHRIST made (long ere seene) admir'd,

Nor *Forme*, nor *Comlinesse* hee did foretell   1285

Should make His outward feature to excell,

No beauty admiration to moue,

For which, wee should Him or desire, or loue.

And so it did succeed : for, who by sight

Of His externall shape, Him knew a-right   1290

To bee the CHRIST, who Man to GOD conceald,

Math. 16. 17.

Such thing of Him, nor flesh, nor blood reveald.

Since CHRIST'S true lineaments set to the eye

(Which any Painter could haue wisht to see)

The bodily beholding of our LORD,   1295

So little force, or furtherance did afforde,

Q

To kindle Men's affections, or to draw
Whom even the *Princ'pall*, not the *Purtrait* saw
To His obedience ; O what madnesse then
What fury strange doth fill the braines of Men,   1300
With dreams deluded, fondly to conceate,
That *lying Pictures* are of powre more great ?
That counterfites of His exterior frame,
Zeale can make fervent, or with *loue* enflame ?
As greater vertue did from *Picturs* flow   1305
Then *Person's* presence they are set to show ?
    Since of a *Servant's shape*, the outward sight,
Which in the flesh did clowde CHRIST's Heavenly
    light
Did, nor with *Motions* nat'rall, nor divine,
Make men to loue, or seeke to Him, incline,   1310
Shall *Motions* by this *Shap's* vaine picture wrought
Iustly, or nat'rall, or divine be thought ?
No certaine : else the *Crafts-man's toole* should proue
On wood, or stone more forcible to moue
Then GOD's owne hand, CHRIST's frame, and featurs
    true   1315
On superfice of humane flesh which drew.

Faith in Christ is necessar, the seing of Christ bodily is not necessar, far lesse is the false counterfitting of his shape necessar.

    However Men conceate that *Faith*, by sight
Is fostred ; thus that *loues* decaying might
Is quickned, yet CHRIST doth the *blessing* giue
To such as *haue not seene* and doe *beleeue*.   1320

The artificiall Crucifixe is a fleshly meane to know Christ after the flesh which the Apostle doth reiect.

    After the *flesh* Paul CHRIST refusd to know
Resolv'd Him thus no more, if ever so :
How should these *Means* of knowledge then content
After the *flesh* CHRIST made to represent ?

Naturall considerations of the art of painting, or graving, may show the artificiall Crucifixe to be but the mockage of the World.

    BVT, of these *Pictures* poysning not a few   1325
With Error, yet to take a nearer view,
Each *Image* should bee like its Patterne made,
From imitating which, it name doth pleade,
And if heereof it no resemblance leaue,
Beholders' Eyes it serues but to deceaue.   1330

The *Painter* then the *Prototype* must see,
Which in his brest must first engraved bee
Before his Pensill, with deserved praise,
Can with its semblance ravisht Eyes amaze.
The Shape, the Lineaments, the Features right   1335
His fantasie must apprehend by sight,
His hand directing, as hee did conceaue,
A viue impression to the Eye to leaue,
Els both deluded is His simple braine
And Men but mocked with an *Idole* vaine.   1340
    For, of the Patterne if through Ignorance,
A bleare-eyed *Leah* hee should draw by chaunce,
A traytrous *Iudas*, being of intent
Rachel's, or *Peter's* purtrait to present,
Needs force the picture (yet) of that must bee   1345
Which it most liuely sets before the *Eye*.
    Though Hee His work should cristen with the Name
Proper to that to make which was His aime,
Yet must it bee that which it truely is,
Not what proposd it was, though nam'd amisse. 1350
    Tho with Apelles' skill, Men now should striue
Pictures, procuring wonder, to contriue,
If from the Patterne diffring, wrought by guesse,
What serue they, fruitlesly but to expresse
And (valued though with vndeserved worth)   1355
Conceptions but fantastick to set forth?
Since these (however by opinion great)
Yet births abortiue of some vaine conceate,
What can they els bee but resemble thought,
The fond *Imagination* them which wrought?   1360
Though Popish Church should authorize the Dead
Church, Painter, picture, all to *Error* lead.
    For, as the braine the *Patterne* doth conceaue
So doth the *Image-Maker* paint or graue:
The Patterns faynd *Idea*, in his braine   1365
First must bee forg't, next the impression vaine

Not of the *Patterne*, but of His conceate,
(A fantasie, hatcht in his head of late)
Finds on the *Table*, or the *mettall*, place,
As arte can his Imagination trace ;   1370
Thus, hold wee must each *Image* of this kinde,

The definition of an
Image made by
arte.

The first Resemblance of the craftsman's minde.
How falsly then doth a mis-shapen masse
Of mettall for our SAVIOUR'S *Image* passe?
How fondlie men perplexe themselues to mixe 1375
Colours most fit to frame a *crucifixe?*
Which when perfited by the best of arte
The most accomplisht *Crafts-men* can imparte,
In no respect with CHRIST resemblance hath,
Triumphing on the Crosse o're Hell, o're death, 1380
No not so much as in His outward frame
By lines which *they* to counterfit doe clame.

The artificiall Cru-
cifixe hath no
ground but the
Craftsman's guesse,
seing never one
that drew Christ's
purtrait saw the
true Paterne.

For, nor the *Paterne* blessd the *Crafts-man's* Eye
CHRIST'S living face who did no living see,
Nor saw He Any who could show by speach   1385
And of our LORD the features truely teach,
But as conceate him ledde, hee boldly gues't,
And, as the *Blind-man* casts his staffe, exprest
Vpon his table : meerly ignorant
Whether in shape, this new-created *Saint*   1390
Lookt liker CHRIST, or either of those *twaine*
Like shamefull death who did with CHRIST sustaine.
But (to giue place to trueth) it lookes like neither,
But, as the Child resemble doth the father,
This new-borne *issue* of the *crafts-man's* braine, 1395
Got by imagination, hatcht for gaine,
Like to the fancie of *his* fond conceate
Who brought it forth, with paine, with labour great,
Must only be suppos'd ; An IDOL right
By Romish definition ; (else but slight)   1400
The Semblance of a thing but faind to bee,
Which no subsistance hath essentially.

Put case, a *Painter*, for a proofe of arte,
Three pictures did most exquisite imparte,
Of Men, streatchd foorth vpon the crosse to
  death,

This *Master-peece* while he accomplisht hath   1406
Is't not to his arbitriment left free
By CHRIST to cristen any of the three?
Or, at his pleasure, all three theeues to make,
Resolving (least they company should lake)   1410
Three other *Christs* to forge? or, to affixe
The Superscription of CHRIST'S *Crucifixe*
Aboue the purtrait of a *Thiefe* of late,
(Adjudged so at least in his conceate)
It calling *Christ?* or, if hee rather please   1415
The superscription new affixt to raise
So make his *Christ* a Thiefe, for some wrong
  draught
Which nearer observation him hath taught,
Can *Pope*, *Priest*, *Prelate*, alter his decree?
Which hee thinks fit, that *Picture Christ's* must
  be.
His *Word* must for a sentence stable stand,   1421
What Hee determins, none can countermand,
None can His worke controule. For, if the sight,
The *Iudge* which onely can decerne aright
Of Picturs, never hath the *Patterne* spyed   1425
How can in such the grossest faults be tryed?
Sense, lacking thus a rule to censure by
In vaine, but in the *Painter's* arte doth pry.
Thus foulest Errors in this kind goe free,
Thus Painters boldly take them leaue to *lie*   1430
Audaciously, with liberty vnraind,
Coosning the world with *Crucifixes* faind,
Them giving foorth CHRIST'S semblances to
  bee,
Which but (at most) His *Superfice* belie.

True IESUS CHRIST the world's *great Iudge,* while
  judg'd,   1435
(At shame^a nor shrinkt, nor at disgrace who grudgd)
An Offring *Holy,*ᵇ *Harmelesse, Vndefild,*
While sacrifiz'd for Man, from grace exild,
While, compted with^c *Transgressors,* lift'd on hie,
(The^d *Innocent* the *Guiltie* setting free)   1440
Loe ! While enduring even the worst of spight,
Strength, Glory, Greatnesse, Majestie, and *Might.*
Brake forth so brightlie through contempt's dark
  clowd,
So (cleare) His *Godhead* did in death, vnshrowd,
That, the *Centurion,* overcome with wonder,   1445

(While HEAVENS their face vaild vp, *Earth* sobt
  a-sunder,
These *glorious Lanterns,* as their lights were spent,
To shine forbearing, while their LORD was shent,
This, to the GOD of *Strength,* while seeming weake,
Its strength resigning, whence it strength did take).
Forc't was, convinc't in conscience, to confesse 1451

That suffer did the SONNE of *Righteousnesse.*
But where's that Splendor darkning *Daye's* bright
  beame,
These Rayes of Glory, shyning even in shame ?
What doe their Popish *Crucifixes* show   1455
Of CHRIST, but shame, death, nakednesse, and woe ?
What greater *Glory* set they to our view
Then to the basest *Malefactor's* due,
That on a gibbet, e're depriv'd of breath,
Endurd like shamefull execrable death ?   1460

True CHRIST, to death while yeelding on the crosse,
(*Life* to giue *life* content ev'n *life* to losse)
Though dead for vs, at all who could no die,
Ceast never living LORD of *life* to bee,
Quickning, converting, strengthning *Soules,* even then
When seeming most contemptible to Men,   1466

While *Bodies* long agoe consumd in graue
Raisd by His pow'r, of Him twice life receaue.
   How doe their *Crucifixes* this expresse
Than a Triumphing CHRIST like nothing lesse ? 1470
Of their owne *Patterns* (yet) true shads they are,
Viue *Idols* of a lifelesse *Corps*, as farre
From any force in working, by their view,
Or bodyes to raise vp, or soules renew
As is the basest Earth, or fondest braine,   1475
Which first gave birth to these *Inventions* vaine.

Christ's bodie was ioined in personall vnion with the God-head. The Popish crucifixe faines a Christ whose body is separate from the Godhead.

   Christ's Bodie (farre above our sin-tost *Masse*)
Not of an onely *Man* the Body was,
But of that peerlesse *Lord*, true *God*, true *Man*,
Whose neare conjunction sunder nothing can, 1480
Whose humane soule, though from its mansion
     forc'd,
Vpon the crosse by painefull death divorc'd,
Yet in the *God-head*, even o'recome by death
The *Body* Being had, while robt of breath,
Which, lying even in graue, His soule possest 1485
In highest Heavens, that *Paradise* of rest,
Inviolable yet the *Vnion* stoode ;
Nor Heaven, nor Earth (one minute) could seclude
The *God-head* from the *Man-hood ; life*, nor *death*,
Nor hellish horror, nor the sense of wrath   1490
Could hinder, still (yet so as none can tell)

Col. 2. 9.

The *Godhead bodily* in *Christ* to dwell :
Which caus'd, (though buried hee behov'd to bee)

Psal. 16. 8, 9 ; Acts 2. 27.

GOD's *Holy-One, corruption* not to see,
Preserving thus (while dead, in coffin layde,   1495
By putrefaction, as all flesh, to fade)
More pow'rfully the *Body* of our LORD
Than all the means the world could els afford.
   What madnesse then to thinke, (though painter's
     arte
Some shadow of Man's *Body* can impart,   1500

Which from its soule may sev'red bee by death,
And turnd in dust, while banished from breath,)
That by the pensill, may resembled bee
The *Sonne of Man*, the GOD of *Majestie?*
Who, having once a mortall shape assum'd,   1505
Can, (without danger) never bee presum'd,
That from his *Manhood* (not in any cace)
His *Godhead* to *dis-vnion* can give place.

If this wee hould (of this as who may doubt?)
How madde are Men, who fondly goe about   1510
Their Crucifixes false, means to appoint,
CHRIST'S Body blest, without the *Godhead* joynt,
To represent; and set before the Eye

The artificiall Cru-
cifixe teacheth a
Christ who is only
man, or whose two
naturs are not
vnite, or who hath
two Persons, as the
old heritickes did.
CHRIST-*Man*, cut short of divine *Majestie;*
The *Word* made flesh denying, or in death   1515
Loosing that *Vnion*, lasting but with breath;
Or, faining such a CHRIST, a Onely *Man*
Even by it selfe subsist whose *Body* can;
Or, of one *Nature*, or of *Persons* twaine,
A CHRIST Imaginary, therefore vaine;   1520
Injuring thus those *ever-blessed Three*,
That *Trinall One*, which was, is, ay shall bee,
Thus venting blasphemies against our *Lord*,
Whose soule abhorreth thus to be ador'd,

Is. 42. 8; 48. 11.
And whom His *Glory* and His *Praise* to giue   1525
To grauen *Images*, doth highly grieue.

Christ's Image
stands in righteous-
nesse and holinesse,
and can not be seen
with bodilie eyes.
CHRIST'S *Image* mockt thus by audacious hands,
In *Righteousnesse* and *Holinesse* which stands,
The object of the soule's spirituall eye
By Carnall sight can not discerned bee: 1530

If it be a filthy dis-
honor to liken the
worke of man's
hands to God the
father, it is no les
disgrace to liken
the work of man's
hands to God the
Son.
And, as no meane presumption 'tis in Man
To liken ought his weake invention can
Produce, to GOD, *Beginner*, *Vnbegunne*,
So to set foorth his *ever-procreat Sonne*,
In nothing to his great *Begetter* lesse,   1535
By ought or toole or pensil can expresse,

No lesser madnesse : if wee GOD esteeme,

Christ's abaising of himselfe giues not libertie to man to abase him more, but obligeth rather to honour Him the more.
That *Holy One* who did the world redeeme,
Who, though for vs, His *Glory* layde asyde,
Did meanly in mortalitie abyde, 1540
Should wee, Himselfe cause humbling, more neglect,
Or should his *Man-hood*, breed him lesse respect?
Though painter's *lines* might possiblie present

Put case it were possible to find out Christ's Linea- ments, and to ex- presse them by art, yet still the glorie of His person dis- charges to doe Him such disgrace as to liken Him to the worke of man's hands.
His *Counterfite* as Hee with shame was shent,
And of his *Servant's-shape* some shadow leaue, 1545
(Or ayming so, at least the world deceaue)
Doth possibilitie a warrant plead,
Or to excuse or Iustifie this deed,
Since every Sinne hath possibilitie,
But none for this as lawfull held may bee? 1550
In humane Shape, if GOD the *Fathers* saw
Yet no Resemblance durst presume to draw,
Why rather now, since *Flesh* the *Word* assumd,
May GOD by *Man* to bee drawne foorth presumd?
Sith that the Law, this madnesse to restraine, 1555
Midst flames of fire was not given foorth in vaine,
Nor now is made lesse valide, than before

1 Cor. 2. 8.
A *Mortall vaile* the *King of Glory* wore.

The Apostles durst not, nor would not draw his purtrait much lese should a profane Craftsman.
If not *Apostles* durst transgresse this law,
Nor cause draw foorth or grave the *Shape* they saw ;
If none of all Our *Lord's* obsequious Trayne, 1561
His *Will* durst write, but whom Hee did ordaine ;

None may preach Christ without a calling from Christ, much lesse make fained pictures of Christ.
Beyond commission ev'n if none of Those
That wrote, His *Shape* might to the World expose ;
If none may, by Himselfe, this honour reach 1565
Except by CHRIST thrust foorth CHRIST yet to preach,
Shall it to painters only bee left free,
CHRIST'S shape and Lineaments to falsifie,
Even though no warrant doth their worke invite,
Nor having seene what to set foorth they sweate. 1570
'Tis like those dreamers, who poore soules deceaue,
CHRIST *crucifi'd* n'ere right considred haue,

Whyle *once* for *all*, and *Once* for *ay* our *Lord*,
Ne're more to bee repeated, did afford

Christ would not
bee seene to suffer
but once, but will
bee heard to have
suffred ever.   His
suffrings Ho will
have set before the
eye of the minde
by His owne ordin-
ances of *Word* and
Sacrament, but not
to the bodilie eye
by man's invention.

Himselfe a living *Sacrifice* for Sinne,   1575
Vpon the Crosse, lost Man from hell to winne,
Himselfe Hee did expose to suffer death,
Shame, paine, and dolour, ev'n the *Father's* wrath,
No more to bee the object of the *Eye*,
Though by the *Eare* oft crucified to bee.   1580
      As death's tormenting throws, as sense of payne,
Hee for a season was but to sustaine,
So was the *Shame* which *Nakednesse* did give,
Not all his other suffrings to sur-vive.
      When therefore having (mortalls to reclame), 1585
Sufficientlie now suffred open shame,
Even at mid-day Hee drew the vaile of night,
About His naked Bodie, so the sight

Christ darkned the
Sunne and made it
as *Night* at *Mid-
Day* while He was
suffring, to show
that hee would not
have men to gaze
vpon his naked
bodie after hee had
suffred   sufficient
shame.   The Pop-
ish *Crucifixes* doe
crosse *Christ's* pur-
pose.

Of gazing eyes (with clowds eclipsd) did stay,   1589
Enlightning Some, who midst those mists did stray,
Them making see, while weakest made, His *Might*,
Sinne's clowds dispel'd, which did their soules benight.
      But (loe) their antichristian *Crucifixe*
With vaine Inventions who God's worship mixe,
Serves to no other end, but as it may,   1595
CHRIST's *Body* naked to the eye to lay.
And to expose His long-past *Shame* to sight,
Hiding the Glorious vaile of darkned light,
By which more honord was that *Prince of Peace*
Than *Nakednesse*, or *Iews* did Him disgrace.   1600
      CHRIST, of the *Cover* Hee drew on, they striue
(Though all in vaine) thus boldly to depriue,
Preassing presumptuously, in CHRIST's despight,
To prorogate the shortned shame of *Sight*.   1604
      But such their CHRIST, such *Crucifixe* they faine,
Such *Paterne*, such the *Purtraite :* both most vaine.
The *Painter's* fantasie the patterne is :
The *Purtrait* only must resemble this,

That lying *Spirit ;* Father of deceate,
That Man true CHRIST should know, who boyles
    with hate,   1610
And studies still to forme in man's fond braine,
False *Christs ;* or of the *True*, conceats prophane,
Doth Parent to this purtrat's Patterne proue,
Hatcht in the Crafts-man's head as hee doth moue.
The *Crucifixe*, *Child* of the Paynter's *Thought*,   1615
Oye to this Lying *Spirit*, thus forth brought
By arte, as carefull *Midwif's* helping hand,
Is from the painfull wretch receiued ; who fand,
And did more labour in this *Birth* sustaine,
As hee opinion did conceiue of gaine.   1620
    This new - borne *Saint* thus being brought to
        light,
See how the wretch doth in his *Worke* delight,
Hee gazeth, wondreth, narrowly doth pry,
Striues if hee can the least escape espy,
Proport'oning by due esteeme its worth,   1625
As longsome paines, and labour brought it forth,
Which in each feature, finding now compleat,
As to adorne some *Temple* only meet,
Hee to the *Preist* presents't, who streight doth giue
It *Name ;* yea, *Holinesse*, as some beleeue.   1630
By *Charmes*, by *Exorcisme* of *Magick* art,
With *Salt*, and *Water* Christned thus a part,
With *Pardons* priuiledg't, with *Odors* sweet
Perfumd, with *Altars* honord, Head and Feet
Anoynted, *Torches* lighted, *Gifts* presented,   1635
Made fitt for *Pilgrimes* now to bee frequented,
Erected last, in place most eminent,
The *Never-Erring-Clergie* giue consent,
That it shall stand to *bee admir'd, ador'd,*
Kiss'd, reverenc'd, crouch'd before, embrac'd, implor'd,
The Holy *Crucifixe* from hence forth cald,   1641
Or, *On His Crosse the KING OF GLORIE nail'd.*

The Blinded people's foolishe superstition,
The base credulitie of their condition,
Approues the *Error*; ratifies the *Deed*,   1645
With them this *Crucifixe* doth credit plead,
Which in affinity or *Shape* more neare
As they conceiue, the *Holier* doth appeare.

The 'devilish ideifying of the Popish Crucifixe.

Loe now the *Crafts-man*, *Priest* and vulgar *Crew*,
Ioyntly fall down, and with devotion due,   1650
As many *Pater-nosters* doe repeat
By number of their beads, as they finde meet,
To this *New-Christned-CHRIST*; and, as acquent
With Tongues their sutes in Latin must bee sent,
To *This* not sparing, with blasphemous breath,   1655
The Honour of *Latria* to bequeath,
Preferring it to all the Heauenly *Quire*,
Or *Crownde* aboue, or *Militating* heere,
Of *Angels*, *Saints*; euen to that *Mother-Maide*,
The *Queene of Heauen*, (of Her if truth be said). 1660

But when for foule *Idolatrie* arraing'd,
Some *shift* in place of *Reason* must bee fain'd :
These subtile *Sophists*, wittie in invention,
Doe pleade by vertue of their good *intention*,
The honour to the *Crucifixe* ascriv'd,   1665
The *Purtrate* first, by Crafts-man hand contriu'd,
Doth hit, but streight sent back, is vpwards driven,

The pretense of good intention doth no more excuse the popish Idolaters, than if a woman should abuse her bodie with every one that she thoght like her husband, and then say shee did so of good intention willing to loue all that were like her husband.

And by *Reflexe* doth sklent hye way to Heauen,
Possessing such as see with others' eyes,
This *By-way worship* CHRIST no lesse doth please,
Than on these *Tables* earst by God's owne hand 1671
Engrav'd, it had beene left th'eleaventh *Command*.

But let those *Doctors* licence me demand,
Who in *Intention* make *Devotion* stand,
If simple *Women* in their *Husbands'* places,   1675
May warrantably yeeld to strange embraces,
And if it passe may for a just excuse,
That their *Intention Them* did not abuse,

Supposing, they did by obedience due
Themselues subject, vnto their *Husbands* true,   1680
And, if those Husbands, wrong'd in such a sort,
Thus to bee mockt and cousind, ought comport,
And over-looke this as a light offence,
Which *Ignorance* doth challenge in defence?
This, without shame, these Clerks can not approue,
Except some *Intrest* having in this *Loue*.   1686

How easily it selfe doth *Error* roote,
In such as on GOD's *Light* their eyes doe shoote,
That on all hazard will goe on Their way,
With them or walke, or stumble, stand, or stray?

NOW, this great *Idole*, set to publick view,   1691
Yet can not serue; all of this numbrous *Crew*,
For private vse *One* must peculiar haue,
To beare about Him, even vnto His graue.
Enricht with gold and Iewels, *These* are borne   1695
The breasts of *Dames* of *Honor* to adorne,
Which not beseeming *Vulgars* (as too deare),
The *Poorer* sort doe *Poorer Christlings* weare
Of polisht *Ivorie*, of gilded *Glasse*,
Of glistring *Horne*, of *Copper*, *Tinne*, or *Brasse*, 1700
Which by the *Priest* if *hallow'd*, so much more
Held worthie are of *Worship*, than before.

If any living *Saint*, heere sucking breath,
Who with our LORD more neare resemblance hath,
To Him more deare, and held of greater worth, 1705
Than all the *Images* art can bring foorth,
In whom this *Spirit*, *Life*, and *Grace* doth shine,
Whom a most neere *conjunction* doth combine,
And whom CHRIST (one day) though despised now,
Shall not think shame *His* ª *Brother* to avow,   1710
Yet if this *Saint* of *God*, adored were,
Cald on, as senselesse *Crucifixes* are,
The World anone the *sacriledge* should see,
Cry out against this vile *Idolatrie*,

Abhorre, to any *Mortall* vnder *Heaven*   1715
Worship, or divine *Honour* should bee given,
But now when greater measure they bequeath,
To *Stockes*, to *Stones*, to *Idoles* voyde of breath,
They neither can, nor will their *Error* spy,

2 Cor. 4. 3, 4.   So darkned hath the devill their Reason's eye,   1720
Or, to damnation poasting on amaine,

Rom. 1. 18.   Dare in *vnrighteousnesse* the *truth* detaine.

Since then those *Wares* so slender are in worth,
To mocked sight *lyes* only setting foorth,   1724
Bookes which pervsd, leaue *Ignorants* more rude,
Gulling the World but with imagind *goode*,
To CHRIST disgracefull, breeding in man's braine
Conceats of Him but carnall, and prophaine,
What Hee left *buryed* preassing to proclame,
His *Glory* darkning with disgrace and shame,   1730
Loosing these *bands* insep'rably *vnite*,
By which both *Natures* in one *Person* meete,
Men's *Faith* diverting from that solide stay

John 14. 6.   The only *Rocke*, the *Life*, the *Truth*, the *Way*,
Vpon a *Shadow* fondly to rely   1735
Which CHRIST shall (one day) to bee His deny,

All the worship and   As being only the *Resemblance* vaine
respect that is given
to the artificiall   And *Birth fantastick* of the *Painter's braine*,
crucifixe is given to
a filthie Idole.   Who, though hee boldly playde the cunning *Ape*,
Did never see, nor could set foorth His shape,   1740
The *Honour* then to This bequeathd, must even
Neids-force, bee to a filthie *Idole* given.

The way to get a   BVT leaving more to stirre this noysome *Sinke*,
right sight of Christ
shining in the mir-   Poysning pure *Soules* with a pestifrous stinke,
ror of the scripture,
and to be changt in   To bee abhor'd, and held in just neglect,   1745
the likenesse of
Christ seene there.   Of all, true CHRIST who truly doe affect,
And on that *Purtrate* long to fixe their eye,
Drawne by his *Spirit*, which the soule must see,
In *Holie Write*, that *Mirror* most divine,
In which His *Image* Gloriously doth shine,   1750

By preaching of His *Word* which set to view
By *Faith* is seene, and doth by *Sight* renew,
So working on the *Soule* which doth behold,
That thus it lookes as from another mold,
Both to the selfe and Others seeming strange,   1755
Turnd in its *liknesse* by a gracious *change ;*
So by the *Spirit* quickned is this *Meane,*
That *heere* if CHRIST thy *Faith* hath truly seene,
Thou shalt His *Shape* take on, bee like *Him* made,
Adornd with *Glorie* which shall never fade,   1760
In Thee this *Image,* whence all *Grace* doth flow,
From *Glorie* shall to further *Glorie* grow,
Each faithfull *Looke* on *This,* of force shall bee
Some gracious effect to worke in Thee.   1764
   Come then, draw neere, *Thou* who to see aspires
Sweete IESVS CHRIST, the *Crowne* of thy desires ;
Come, *Thou* who loues on *Him* to looke aright
(Abhorring *Counterfits* which mock the sight)
Whose face alone doth true content afford,   1769
Come, heere behold thy *Loue,* thy *Life,* thy LORD.
   BVT if thou *Him* wouldst to Salvation see,
Thy *Soule* must glas'd in this same *Mirror* bee,
Thy breast's most inward *Cabins* must bee sought,
Thy selfe made *Center* of thy *Circling* thought :
Thou must not skarre vpon thy *Soares* to looke,   1775
To read thy *dittay* in that sacred *Booke,*
As thou by *Nature* art from *Grace* exild,
With *Miserie* surcharg't, with *sinne* defyld,
Procliue to *fall,* to *perish* by and by
Without remeed, if *pitty* CHRIST deny ;   1780
As dead in *Sinne,* till quickned by His *Grace*
Already damn'd till Hee the *doome* deface ;
Lost, on His shoulders till Hee home *thee* take,
GOD's *Enemie* till Hee the *friendship* make,
The *Devill's* bound *slave,* still ragging on in Ill   1785
Till He redeeme thee, and *renew* thy *Will ;*

Marginal notes:

1 Cor. 15. 49.

A man must see his owne vglines in the glasse of the law before hee can see Christ's beautie in the Gospell.

Ezek. 16. 3, 4, 5.

Rom. 5. 12, 14.

Ep. 2. 1, 5.

Rom. 6. 17.

Eph. 5. 8, 14;
Ibid. 4. 18.
An *Atheist* vile, *Erroneous*, short of *sight*,
Till Hee *thee* teach to know thy GOD aright,

Gen. 6. 5;
Mat. 15. 19.
Thy heart a *Seminary*, which doth breed
And nurse of all kind wickednesse the seed   1790

Eph. 2. 3.
Till by his *Spirit* purg'd ; a *Child* in short
Of *Sathan*, miserable in each sort,

Iohn 3. 5.
Till hee *Regenerate*, thy soule endue
With *Grace*, and make of thee a *Creature* new.

If the sight of thy
owne sins doo not
humble, yet the
terror of an Iust &
angrie Iudge may
bring the low.
Deut. 9. 3.
BVT if this *Sight* doth vertue lacke to lead   1795
Thee, thy estate to mourne and seeke remeed,
Behold that *Lambe* a *Lyon*, full of Ire,
An angrie *Iudge*, a hotte consuming *Fire*,

Heb. 12. 29.
Thee citing, whom no *misery* can draw,
By terrifying *Trumpet* of His *Law*,   1800
Araign'd, before His fearfull *Throne* to stand,
Condemn'd in *Conscience*, trembling foot, and hand,
His awful *Eyes*, which *Flames* and *Lightning* dart,
The deepest *Darkes* of thy deceaved heart   1804

Iohn 2. 24, 25;
1 Cor. 4. 5.
Heb. 4. 13.
Shall search : none needs to tell Him what thy breast
Keeps buried from the World : the *Most* the *Least*
Nor of thy *Words*, nor *Deeds* can *Him* escape :
The *Thoughts* most secreit, which thy *Soule* did shape,
Even ere outbreaking wilfull *Involution*
Thee guiltie made by *Actuall* pollution,   1810
Before Him muster : He can open lay
All that make vp thy dreadfull *Dittay* may.

Though *vse* of *Sinning* Thee secure hath made,

Psal. 53. 1.
Though with the *foole* Thou in thy *Heart* hast said
There was no GOD thy foule *Misdeeds* to marke,
Thy *Words* to view committed in the darke,   1816
Or to avenge the wrongs thou boldly wrought,
As to a reckning never to bee brought ;
Though while the LORD did patiently forbeare,
But like thy selfe, Hee did to the appeare,   1820
Thou shalt Him comming vnto *thee* behold,
These sinnes which thou committed vncontrold,

In order ranking All before thy face,
No *circumstance* omitted ; *Time* nor *Place*.   1824
    These grosse *Offences*, which (to thee but slight)
Thy *Nat'rall Conscience* rub'd, by *Nature's* light,
In their commission, beeing set to view,
Then, shall another *sight* of *sinne* enswe :
    Thy former *actuall Roll* Hee shall enlarge
Sinnes of *Omission* laying to thy charge,   1830

Math. 25. 42, 43. The *Good* vndone requiring at thy hand
Which to performe, or *Law* or *duty* band,
Thus shall hee judge thee guiltie of neglect
Of *things* which thou didst never wrong suspect ;

Mat. 12. 36.   Thy Idle *Words* shall not vnchalleng't slide ; 1835
The vnadvysed *Passions* of thy *Pride*
Which thou couldst never curbe, a cause thou must
Acknowledge now of thy *Damnation* just.
    Thy *heart* exposing lust-intangling *Hookes*
By wanton *gestures*, by lascivious *lookes*,   1840

Mat. 5. 28. Thee shall Hee make convince, a *Wretch* most vile
Whom *Whoredome* and *Adultery* did defile.

Ibid. 22.   Each *Word* from thy deceatfull *lips* sent foorth
To wound thy *Brother's fame*, or wrong his *Worth*
No *light* or *veniall sinne* (as men now speake)   1845
Hee shall admitt, but such as *Wrath* shall eake,
Thee rendring worthy of eternall *Ire*,
The wofull *object* made of quenchlesse *Fire*.

Numb. 16. Behold *Him*, charging *Earth* with open *Wombe*
To swallow over and aliue entombe   1850
Thy proud ambitious *Spirit*, still repining
While thou in *Darknesse* art, at others *Shining*.

Gen. 19. 24.   Behold IEHOVA from IEHOVA sent,
Thy filth to clenge with *Fire* and *Brimstone* bent,

Act. 5. 5. Readie to strike to death thy guilefull *Heart*   1855
Which, with thy double *tongue* confed'rat, parte

Act. 12. 23. Taks gainst the *Truth :* Thee readie to devowre
With *Vermine*, (creatures though of meanest pow're,)

R

Of sacrilegious *Pride*, while in the hight,   1859
Thou crownst thy selfe, GOD roabing of his right.

Mat. 23. 13, 14, 15.

Him shalt thou heare denuncing *Wrath* and *Woe*

Against thy base *Hypocrisie*, in show
Who other seem'd, then ever in effect
Thou was, or truly didst to be, respect,
Even to thy face, not mongst thy least offences, 1865
To thy disgrace discou'ring thy *Pretences*,
Whom wordly aymes, whom private ends did leade
Religion but to follow, for thy bread.

Luk. 14. 18, 19, 20.

Hee, nor thy *Mariage*, *Oxen*, *Farme* nor ought
Which thou a fit *Apologie* hast thought,   1870
Shall for a just excuse admitt, for thee
More slacke in serving of thy GOD to bee.

To him all *Iudgement* hath the FATHER given,

Mat. 25. 21.

Him shalt thou (on day) in the *Clowds* of Heaven
See, seperating soules Impenitent,   1875
Such *Goates* as Thee, to all vncleannesse bent,

Iohn 10. 3, 4.

From His owne *Deare-Ones*, His selected *Sheepe*
His voice decerning who his ways did keepe.

Thine Eares what then thy *Doome* shall bee, may
     heare,
If thou from *sinne* doe not in time reteare ;   1880
Once Hee hath sayd, and yet againe will say
Depart Accursed, to be damn'd for ay,

Mat. 25. 41.

Yee Workers of Iniquitie, (and none
More guiltie than thy selfe thou maist suppone),
In endlesse *Fyre*, in everlasting *Paine*   1885
Prepared for the *Devill* and all his *Traine*,
Of which are all, who drencht with sinfull spaite,
Lye buried in their *Naturall* estate,
Even thou, as long as *Vnrenew'd* by grace,
And dost *vnchangt* continue in this cace   1890
Deferring to that gracious *Iudge* to sue
The SONNE of GOD, by *absolution* true,

Who only can thy free *Remission* seale,
Cancell thy debts, thy *Conscience* calm'd make feele
The fruit of his *forgivenesse;* give thee *Peace,*   1895
That true *Tranquillity,* which finds no place
In *Pardons* given by men, for gayne procuird,
In *All* at least, who ever haue endurd
The Inward tempest of a sin-tos'd soule,
Looking aright vpon that fearefull *Scroule*   1900
Of *accusations,* having layd to heart
The Nature of GOD'S *Iustice, Sinne's* desart.

If a man be humbled in the sense of his sin, & God's deserved wrath, then may he get a comfortable sight of Iesus Christ in the Gospell.

If in thy selfe, thou hast this vgly *Sight,*
Perceav'd, the *Vengance* due to Thee by right
If thence, thy soule with inward *Terrors* shaken,
By *Iustice,* trembling stands, to be o're-taken :   1906
If feele thou dost a gnawing *Worme* torment
Thy vexed conscience, but with ease acquent,
Stinging thy heart, which with remembrance bleeds,
Of long-long buried, and of late *Misdeeds,*   1910
Kindling in thee sparkes of that quenchlesse *Fire,*
Sent foorth as Messingers of further Ire
In time to warne Thee what abids for ay
All, that in *Sinne* without *Repentance* stay ;
If from *Aboue* some sharpe correcting *Rod*   1915
Hath made thee see an awfull angrie GOD
Quickning in thee some *Spunke* of true desire
His *Peace* to haue, gainst whom thou didst conspire,
Renouncing henceforth to bee Sathan's slaue,
In life renew'd resolv'd thy sinnes to leaue,   1920
In this pure MIRROR thou mayst then make bold
Sweet IESUS CHRIST thy SAVIOUR to behold

Heb. 8. 6.
Ibid. 9. 15, and 12. 24.
Zach. 18. 1.
Apoc. 22. 6; Ibid. 7. 17.
Mat. 9. 12;
Luk. 10. 35, 43.

A readie MEDIATOR full of *grace,*
Pleading thy *Pardon* and eternall *Peace ;*
A *Fountaine* open'd, living streams distilling,   1925
In *David's* house, with *Heavenly water* filling
Thy thirsting Soule. That true *Physitian*
The precious *balme* of *grace* who only can

Powre in thy wounds, THEE can alone make cleane,
Though nought but *leprous* spots in thee bee seene ;

Mal. 3. 1.

The *Angell of the Covenant*, who brings   1931

Ibid. 4. 2.

To *Sinners*, healing vnderneath His wings,

a Exod. 25. 21.

A *Mercie seate*, the ^a *Tables* of the *Law*
To hide, whose challenge Thee in *Iudgment* draw.

b 1 King 1. 50.

An *Altar*, from whose ^b *Hornes* of safe *protection* 1935
GOD's justice most severe gainst sinnes infection

c Iohn 6. 37.

Man never banish'd, for ^c *refuge* who fled,
Or whom to Him the *Hope* of *Mercie* led.

d Numb. 35. 6 ;
Deut. 4. 41.
Ios. 20. 2.

A ^d *Citie*, where in safety to reside
And beare the *Devill* and all the *World* at fead,

e Apoc. 21. 25.

Whose ^e *Ports* shoote never, ever patent bee   1941

f Esa. 60. 11.

To all, that from persuing ^f *Iustice* flee.

g Genes. 6.

A saving ^g *Arke* where thou secure mayst rest
Where inward *feares*, nor *foes* can thee infest,
Where thou most safe mayst ly, though *Heavens*
    should weepe   1945
Even floods of wrath man from Earth's face to
    sweepe.

h Numb. 14. 46.

A *gratious* ^h *Aaron*, reaching forth his hand
Who doth with *Incense* in his *Censor* stand
To stay the *Plague* of *sinne*, on thee begunne
(Without Remeed) ere thou bee over-runne.   1950

Draw neare in time, and labour to perceaue
How such as went before Thee furthred haue :

i Math. 9. 10.

To ⁱ *eate*, to *drink*, Loe ! He did not disdaine

k Luke 7. 36.

With ^k *Publicanes*, with *persons* most prophane, 1954

l Luke 4 ;
Iohn 8. 3.
Luke 7. 38.

Curing their sinnes : vile ^l *Whoores*, adultrous *Goates*
Hee gathers in, and purgeth all their spots.

m Luke 19. 5.

Most covetous ^m *Extortioners* find grace,
None are debard who mourne to Him their *cace*.

Behold as He doth stand ! Doth sweetly call,

n Math. 11. 28.

Come, O yee ⁿ *Weary*, *Come* yee *loaden* all,   1960

o Math. 11. 29.
Ierem. 6. 16.

Draw neare my ^o *Deare-Ones*, I will giue you *rest*,
Your Soules in *peace* shall *hence-foorth* bee possest ;

"Who come to Mee faint, comfortlesse, and
 weake
" For succour, in no cace I can forsake."

If thy conscience be not quieted at the first looke on Christ, yet a continuing to looke vpon Him, and His offices, and natures, and gracious working with others, may doe it.

But YET, if still thy *faults* thy *conscience* vexe, 1965
If still the sence of *Wrath* thy Soule perplexe,
If still the hope-exyling *feares* remaine
That *justice* shall, with never-ceassing paine
For sinne, at last, sease on thy guiltie Soule,
A righteous GOD, who boldly durst controule: 1970
And, if thou canst not yet be brought to see
How GOD can pardon such a wretch as thee,
So vile a worthlesse wormeling, by desart
Who worthie of hel's deepest dungeon art,
Looke on the *Mirror* then ; *See*, from aboue, 1975
Of GOD the FATHER the vnbounded loue,
Who, when He All haue damnd in *justice* might,

a Iohn 3. 16 ;
1 Iohn 4. 9.

So lovd a *the World*, that He His chiefe delight
His SONNE Eternall, *Second* of these *Three*
Which still make vp a *Trinall Vnitie*, 1980
To mortall *Man* did gift, in time a *Child*
Heere to be borne, to *Man* from grace exild,
Whose *Name* and *Nature* thereto made agree

Esay. 7. 14 ;
Math. 1. 23.
b Esa. 9. 6.

Our blest IMMANUEL, GOD *with vs*, should bee,
The Mightie b GOD in humane flesh, and feature,
GOD reconcealed vnto manly *Nature*, 1986
That Hee man's *Persons* might to GOD conceale,
And that through *Him* GOD'S friendship *Man* might
 feele :
Whose searchlesse *Wisdome* so profound appeares

c Ibid.

That thence the name of c WONDERFULL He beares,
For, wonderfully Hee found out a *Way* 1991
Man to set free, and fully to defray
His debts, the *Iustice* Infinite contenting,
And of an angrie GOD the rage relenting ;

d Col. 1. 21.

A *Way*, to make on Thee, while *even* d *God's foe*
The boundlesse *Fountaine* of His *Mercie* flow, 1996

While thou (deservedly) groaning lay'st beneath
Sinnes pressing load, and GOD's Eternall *Wrath*.

a Iohn 1. 14;
Math. 5. 17.

Behold for Thee He ^a MAN becomes, GOD's will
In ev'ry point compleetly to fulfill,   2000

b Heb. 7. 22.

Thy ^b *Cautioner*, who to procure thy Peace
(A bankrupt vnthrift, prodigall of grace)
That from *Rebellion* thou relax'd might bee,

c Heb. 9. 14.

By ^c *satisfaction* full did set thee free,

d Heb. 7. 27.

Himselfe for thee a ^d *Sacrifice* presenting,   2005

e 1 Ioh. 4. 19.

Ere loue thou couldst Him, thee with ^e *loue* preventing.

f Math. 3. 13.

See how He stands, as if with ^f *sinne* defild,

g Mark 1. 8;
Luke 3. 21.

Even in thy ^g *Name* and *Roome*, by *sinne* exild,
Washd as a *Sinner*, by the clenging streame
Of *Baptisme*, sinfull in the world's esteeme,   2010

h Math. 17. 5;
2 Pet. 1. 17.

The ^h *Father* audibly from HEAVEN expressing,
And fully pleasd in HIM, HIMSELFE professing
That Hee should *Suretie* bee, thy *burden* beare,
And charging thee againe *His voice to heare*.

How canst thou then, (while lying vnder ire), 2015
But boile with flames of vehement desire
To heare Him calling, *Come*, O weary wight
If vex'd with inward *feares*, or outward *spight*,
Come mourning Soule, in *conscience* opprest,
Vnder my *wings* securely take thee *rest*?   2020

If thou belieue, if thou in *faith* doe heare
And follow Him that cals, thou needst not feare
That thou assaulted, shall a *shelter* lake,
That wrath shall thee persue, or overtake.

Why still then trembling stands thou? still agast?
Twixt GOD and CHRIST (now) *covenant* is past 2026
In thy behalfe: and CHRIST accordingly
Hath *suffered*, *absolv'd* and *ransond* thee.

Since then of GOD the free, and endlesse *Loue*

i Iohn 3. 16;
1 Iohn 4. 9.

Thou for thy ⁱ *Warrant* hast, what should thee
moue?

ᵃ Ezek. 37. 26.

Since of that ᵃ *Covenant* new which lasts for ay, 2031
The *Truth* and *Strength* not subject to decay
Twixt GOD and CHRIST for *Man*, twixt GOD and
    Man
In CHRIST, which nothing change, or alter can,
Doe thee secure ; what need'th thee doubt or feare ?
That thou shouldst perish, CHRIST thee bought too
    deare. 2036

What lackst thou ? what deficient is to found
And build thy *faith* on a most solide ground?

ᵇ Act. 20. 28 ;
Heb. 9. 14.
ᶜ Philip. 2. 10.

The MAN, who doth thy ᵇ *Mediator* stand
Is ᶜ *also* GOD : doth all this *All* command. 2040
Hee, worthy pardon is for thee to pleade :
When Hee maks sute for what thou standst in neede,
The FATHER can not what Hee asks forsake :
Hee Greater is than a repulse to take.
Hee *High is as the Highest* to appeare, 2045
And GOD for *sinne* offended, to draw neare,
Before whose face no creature dare be found,
When frowning, Hee His anger doth vnbound.

ᵈ 1 Tim. 2. 5 ;
Heb. 7. 24.

Againe, that GOD, thy glorious ᵈ MEDIATOR, 2049
Man likewayes is, *Man's Sonne*, and *Man's* CREATOR.

* GOEL. So
stiled by
Iob 19. 25.
ᵉ Esay. 57. 15.

Thy * *Kinse-Man in the flesh*, to thee more neare
Than any *Saint*, or was, or can bee, heere.
Though He that *Loftie* ᵉ *One*, that *Great One* bee
Who *Ever-blest*, endwelth *Eternitie*,
Yet daind He hath (thee to lift vp and saue 2055
Though even the basest and most abject slaue)
Himselfe to humble, and stowp downe more low
Then any other able was to doe,

ᶠ Iohn 19. 17 ;
Philip. 2. 7.

Himselfe Hee ᶠ *emptied*, did the *Crosse* take on,
Was made of *reputation* small, or none, 2060
Was *peircd*, was *presd* with paine, to clenge thy score,
A shamefull death endurd : *What wouldst thou more?*
Behold Man's *Nature* wondrously combind
(By vnion such, as nature can not find)

Vnto the *Godhead*, in His *Person:* so   2065
How easie thing it is for GOD to doe
Thence see thou mayst, tho *Sinne* hath made *dis-*
      vnion,
To make thy *Person* haue with Him *Communion.*
Behold, how by this *vnion personall*
Of *Persons* not, but *Natures:* naturall   2070
Sense all transcending, *Sathan* conquered lyes,
Even by that *Nature* He did first entyse.
Thy LORD on Him assum'd thy humane *Nature*
That Hee of thee might make a divine *creature*,
Abaisd *Himselfe* the *Sonne* of *man* to bee,   2075
To make to GOD a chosen child of thee.
      Behold His Worthinesse who pleads thy *peace*,
Thus shalt thou see how thou, vnworthy *grace*,
Mayst bee receav'd, through *Him* mayst favour find
Who, though thou faultie, *loving* is and *kind.*   2080

ᵃ 1 Tim. 2. 4.   *Behold*ᵃ how GOD, in CHRIST, most willing is
To saue, to comfort, and to cherish *His;*
The soules of trembling *sinners* doth sustaine
While seeming swallow'd vp, with sense of paine,
With inward anguish, and thou nought shalt see 2085
In GOD from grace to let or hinder thee.
      Behold thy LORD, how not without *delite*,
The Worke of *Man's salvation* to perfite,
Such *Offices* did daine to vndertake
As for thy well and safety best did make.   2090

ᵇ Heb. 4. 16.   Thus strengthned thou more ᵇ boldly mayst draw
      neare
The *Throne of grace*, to bee ex%md of feare,
Set free from thy rebellion, so eschue
The *Vengance* to thy *disobedience* due.

ᶜ Esay. 9. 6.   *Behold* how *Hee*, as ᶜ *Counseller* most wise,   2095
To the Eternall *Monarch* of the skies,
ᵈ Iohn 1. 18.   While in the *Father's* ᵈ bosome, GOD alone
Man's flesh as yet not having taken on,

·

By *Patriarchs*', & *Prophets*' mouths, did breath
GOD's *Mysteries*, to man deserving death, 2100
His *Counsells* deepe reveald, His *secreets* spred,
And *Man* againe to know His *Maker* led.

Luke 13. 23.   *Behold* how in His ^a*flesh* He went along
The holy land, and (even His foes among)
In proper *person* preacht in ev'ry place 2105

Isa. 61. 1;
Math. 5. 4.
Iohn 15. 15.

Glade ^b*tydings* to the Soule that mournd for grace,
And yet by ^c *Preachers*' mouths continues still
Revealing to the world *His Father's will.*

Behold, to HEAVEN how having taught the way

1 Pet. 1. 19.
Hebr. 7. 27.

A ^d *Lambe* vnspotted, *Once* for ^e*all*, and *ay*, 2110
Hee offred vp *Himselfe*, the world from *sinne*

Col. 2. 15.

To purge, o're hell the ^f *Victorie* to winne,

Heb. 7. 25.

A ^g *Sacrifice* most *perfitly* to saue
And *sanctifie throughout*, no spot to leaue
Vnpurgt, in *all*, through *Him* who accesse clame
To GOD, *salvation* vrging in His name. 2116

Levit. 16;
Exod. 13. 10;
Heb. 9. 12.

Looke how our ^h *Aaron* with a purpure flood
All over-sprinkled of His owne deare blood,

Heb. 9. 24.

Enters the Holyest ⁱ *Sanctuary* of HEAVEN
To repossesse *Man* thence most justly driven, 2120

Exod. 28. 29
& 9.

Our ^k *Names* vpon His *breast*, and *shoulders* bearing
With *heart's affection*, and with *strength* appearing
His owne poore mourning *Weake Ones* to sustaine,
That they with GOD may still in grace remaine. 2124

1 Pet. 3. 22;
Heb. 1. 3;
Psal. 110. 1;
Math. 22. 44.

Behold thy LORD set downe, on ^l GOD's right hand
O're HEAVEN, o're *Earth* o're *hell* to beare command
As *King*, as *Conqu'ror*, *captiues* to rescue,
The *tyrannie* of *Sathan* to subdue,
From thraldome to set free *all* that desire 2129
To bee releev'd from *wrath*, from *Sinne's* Impire.

Behold Him gifted with *Dominion* free

1 Tim. 6. 15.

MONARCH of *Monarchs*, ^m KING of *Kings* to bee,
With vniuersall pow're, to *rule*, to *raigne*
GOD over *All*, *All's* onely *Soueraigne*,

Of all things at his pleasure to dispose,   1352

a Mat. 18. 6.

For well of *His ;* those a *Proudlings* to oppose

Who boldly dare presume to vexe or wrong

The meanest *member* that doth *Him* belong,

b 1 Sam. 2. 6.

To whom Hee lists eternall b *life* to giue,

To damne to *death,* from *death* or to reuiue,   2140

Psal. 2.

His *foes* to make his *foot-stoole :* pestring downe,

All godlesse *Atheists,* traytors to his crowne

That Him contemne, or dare His *Scepter* slight

Them making feele His powre, His boundlesse
might.   2144

No inlake in thee
but thou may see
how it is supplied
in Christ.
c Hosea 14. 4.

What fearst thou then, if thou thy *Sinnes* foosake,

And seeke that Hee in *friendship* thee may take?

GOD's *loue* is *free,* and c *firme ;* no change admits,

Continues to the end, and never flits ;

His *Truth* both *seald,* and *sworne,* doth thee secure

d Esa. 54. 10.

By way of *Cov'nant,* d which shall ay endure.   2150

The LORD of *lyfe,* CHRIST IESUS set to sight

In this cleare *Mirror, Thine* by *double* right

Is made, to thee *twice sibbe* who groanst for grace,

The *Sonne* of GOD, the *Seede* of mortall race,

Twice *Brother's* Hee become ; by *Incarnation*   2155

Himselfe for thee to make a fit *Oblation :*

By thy *adoption ;* even with Him to *share*

e Rom. 8. 17.

The *Heritage,* of Heaven to bee made e *heyre.*

If *Blind* thou bee, and of a *guide* hast neede 2159

From *Sinne* and *wrath* thy straying soule to leade

Deut. 18. 15, 18 ;
Eph. 2. 17.
f Iohn 14. 6.

Loe, Hee a *Prophet* is, who f *peace* doth preach

Draw neere, Him hearken : Hee the way shall
teach.

Twixt GOD and *Thee,* if thou the *feade* dost feare,

g Heb. 7. 17.

Behold, a g *Priest* Hee doth for thee appeare,   2164

Who all His *friends,* or *friends* that seeke to bee,

Hath by one *Sacrifice,* for ay, set free.

If *Lame* and *Impotent* thou art, vnmeete

To runne to God, or flee from *Sathan's* feete,

To strengthen thee, hee is a *Mightie* ^a KING,

Who can rayse vp the weakest *vnderling*.   2170

    What long agoe, as *Priest*, hee hath procurd,

As *Prophet* Hee expones, perswads; assurd

To make His owne of safety : shall at last

As *King* apply, conforme to *Paction* past.

    What Hee, as *Priest* hath purchast, foorth hee

      drawes   2175

From *God's* great *Treasure*, opned for his cause

To our behoue, who as he *dayly* pleads

For vs, by ^b*priestly Intercession* speeds.

    What Hee as *Prophet* hath expond, by *Word*

In holy *Write*, as *Prophet* doth afford   2180

Perspicuous, by his *Spirit* made most plaine,

That Gratious *Doctor*, *Teacher* of His Trayne.

    What Hee as *King* hath gifted and applyed,

(And what in Him can bee by GOD denyed?)

Hee doth as KING gainst all thy foes maintaine 2185

To settle thee, in peace with Him to raigne.

    Now, if to Him His weaklings bee so deare,

Courage dejected soule ; thou needst not feare ;

Ryse, follow on, Thou in this Glasse shalt see   2189

CHRIST'S GLORY *shining more and more to thee.*

    If Thou from *feare* bee in some measure fred,

If hope of mercie thee to feele hath led

Some   spunk   of   *life*,   some   woontlesse   *warmnesse*

    glow

Within thy bosome, making *tears* to flow

Of godly *sorrow*, mixd of *Griefe* and *love*,   2195

Thy frozen heart begunne to melt and moue ;

Behold how hee hath *breath*, as thou dost *Mourne*

To make thy ^c*faintly-smoaking flaxe* to burne,

And tenderly, till greater strength it breed,   2199

Of thy weake *Fayth* doth touch the *bruised reed*.

    Behold how ^d One, brought in his bed, by force,

Layd at his feete, his *pittie* doth enforce,

Departs, of *sickenesse* and of *Sinne* made cleane,
Rejected not, because despisd and meane ;   2204
How much more thee shall Hee receaue in *grace*
Who running comst, layst out to Him thy cace,
With bleeding heart dost His *compassion* plead,
Seeking to thy diseased *Soule* remeed ?

Thy LORD thou mayst, with thee a part who
  beares,
Behold His *bottle filling* with thy *teares*,   2210

a Luke 7. 38.

With that Sweete SAINT, for sinne, in *sense* a *of wrath*
With luke-warme *floods* when thou thy cheeks dost bath,
With *Her* sitts mourning, powring from thine eyes
In heartie *love*, thy greeved LORD to please,
Streames to be-dew and washe His sacred *Feete*, 2215
That Hee may cleanse, and for Himselfe make meete
Thy spotted *Soule*, who nought esteemest too *rare*
Too *pretious*, on *Himselfe*, or *cause* to ware.

Though men doe *mock*, and with *contempt* doe prise
Thy *mourning*, thy *devotion* doe despise,   2220

b Mat. 5. 4.

Thy LORD, who (one day) shall thy b *paynes* com-
  pense,
Thou speaking mayst perceaue in thy defence :

c Cant. 2. 4.

Loe Hee, a *Banner* c *of His love doth spread*,
And to his owne *Wine-sellers* thee doth leade,

d Cant. 2. 5.

That by his d *flagons* comfort thou mayst fynd,   2225

e Ih. 16. 20. 22.

Hartning thy sorrow with his e *favours* kynd,
The *earnst* thee giving of that gratious day

f Apoc. 7. 17;
Ibid 21. 4.
g Ez. 9. 4. 5. 6;
Apoc. 7. 3.

When from thine eyes, *teares* f *Hee shall wipe away.*
Hee shall his *Seale* vpon thy g *forehead* set
That the *Destroyer* thus may warning get,   2230
The wicked *World* while *floods* of *vengance* bath,
Thee to discerne, from mongst the *Sonnes of wrath.*

How hee who be-
leiueth must looke
to *Christ* present-
ing his burthen and
his yoke.
h Mat. 11. 30.

Hold to thy shoulder, sturre not to take on
His lightsome h *burthen ;* which repenteth none
That ever it did beare : which all makes glad   2235
On whomsoever Hee the same hath layd.

Behold Hee stretcheth foorth His hand, to lay
His *Law* vpon thy back, thy sinnes to slay,
So to presse foorth thy old impostumd *soares*,
But not to harme thee, who his *Peace* implores. 2240
Thy *flesh* and vitious *Nature*, must bee slayne :
Thou must not shrinke at sense of outward *Payne*.

a Mat. 11. 29.

    Behold, His ^a *Yoke* Hee brings ! *How loath to part ?*

Stretch forth thy *necke*, thy *hands*, thy *feete*, thy *heart*,
That Hee may bind it on : that, (hence) for ay 2245
None, saue thy LORD, thy *service* challenge may.
Loe ! that thy *yoke* may *light* and *easie* bee
Hee goes before *Himselfe* and drawes with thee,
Yea both thy *yoke* and *thee* Hee drawes ; and beares
Thee, wrestling with thy *burthen* who appeares. 2250
Goe on : O never, never leave thy LORD
Where ere Hee leads thee ; Hee will strength afford.
Hee no where els *Thee* shall invite to goe
But where before, the way *Himselfe* did show. 2254

How a man under tentation may looke vpon Christ in the mirror of His word.

BVT NOW doth *Sathan* rage with greater spight
Then when secure thou layst in *sinne's* dark night,
Redoubling his assaults, *Thee* vexing more,
Presenting *bayts* more frequent then before ?
Behold thy LORD, whom HEAVEN, whom *Earth* obeys,

b Mat. 4 :
Mark 1. 12.
Luke 4. 1.

In ^b *Wildernesse, alone,* twice twentie dayes 2260
With *apparitions* visible frequented,
Not from that *Ill-One's* firie *darts* exempted.
If CHRIST hee durst attempt to make his *Thrall*,
Whom gainst his *dints* Hee knew a *brazen wall*,
What wonder thee a *weakling* hee entyse, 2265
To his *persute* whose *soule* oft guardlesse lyes ?
    But seest thou CHRIST prevaile ? His *powre* confine ?
Him streight dis-arme ? The *Victorie* is thine.

a Ex. 14. 13.

O stand!   O heere *behold* ᵃ *the LORD'S Salvation!*
This Combate to thy *safety* hath relation,   2270
Heere *Sathan* also made before *thee* flee,
Thy selfe in CHRIST victorious thou mayst see.

Sathan is not af-
frayd though some-
times hee faine
feare, for holy water
or crossing.

But *holie water* in the Ayre to tosse,
And with the finger *heere and there* to *crosse*,   2274
Scorne thou, as fruitlesse freets, least *Sathan* slight
And scorne such *weapons* should resist his *might*.

How a man vnder
cōtempt of the
world, or despised
of his friends may
looke on Christ.
b Psal. 38. 11.
c Iohn 15. 19.

Doth now the World a *mocking-stock* thee make?
Thy ᵇ *friends* (before) thy *fellowship* forsake?
Now art thou hated, since by gratious ᶜ *change*
Thy former *life* become to thee is strange?   2280
Now pointed at? because to sin thou shunnes

d 1 Pet. 4. 4.

And no more to thy wonted ᵈ *ryot runnes?*
Now doe the wicked louse their tongues to *lyes*,
Traducing thy *profession* as they please,
Not sparing even thy *person*, cens'ring *thee*   2285
Or *madde*, or *foolish*, or *precise* to bee?
Behold thy LORD, exposd to like despight,
Vexd, mockt, persued, with *malice* greatest *might*,
Despysd, opprest, the marke of *envy* made,
A common *foe* for all men to invade.   2290

e Iohn 1. 11.

See ᵉ how Hee comes vnto His *Owne* by *Blood*,
By *bonds* of *nature*, even by *them* withstood,
Rejected, not receiv'd, but mett in place
Of kindlie acceptation, with disgrace.
A Man, beside *Himselfe*, in their esteeme   2295
Behold the SAVIOUR of the world doth seeme :
Him they mistake, and seeke to apprehend

f Luke 23. 2.

As if His countrie's ᶠ *foe*, not *Cæsar's* friend,   2298
Even one whose *course*, (which they not rightly saw)

g Iohn 11. 45.

Their ᵍ *State* might touch, *themselues* in danger draw.
Each day that did His *life's* short terme compleet
Heere, with a severall affront did meet.   2302
But while His *course* Hee closd, *O griefe! O teares!*

h Is. 33. 3;
Mat. 27. 41. &c.

See how ʰ *vnmov'd*, what bitter *taunts* Hee beares.

With what vnvtterable *anguish* torne,

While suffring midst His *Paines*, the *Hight* of *Scorne*,

Which more than all the *Stripes*, His *Soule* did racke,

Which scourging *Burrio's* layd vpon His backe. 2308

^a *Ibid. 27. 29. 30.*   *Behold*, they *nod* ^a *the head*, they *bow the knee ;*

Who *Wisdome* was, to them a *foole* must bee.

The Honorable SONNE of GOD they floute,

^b *Math. 27. 28.*   And put a *Purpure* ^b*garment* Him about,

A *Crowne* of *Thornes*, vpon His holy head,

And in His harmelesse *hand* a brittle *Reede*

Worthy no other *Scepter*, in their thought :   2315

With *shame*, with *scorne* to death He thus was brought.

    " *LORD Thou, that I should liue, who daind to die,*

    " *Thy servant and disciple make of mee,*

    " *Though I with Thee should suffer, even while heere,*

    " *Scorne, spight, contempt, wrong most vnjustlie beare,*   2320

    " *Which, to my sight, thou standst, by my procuring,*

    " *Before the eyes of liuelie faith enduring.*"

How a man vnder povertie may looke vpon Christ in the mirror of the Word.   If *Povertie* thee pinch, if *want* thee vexe

Looke on thy LORD, whom care did ne'er perplexe

Of wordly *Wealth;* who heere did liue content 2325

To serue *Himself* with what His *servants* lent ;

^c *Luke 8. 3.*   Those holy ^c *Matrons* who did Him attend

Vnto His death, who did permit to spend

Their proper *goods*, forth for His vse to lay,

The charges of His *Iourney* to defray.   2330

^d *Mat. 17. 27.*   Who being *tax'd* did ^d *Tribute-money* lake :

^e *Mat. 8. 20.*   Whom ^e *house*, nor *hold* did ever *owner* make :

^f *Luke 2. 7.*   In poore estate most meanely who was ^f *borne ;*

^g *Ibid. 24.*   Whose *offring*, which the ^g *Altar* did adorne

ᵃ Levit. 12. 8.

In *His* behalfe, instead of fatned ᵃ *droaves*,   2335
The poore-man's *Pigeons* was, the *Turtle doves* ;
In *Ioseph's* house his *life* not *Rich* could bee :
A poorer spoyle the *Sunne* did never see
Than at His *death* His *foes* did part by lote,

ᵇ Iohn 19. 23.

His greatest wealth a ᵇ *sober seamelesse coate*.   2340
    If this *communion* with his *povertie*
Griefe of all *straits* can not asswage to thee,
Looke on the *riches* of spirituall *grace*   2343
Which hee on all bestowes, His steps who trace.

ᶜ Heb. 1. 2.
ᵈ Rom. 8. 17.

Loe, heyre Hee is of ᶜ HEAVEN and *Earth :* of all,
And with Himselfe ᵈ *Co-Heyre* annexe thee shall,
Yea will not (heere) with thee so sharply deale
But (as best sutes His *Glorie*, and thy well)
Both will, and can provide, that thou nor lacke
Foode for thy bellie, *cloathing* for thy back.   2350
And, though thou seest not how, yet take not *care*,

ᶜ Luke 12. 6.

His providence to ᵉ *Sparrowes* in the ayre,
To *Lillyes* of the field, to every thing
Which His *eternall Word* to life did bring
Extended is, and (as to him seemes best)   2355
Thy *Portion* furnish shall amongst the rest.
    By speciall care, thy LORD can make thee feele,

ᶠ 1 King 17. 14-
16.
2 King 4.

Enlarg't, the *lytle* measure of thy ᶠ *Meale*,
Thy *Cruise of Oyle* sufficient, thee to feede
Till more Hee send, to *last* as thou hast need,   2360

Deut. 8. 4.

Can in thy greatest troubles thee vphold,
Cause that thy *Garments*, nor thy *shoes* waxe old,

Dan. 1.

And if Hee but a dish of *Pulse* propine
Aboue thy fellows can thy *face* make *shine* ;
Hee multiply thy *lytle*, even thy *least*,   2365
Can, though a daye's *provision* thou but hast,
As easily it makes to hundreths streach

ᵍ Mat. 14. 19 :
Iohn 6. 11.

As for *fiue* ᵍ *Thousand Soules* hee earst made reach
(With plentie fed,) those *Loaues* and *fishes* few,
For *Fyue* alone which els were but enew.   2370

If thou for Him doe *thirst*, by manner strange

^a Iohn 2. 8.

He, for thy vse, *in wine* can ^a *Water* change :

^b Iohn 4. 14.

Yea *living* ^b *streams* can give thee, if he list,

Which tasted once, thou never more shall thrist.

Mat. 17. 27.

A *Fish*, with money in its mouth, be driven   2375

^c 1 King 17. 6.

Shalt on thy *Hooke*, ^c *Ravens* feede thee *Noone* and *Even*,

^d Ex. 16. 14 ;
Psal. 78. 27.
^e Exod. 17. 6 ;
Numb. 20. 9.
Psal. 78. 15.

Heaven's ^d *Manna* rayne, the flintie ^e *Rocke* shall serue

Thy thirst to quench, ere thou for want doe starue.

" *O that I may* (LORD) *for thy Kingdome care,*

" *Thee aboue all things serue ; so shall I feare*

" *Adversitie nor want : thus what may ayde*

" *My vext estate, shall to my hand be layde.* 2382

^f Tim. 16. 17.

If *Rich* thou bee, take heede *vncertaine* ^f *wealth*

How a man in
wealth & prosper-
itie may behold
Christ with profite.
^g Prover. 23. 5.

Steale not thy heart, thy soule deprive of health :

Trust not therein ; be not puft vp with pride   2385

Of things, on ^g *Eagles'* wings which swiftly slyde,

Fixe thou on *Him* alone thine *heart*, thine *Eye*,

2 Cor. 8. 9.

To make *Thee Rich*, who *poore* did chuse to bee.

O ! let thy *humble* Cariage, *modest* mynde,

Thy thoughts with *moderation* confind,   2390

Beare witnesse, that thou *pure* in *Spirit* art,

That thou dost *thirst* and *hunger* in thy heart

To bee inriched with that *Righteousnesse*

Which CHRIST still gifts, yet never is made lesse.

Bee greedie of His *golde ;* O begge to weare   2395

His *Garments*, that thou glorious mayst appeare,

That truly *rich*, thou mayst thy selfe present

^h Phil. 4. 11.

To GOD ; ^h *in wealth*, in *want* alike content.

These earthly things, but solide as a *dreame*,

More worthy than they are, doe not esteeme,   2400

But for thy LORD's vse, seeke to vse them, so

That on their *Owner* thou mayst them bestow :

Whom if thou see, or in his *Churches* neede

Or *Any* of his *Saints*, thy pittie pleade,

S

O then thy *superfluitie* to spare   2405
To help the cause belonging to *His care*,
His poore distressed *Brethren* to relieue
In whom His *grace* and *Image* shineth viue,
A horrible *Ingratitude* must bee,
Yea even a damnable *Impietie*.   2410

How a man in sick-
nesse may get a
helpfull sight of
Christ.
If *sense* of *payne*, if *soares* of any sort
Thee so assaile, as hard is to comport,
Looke on thy LORD, how *torturd* for thy sake,
Scourg'd backe and sides, GOD's *wrath*, thy *paynes* to
      slake,
See how his pretious *bloode* for thee is shed,   2415
To *Calvary* with shame, along while led,
With which the senselesse streets all red, seem'd
      blushing,
While bath'd with *Rivers* from his *woundes* foorth
      gushing.
Behold the *Nailes*, driven both through foote and
      hand,
Not in a *masse* of *mettell* which doth stand   2420
Him suffring to set foorth : a *living Man*
Thy object is ; what *spight*, what *malice* can
Enduring on the *Crosse ;* a publicke wonder,
Whose *Legs* and *Armes* streatchd foorth, neere rackt
      asunder,
Not suffered were to stand, as to His griefe   2425
The least-least meanes afford might of reliefe,
But as most obvious to the *Souldiers'* minde
They might bee found, His *Bones* to *breake* combinde.
Behold, by burthen of His *Body* blest,   2429
His flesh doth yeeld (while being down-ward prest)
Gaping and growing *Wounds*, still made more large,
As more His *Weight* His tender *Hands* doth charge.

¹ Iohn 19. 28.
Harke, how He cryes I ª THIRST, complaines of
      drouth,
For other *Paines* who *opned not His mouth*,

Though passing great, most sensibly though felt,
With this of all most vehemently delt.   2436

O see, how *He His* weary *Neck* extends
And languishing, with ready *mouth* attends
To drink the offred *Vinegar* and *Gall*,
His burning *Thirst* to quench, to FINISH ALL,   2440

Of which the bitter *sowrenesse* proving, straight
A very *Tast* to *Him* becomes a draught.
This Ruefull sight presented to thine eyes,
Inward or outward *Paynes* may serue to ease,
Grieues all allay, giue *Patience* to comport,   2445

Till GOD thy *Dolours* slaken, in some sort.

If *healthy*, *sound*, and *strong*, from trouble free,
Looke on the *Price* that purchast *All* to thee,

His *Stripes* did make thee whole : thy LORD did
beare
Thy *Maladyes*, that thou mightst sound appeare.
Hee thy *Infirmities* on Him did take,   2451
Thy *Health* to thee a *Blessing* thus to make,
And that thy sicklie *Soule* might whole bee found,
Whose stat's oft worst, thy *Body* while most sound.
    " *O that I may* LORD *whollie heere imploy*   2455
    " *My selfe, while health, while strength I doe*
        enjoy,
    " *In serving Thee ; and, to my dayes as length*
    " *Thou addst, I loue Thee may with greater*
        strength,
    " *That so, while health and strength, as shads*
        shall flee,   2459
    " *Both sound and strong I may bee found in Thee.*"

Doth long *discent*, vn-discontinued *race*
Of hon'rable *Ancestors*, make thee place,
Worldly *Preheminence* to thee beget
Aboue the *Simpler Sort*, below thee set ?
Art thou a *Noble*, or some speciall *Peere*   2465
So *Great* as thy *Inferiors* thee admire ?

Or, (tho *Enobled* not by *Place*) doth *blood*
From the Ignoble Vulgar thee seclude ?
In this forbeare to *glorie ;* but *behold*
Thy LORD of *Royall Linage, Race* most *Old,*   2470
A BRAUNCH whose *blood* deriv'd from *David's*
  stemme
Did make Him right to weare a *Diademe,*
A KING, respecting even His *Manhoode,* borne ;
Yet, all proud thoughts of *Pedegries* to scorne,
Himselfe abasd, in *Grace* to make vs *Great,*   2475
And (though a *Personage* of *High estate*)
Became most *low,* vs *Hon'rable* to make
Even our *Dishonour* on *Himselfe* did take.
  " *O seeke Nobilitie, which ne'er shall fade,*
  " *Honour from which thee no man can degrade,*
  " *By seeking right in Him, a Child to bee*   2481
  Of GOD ; true Honour's most supreme degree.
Art thou by birth *Ignoble, Base, Obscure ?*
Behold thy *Glorious* KING in state as poore,
As *meane* as thou, descended, *thee* to raise,   2485
Even with *Himselfe* thee to possesse and *scase,*
Not in a *State* but lasting for a day,
But of a *Kingdome* made secure for ay,
Vpon a Throne thee freely to set downe
To swey a *Scepter,* and to weare a *crowne.*   2490
  If *Base* thou bee, yet still to *climbe* assayes
The bruckle *braunches* of *vaineglorious* wayes,
If *Noble,* yet to swell with *Pride* doth chuse,
And seekst *ambitiouslie* all meanes to vse
To proppe thy worldlie *Credite,* with profane   2495
And worthlesse wretches, who no *Course* disdaine
May further their base *Ends,* affecting *Praise*
Of *Men,* their *Names* upon *Fame's* wings to raise,
Blind to behold that *Glorie,* to bee found
With GOD, which seene, all such *Desires* doth
  bound ;   2500

O study then more steadfastly to stare,
And on thy LORD to looke with greater *Care;*
Yea, neede thou hast to *Touch*, from Him that so

a Luke 8. 46. *Vertue* to heale this a *Vanitie* may flow.

How a man may learne humilitie looking on Christ in the Scripture. *Behold*, he sits as *Doctor*, teaching thee   2505
(*Himselfe* thy *Patterne*) true *Humilitie;*
Inviting thee who to His *Schoole* dost seeke

b Math. 11. 29. To learne of b *Him*, who *lowly* is and *meeke*.
See, how to purge thy Soule of stinking *Pride*,
The God of *Glorie*, *Glorie* layes aside,   2510

c Philip. 2. 7. A c *Servant's shape* assumes, a *Man* most meane

Math. 9. 10. Becomes; mongst *Publicanes* and *Sinners* seene,
To winne them home : *Himselfe* associating
Even to the *Basest*, *Good* to them to bring,
Accesse and speech to None, when askd, denying,
Most homelie with *His friends*, on *Him* relying. 2516
   Behold, (not pampred with delicious fare,)
With these Hee sits whose *Table* turnes their snare,
His traine attending, till He baselie haue
By surfetting become his bellyes slave;   2520

d Math. 21. 18. But d *hungring* oft, and *thirsting* for thy sake,
His sober *Trayne* doth His *Companions* make,
Serv'd at one *Table*, feeding even as *Hee;*

e Iohn 13. 5. Whose e *feete* from *filth* that *He* might *wash*, O see
How with a *Towell* girt about *Hee* stands,   2525
And stowping downe, with *Basen* twixt *His* hands,
With humble *Heart* performs that *service* meane,
And wipes them with the *Linnen*, thus made cleane,
The Greatest teaching who *His* Schollers are,
For *Him* their *Pride* to *mortifie* so far   2530
That to *His Least-ones*, though despisd they lye,
The meanest charge in *loue* they not deny.
   If *He*, thy LORD and KING, became so low,
Wilt thou, to be *His Servant* who makes show,
Lodge in a haughtie heart soule-poysning *Pride*,
Who glory canst, as thine, of nought beside   . 2536

Sinne, Miserie and *Shame?*   Thy *Pride* disclame,
Or in thy *Lord* no part thou needst to clame.
Humble LORD IESUS mongst *His* lowlie traine
Doth no ambitious servants intertaine.   2540
Both *Paradice* and *Heauen* spew'd out once haue
The *Proud*, and such can never back receaue.

If *Honour's* smoakie vapour blind thee so,
Thy GOD, thy selfe nor suffring *Thee* to know :
Thee, if *High place* so please, that nought beside
Can serue to feed the *fire-brand* of thy *Pride*,   2546
Why thus O Foole ! art thy affection fird
With what thou canst nor haue, nor keepe, acquird ?
Why doth their worldly *Greatnesse* thee intyse,
Who nothing lesse than *Vertue's worth* can prise ?
Why pin'st thou for Preferment ?   Casts thy care
On things which may thy inward *Peace* impare ? 2552
Is earthlie *Dignitie* to Thee so deare,
In it thy *Happinesse* esteeming heere,
That, (with all danger) thou darst it imbrace,   2555
By this prejudg't though of a better *Place ?*
Vaine *Glorie-hunter* change in time thy course,
Leaue taynted *Streams*, seeke *Honour* in the *Source.*
If meanes thou vse, with CHRIST thou mayst
        obtaine
In *Glory* which shall never end to raigne.   2560
His *Crosse* to *Climbe*, by *suffring* bee content,
The *Seale* by which the *Saints* to *Heauen* are
        sent ;
There shall thy *Honour*, (never to take flight,)
By GOD bee given, in *Men* and *Angels'* sight,
Where Time discourt, nor *Envie* thee can harme,
Nor flattring *Straines* of *Sycophants* can charme 2566
Thy *Prince's* eare, *from Honour* to degrade
Thee, *Great* but for *thy greater* ruine made,
Nor *Life* bee short, toile-conq'red *Sutes* to brooke
Some anxious *Dayes*, but lasting as a *Looke.*   2570

a 1 Tim. 6. 10.
How the avaritious man may be healed by looking on CHRIST.

If *Loue* of *Money*, whence all a *Evill* springs,
Thee, (*prickt with thornie cares*), in bondage brings,
Moue thee to *scrape*, to *scart*, to *pinch*, to *spare*,
To *rake*, to *runne*, to *kill* thyselfe with *care*,   2574
Things most secure to *doubt*, to *waite*, to *watch*,
Of *Penny*, or of *Penny-worth* to *catch*
Some *Gnat*, by chance, in *Spider-web* arriv'd,
Of *Bowel-wasting-wretched wayes* contrivd,

b Math. 6. 34.

Draw neere, heere learne but for the b *Day* to care,
Vncertaine to suck vp *To-morrow's* Ayre :   2580
Come see thy LORD and *His* poore *Traine* preparing
Things for another *life ;* no travell sparing
About this *Task :* for worldly *goods* content
With what by GOD to serue the *Time* was sent,
Like *Pilgrims*, passing to their blest *aboade*,   2585
Not over-charged with superfluous *loade*.
Alace ! what meanst thou, (while in soule most pore,)
Thy selfe to toile, to conquesse cankring *Ore ?*
Heaps to hoarde vp of *Pelfe*, whose *Rust* at last

c Iam. 1. 2. 3.

Shall *Witnesse* bee, that c *Sentence just is past   2590
Of thy *damnation ?*   O ! in time forbeare
On *drosse*, on *dunge*, still to bee *doating* heere ;
Care for these *Treasures*, which in CHRIST are found,
In which all *grace*, all *wisdome* doth abound :
That *Pearle*, Himselfe, aboue all *price* who is,   2595
Than all the world beside, more *deare* to *His ;*
If thou enrichd wouldst by some *Good-thing* bee,
Sell all thou hast ; and with *affection* free
Prefer to *part*, with all things earthly twinne,

d Mat. 13. 45. 46.

Losse even thy *lyfe*, this peereles d *Pearle* to winne :
And though no *Coine* thou dost command, nor *ware*
With this *Equivalent* thou canst compare,   2602

e Isa. 55. 1 :
Apoc. 3. 18.

Hee without e *price*, or *money* will bestow,
(As thou thy *wants* and *Indigence* doth show,)

f Ih. 6. 33, 35.

Both *gold* and *garments*, f livelie *foode* and *all*   2605
What wish thou canst, yea even *Himselfe* withall.

How the Licentious
may learn Temper-
ance by looking on
Christ.

Mongst those *diseases*, to thy soule which sticke,
If of the *fever* of *Intemp'rance* sicke,
Selfe-rotting fleshlie *pleasure* it affect,
Thee carying headlongs to eternall wreake,   2610
If with this beastlie *Sensualitie*,
This soule-besotting *sinne*, thou grieved bee,
That *poyson* casting vp, which (late) seemd sweete,
And with delight thy *senses* did invite
Even to a *surfet*, Longing for *remeed*,   2615
Looke on thy LORD, who all *His dayes* was dead

Isa. 33. 3; ibid.

To Earthlie *pleasures :* who, with *grieues* acquented,
A man of sorrowes liu'd, heere vnlamented,
Whose *breast* did beare, brash't with *displeasure's*
     dart,

a Mark 8. 12.
b Psal. 69. 20.
c Mat. 26. 38;
Mark 14. 33 and
34.

A *bruised* [a] *Spirit*, and a [b] *broken heart*,   2620
On whose sad [c] *soule did heavie sorrowes* light,
When *wrath* sustaining, (due to vs by right,)
In Him our sinfull *pleasures* were persued,
Eternallie which wee had not eschued
If GOD and *vs* Hee had not stept betweene,   2625
Even with his owne *Heart-blood* to make vs cleane.
Hast, sensuall *slaue*, thy filthie *soule* to hyde
Vnder his *shadow*, least thy daring *pride*
With *wrath* bee punisht : who *forbidden Tree*
Of false *delights* durst taste, defended thee.   2630

d Heb. 5. 7.

Behold [d] Hee *mourns*, for what thou madst thy
     sport,
While check't in *Conscience ;* O ! with *tears* resort
To Him in private, lest for lightlie prising
His *Tears*, for want of *tears* in thee arising,
Anguish and *sorrow*, which shall never slake,   2635
Teares never finding *truce*, thee overtake.

Behold, how *Horror* on his *soule* doth sease,
Forth-wringing *sighs* and *sobs*, for thy *disease*,
With *wrath* brunt vp for *sinne*, in which of late
Thy foolish *soule* did false *content* conceate.   2640

" *O change thy mind: Thoughts sometime seeming
        sweete*
" *Iudge causes now for which thy cheeks to weete.*
See, how all *baithd* in His owne *blood* Hee lyes,
Thy lewd *delights* how He most *dearely* buyes,   2644
Torne, beaten, stabt, with *thorns, nailes,* cruell *speare ;*
Stript naked, Sham'd and *slayne ;* yea more, doth
        beare,
Persuing *wrath,* to *expiate* thy *Crime,*
Thy *beastly swine-like bathing,* all thy time,
In brutish *lusts,* still *wallowing* in the *myre*
Of *fylth,* no *limits* set to thy *desire.*   2650
    O ! See his *veynes* their pretious *Treasures* spend-
        ing,
His *heart* yet hot, a *double streame* foorth sending
Of *blood* and *water.*   *Quicklie, quicklie* haste
With mournefull *soule,* which truely doth detaste
Thy vile licentious life : most humbly craue   2655
Those guiltlesse *streames* in thee no *guilt* may leaue,
That (hence) by vertue of this *Ransome* fred,
Tears thou to Him, who *bloode* for thee, mayst shed.
Soft *case* exile, till, by vnfaind *confession,*
Thy pittying LORD for thee make *Intercession.* 2660
Those pois'nable *delights,* disgorg'd now having,
Once greedilie drunke in, thy *soule* deceaving ;
Resolving (hence) by *action,* nor *consent*
More to licke vp thy *sins'* loathd *excrement,*
To *sense* though seeming *sweete,* which now turnd
        sowre,   2665
A *flood of bitternesse* on thee doth powre,
Thee, stinging with soule-wringing sad *remorse,*
The more represt *repining* with more *force.*
    But, gainst this *Tyrant* having now prevaild,
By time, this *hundreth-headed Monster* quaild,   2670
Beware, once *foyld,* thou never set it *free,*
Once *damn'd,* ne're after it *absolued* bee,

Least by that Righteous *Iudge*, whose *sentence* stands,
Thou bee adjudged to eternall *bands*,   2674

Whose trampled *blood* Hee shall at thee require,

A *Sow* turnd backe to *wallow* in the *myre*.

If with thyselfe, for *Sinne*, to live at *strife*
In *detestation* of thy vitious *life*
Thou truly dost desire, to find true *peace*,
Looke, looke upon thy LORD'S most lovelie *face*,
Perpending, pond'ring, laying deepe to heart,   2681
No midst there is, but thou with Him must part,
For *ever* sev'red from His *Holinesse*,
To pyne in *Torments* which no *time* makes lesse,
Thy *Back*, in time, or turning, with thy Sinne,   2685

(As thy ^c *right hand* or *eye* though deare,) to twinne.

'Tis base to thinke (if *soules* not to betray)

That CHRIST and ^d *Belial* can together stay,

Thy LORD'S chast *loue*, and thy licentious *lusts*
From thy divided *soule* one other thrusts.   2690
Pleasure in Him and fleshlie *pleasure* fall
So foull at *strife*, they can, nor *mixe*, nor *wall*.
To bee conform'd to Him take *pleasure ;* so
As thou makst *progresse* shall thy *pleasure* grow,
Pleasure without compare, which thee shall make
Sinne's deare bought seeming *pleasures* soone forsake.

No *Concupiscence* e're defild his minde,   2697
Nor sinfull *Motions* least-least place did find
In His *affections*, Him to lead astray,
Darkning in Him the weakest shining *Ray*   2700
Of perfite *holinesse*, mou'd but draw neare
That beastly *Idole*, as thy *life* held deare,
The which to *serue* thou all thy *dayes* hast doted,
To sinfull, sensuall *delights*, devoted.

O runne to Him for *grace ;* ^e Hee can deny   2705
None, who in *patient hope, knock, seeke*, or cry.
If thou but *mourne* to Him with *sorow* true
Of *lusts* vncleane, thy *Devill* hee will subdue.

His *Father's* service, Him in such a fashion
Did ravish with continuall *meditation*,   2710
Wholly with *This* tane vp, that in his *minde*
No idle *Rav'ryes* place besids could finde,
Such as thy *time* doe waste, *doores* open make
To *Sathan* and his *Trayne ;* who course doth take
On *Wings* of vaging *thoughts*, before to send   2715
His *Messingers ;* comes then *apace* in end
Himselfe ; These in *securitie* possest,
And having rowme prepaird for him to *rest.*

His *Calling* painefully hee did persue
At all *occasions :* teaching *thee* thy due,   2720
To *watch*, to *fast*, to *pray*, Hee giues the ground,
Least thou by *Sathan* shouldst bee *Idle* found.
Hee vs'd the *meanes*, of which hee had no neede,
But by *example* that He thee might lead.

a Luke 28. 37 ;
Mat. 14. 23.
Mark 6. 46.
In solitarie ᵃ *mountaines*, all alone,   2725
Hee oft for thee hath *mournd*, till *night* was gone,
b Iohn 8. 12.
Hath all the *day-long* in the ᵇ *Temple* stood,
Feeding the *famisht soule* with HEAVENLY food,
Delighted more his FATHER to obey,
His *will* to doe, to HEAVEN to teach the *way*,   2730
c Iohn 4. 31. 32.
33.
When ᶜ *Thirst* or *hunger* vrg'd, then *drink* or *eate,*
Though length of *Time* and *travell* did invite.

"Now if a *Patterne* this to make, thee please,
"A *Scope* to ayme at, standing not for ease,
"Bee diligent to *follow*, spare no *paine*,   2735
"Thus are thy *lusts* subdu'd, thy *sinne* is slaine.
O giue me LORD, with floods of teares vnfaind
To bath my bosome, with vncleannesse staind ;
Looke on a sorrie wight, in mournefull state,
A Lazare lying at thy mercie's gate :   2740
Ezek. 16. 8.
O passe not by : let mee thy pitty proue,
Cast over mee the Mantle of thy loue :
Though I bee out of measure vile, yet LORD,
I cleane shall bee, if thou but speake the word.

Thou who hast proudly the oppressor played,   2745
A rav'ning vulture on the Pigeon preyd,
The faces of the poore hast grunde, laid watch

The Tyrannizing extortioner, by turning to Christ procureth pardon. Luke 19.

The very morsels from their mouths to snatch,
Runne, runne, make hast, thy SAVIOUR comes along,
Climbe with *Zacheus* to eschue the throng   2750
Of *sinnes*, which happily in silence lye,
Yet to the Heavens for wrath and vengance cry,
And, on thy selfe if lookt thou hast aright,
Thou canst no misse a comfortable sight
Of Him, the lost who came to seeke and saue,   2755
Of whom thou shalt not a repulse receaue.
      " None ask in fayth and do vnpardond part,
      " Those suts alone lack successe which lack
            heart.

Behold, no readier thou art course to take
Due reparation for thy wrongs to make   2760
Than *Hee*, to bid himselfe thy guest to bee,
Salvation offring, even vnaskt of Thee.

How the Envious may be helped by looking on Christ.

If *Envy*, harbord but in worthles breast,
With *plentie pind, disquieted* with *rest*,
Evill with *good*, with soundest *health* most *sicke*,
With *wellfare wretched*, doth thy *soule* afflict,   2766
Looke on thy loving LORD, and *blush* to see
Him for his *Foes*, in *loue*, content to *die*,
While causlesly, thou dost thy *Brother* hate,
Who harmd thee never, but in thy *conceate*,   2770
Or, as the bleard-man's *eye* the *light* offends,
Whose *hurt* upon his owne *defect* depends.

Impatient passions healed by looking on Christ.

Thou, whose proude heart doth boyle with *furye's*
            flame,
Who canst not thy vndaunted *Passions* tame,
O, bee ashamd the *Mecknesse* to *behold*   2775
Of thy provoked LORD, *betrayd* and *sold*,
By *words*, by *deeds* injurd ; in whom did shine
Such *patience*, that even *those* who did repine

To see Him *liue* he *pittyed*, yea *procur'd*

Luke 23. 34 ;
Isa. 53. 12.
For *them*, by whom Hee cruell *death* endur'd.   2780

Learne, as thou lookst, thy beastlie *rage* to bound,

To bridle *Furie*, least it thee confound,

Which as a *fire*, still readie is to *burne*,

As to *revenge*, or *malice* thou dost turne,

Yea to *devoure*, if finding once a *vent*,   2785

Though for the least conceated *discontent*.

Feare to doe right,
in evrie estate,
cured by looking
on Christ.
Base FEARE, who darst not in thy *place* discharge

Thy *duetie, lesning* what thou shouldst enlarge,

Looke heere, and learne wise *Courage*, to persue

Thy righteous *Ends*, what's to thy *Calling* due,   2790

For *fead* nor *favour*, which thou canst no spare,

Thy LORD'S *Commission* if thou not empare.

Hath GOD thee cald his *Counsels* to disclose,

a Ezek. 2. 6.
His *will* to publish? [a] standst thou who oppose

b 1 Sam. 17.
Thy message?   What [b] *Goliah* thee assaile?   2795

c 2 King. 18. 17.
What raging [c] *Rabsaketh* against thee raile?

d 1 King 22. 27.
Fearst thou *distresse?* [d] what though constraind to *feed*

Thy famisht *Bodie* with *affliction's* bread

While heere thou breathst, wilt thou to *speake* for-beare

e Ibid.
But what may pleasing be to [e] *Achab's* eare.   2800

f 2 Chr. 18 ;
1 King 13. 1.
g Ez. 3. 18, &
33. 7.
Art thou a [f] *Man* of GOD, a Prophet true?

[g] It lyes thee on thy *life*, what ere ensue,

Wrath to denounce gainst a revolting Land :

h 1 King 13. 4.
Though [h] *Ieroboam* should streatch foorth his hand.

Nor *death* nor *danger*, thou by *sense* must scan.   2805

i 2 Sam. 12. 7.
Thou must not shrink to say, [i] *Thou art the Man*.

k Heb. 4. 12.
Him, whom thy hand hath charged, [k] of his *word*

With the two-edged soule-dividing *sword*,

Thou canst not but to *Indignation* moue,

If Thou a *Coward* in His *cause* shouldst proue.   2810

To speake doth thy *commission* warrant beare,

And dost thou of the *Arme* of *flesh* take *feare?*

ª 1 King. 19. 4,
5, 6, 7.

Behold, though to the ª *desarts* forc'd by flight,
To shield thy *life* from tiranizing *spight*,
Thy LORD can send, who best doth know thy neede,
An *Angell*, in thy *Famine* thee to feede.   2816

ᵇ Ier. 40. 1.
ᶜ Ibid. 20. 2.
ᵈ Ibid. 32. 3, and
38. 6.

Can strengthen thee, that ᵇ *Chaines* nor ᶜ *Stockes* nor
        ᵈ *Iaile*
Shall in His *Service* hence thy *Courage* quaile ;

ᵉ Act. 16.

Even for thy cause, can make the ᵉ *Earth* to quake,
All the *foundations* of the *prison* shake,   2820
Thy *boults* of *brasse*, thy *bands* to brust asunder,
Thy *keepers* overcome with *feare* and *wonder*,
To *stoupe* before thee, and to *wash* with *teares*
Thy *strips*, the *badges* which for CHRIST thou beares.
If GOD bee for thee, panse no who oppose :   2825

ᶠ 2 King. 19. 18.

His ᶠ *Hooke* can *haill* the *haughtiest* by the *nose*.
    What ere thou art, beware for *Feare*, to wrong
Thy LIEGE or *Lord*, to whom thou dost belong,
Least for a *Counseller*, of faith vnfaind,
A *Servant*, with no imputation staind,   2830
Disloyall and *Vnfaithfull* thou be found ;
To thy base *Ends* to lay a sliprie *ground*
While thine owne *Ease*, (of all true worth denude,)
Thou setst before GOD'S glorie and their *Good*,
And, from the *Right* made slavishlie to swerue, 2835
Stoupst downe their *Will*, though not their *Well* to
    serue.
    Although, (transported with the *Times* disease,)
Thy *selfe* and *Men* thou for a space mayst please,
Base *Temporizer*, yet when better *Light*
The *Weaknesse* of thy *wayes* shall set in sight,   2840
In thine owne *Colours* then bee seene thou must ;
For loyall *Subject*, *Servant* worthie trust
To GOD, thy PRINCE and *Lord*, thou shalt apeare
A slavish *Drudge* alone to servile *Feare*.   2844
    Behold, that No man's face should breed *affright*,
Or turne thee but a haire-bredth from thee *right*,

Thy LORD Himselfe doth in the *Mirror* show

Mat. 10. 32, 33;
Mark 8. 38.

As to his faythfull *Servants* friendlie, so

Most terrible to *All*, whom *Feare* doth draw,

Of *Man* than GOD to stand in greater aw.　　2850

　THOU whose leud *tongue* and lips to *lyes* did moue,

To looke on Christ
for bridling and
ruleing of the
tongue.

Looke heere, and learne the *Truth* to speake, to
　　loue.

No guile was in his mouth.　No faire *Pretence*

Of *Complementall* kindnesse mockt the *sense*

Isa. 53. 6.

Of *Any*, His *Societie* who sought ;　　2855

His *speaches* never varyed from his Thought.

a 1 Pet. 2. 22.

None Hee did a *cousin*, none with *lyes* deceaue,

Did *flatter* none, of none would *flattery* haue,

b Mat. 11. 19,
and 12. 24.
Iohn 8. 48.
c 1 Pet. 2. 23.

While foul b *reproach* His *Patience* did assaile,

His *peace* He keept : c *raild on*, He did no *raile*.

Hee No-man *slandred*, but who did offend,　　2861

In *time* and *place* most fit did *reprehend*,

In All rebuking *sinne ;* Hee *Cursed* none

But when of *Heaven* and *Earth* as *Iudge* alone,

Gainst *Hypocrits, Professors* but in *show*,　　2865

Hee thundred foorth *damnation, wrath* and *woe*.

　Chast were His *speeches, sober* were His *words*,

To nought vndecent His *discourse* debords.

No *Time* Hee did in idle *purpose* spend

But such as did to *edifying* tend :　　2870

Hee knew, in things committed to His care,

The fittest *season* both to speake and *spare*.

By hurtfull *Silence* He did *Nought* conceale,

His FATHER'S *Glory*, or his *People's* well

That might prejudge ; in *speache* nor *word* at all

Vntimely vttred from his lips did fall.　　2876

　　" Thus to thy *Good*, as Hee did frame His *speach*,

　　" Him make thy *patterne ;* speak as He doth
　　　　teach.

　　" What by *exemple* hee doth set thee to,

　　" According to thy *measure*, ayme to doe.　2880

Everie maladie of
soule may be helped
by looking by faith
on Christ in the
Scriptur and everie
vertue may be got-
ten this way.

IN SHORT, cause *All* heere can not reckned be,
To reade thy *life's* past *legend* leaving *Thee*,
So, in the *Mirror*, for thy help to looke,
To turne the *volumnes* of that sacred *Booke*
Where CHRIST is seene *aliue, dead, rais'd againe*
To *life*, for *sinne* ne're after to bee *slaine*,   2886
That looking heere, *faults* of what ever kinde
By light of *Scripture* in thy *selfe* thou find,
CHRIST thy *Consulter* thou alone mayst make,
What course most meet for thy remeed to take.

What ever *Sinnes* thy *Conscience* on thee draw,
By looking in the *Mirror* of the *Law*   2892
CHRIST make thy *glasse*, (tho with thy faults offended,)
To show thee how thy *misses* may bee mended.
What ere *deforme* doth in thy *soule* abide,   2895
In Him looke *something* that *defect* to hide,
No leprous *spot* vnpurgt in *thee* is seene,
The which in *Him* thou mayst not haue made cleane,
How ere in thee *Sinne's Plague* its *poison* spread,
Seeke out, in *Him*, and thou shalt find *remead*.

To GOD, to *Man*, by whatsoever bands   2901
What thou to *doe*, or *suffer* oblisht stands,
How e're extended bee thy *dutye's* lines
Looke still on CHRIST, as in His *Word* He *shines*,
By *light* of which thy *minde* lift vp to see   2905
HIM in the HEAVENS, dispensing vnto *thee*
These *vertues* which hee craues ; and what hee showes
By *Life's* rare *Patterne*, working even in *those*
In whome His *loue* a true *desire* doth bread
To bee *conforme*, made like *Himselfe* their *Head*.

Truth of religion
may bee learned of
Christ seene in the
Scriptur.

True *faith*, not *firme* but for a *day* or *houre*,   2911
But such as stedfast stands, in ev'ry stoure,
True *Loue*, possessing all the *soule* and *senses*,
The *powrs* all drawing, (free of faind *pretences*,)
To GOD, in full *obedience* to His *will*,   2915
In *absolute submission*, suffring still

With patient *heart* as pleaseth Him to deale,
Who best doth know what best is for thy *well ;*
Pure *worshipping* of GOD, in maner *chast*,
For *warrant* as His *ordinance* thou hast,   2920
Without all *mixture* of *Inventions* vaine,
The *bastard broode* of man's presumptuous *braine*,
Him teaching thou shalt *heare*, *Him* showing *see ;*
Himselfe in *Person* even preceeding thee,
A blest *exemplar*, a most gracious *guyde*,   2925
And if thou loue, (*sinne's* luggage layde aside,)
To follow on, to thy eternall *well*
In *thee* the like *Him* working thou shalt feele.
      Whatever bonds of *neighbourhood* doe clame

Dutie to parents and friends how to be learned at Christ. Thy LORD will fitt, and by *degrees* thee frame   2930
Thy *Duty* to discharge, to *Great*, to *Small*
As *equity* requires to doe to *All ;*
Mercie to show vnto the *miserable*
As *neede* in them exacts, as thou art *able :*
As *Lazarus*, as His *Disciples* deare   2935
Hee did *esteeme*, *loue* to thy *friends* to beare,
Kindred and *bloode* with due *respect* to prise,
But those whom *Nature* thee more nearlie tyes
Most to regard, thy *Parents*, who did spare
No *paynes* for thee, while for thy selfe to care   2940
Thou couldst not, in more *speciall* degree,
In greater *measure*, loe *Hee* teacheth *thee*

Io. 19. 26, 27. While from the CROSSE, to IOHNE, his loving *friend*,
Now in *His* place, HER hee doth recommend
Who gaue Him *birth*, *His Virgine-Mother blest*, 2945
By speciall *care* HER singling from the *rest*.

Servants may learne their dutie by looking on Christ.   *Servants* may looke, in *servant's shape*, how Hee
Good proofe did give of his *fidelitie*
And diligence to HIM did *Him* employ,
So, follow on with *cheerefullnesse* and *Ioy*,   2950
That to what ever *Charge* their *Place* them call,
Eph. 6. 5, 6.   As done to CHRIST their *service* may bee all.

T

And masters their dutie.

Maisters, remarking how their LORD did lead
These *twelue*, who speciall *priviledge* did plead
To serve Him as *Disciples :* how most *kind*,   2955
Most *affable* Him all of them did find,
Their *faults* so *wisely* checking that no eye
Did no their *well* sought in His *service* see,

Eph. 9. 6.

May learne in *meeknesse, lenitie* and *loue*
To *rule* aright, not *Tyrannizers* proue,   2960
Their *servants* in *obedience* due to draw,
By *wisdome* more than *force, loue* more than *awe*.

And the maried their dutie.

The *Maryed* may that strait *conjunction* see,
Of matchlesse *loue*, that sacred *mysterie*,
CHRIST and His *Church* combining, thence to *loue*
May learne, as *wedded* to a LORD aboue   2966
Who *lov'd* them *first*, so from this *patterne* draw
In earthly *wedlock* a religious *law*,
Of holy *loue* a *lesson*, how to frame
These *dutyes* chast which *mariage bands* do clame.

The fitted *Soule*, which hath its *lusts* subdued,
Singly to *liue* with *strength* of *grace* endued,   2972

Mat. 19. 11, 12.

A NAZARITE to GOD to which is given
To liue, an *Eunuch* consecrate for HEAVEN,
Hath for a *Guyde*, to follow who invits,   2975

Iohn 1. 45.

IESUS of *Naz'reth, prince of Nazarites*.

And parents their dutie.

Heere carefull *Parents* how to trayne may see
Their *Children, Them* how nurse in pietie,
How in their hearts to sow the *seeds* of *grace*,
How *vice* and inborne *Error* to displace,   2980
Hereditarie *Evils, faults* foreseene,
Sinnes ready to break foorth how to preveene,

Mat. 16. 6-12.

How keepe from leavenning with *doctrins* vaine,
From *course* of *life* corrupt how to restrayne.

By looking on Christ as Hee shines in the Mirror of the Scripture Subiects may learne their dutie to Magistrats and namelie Churchmen.

Heere *Subjects* study may *subjection* true,   2985
Submissiue *loyalty, obeysance* due,
But *Church men* chiefly, by *ambition* blind,
Whom CHRIST fore-seing should affect to find

Worldlie *Preheminence, Respect* and *Place*,
Aspire the steps of *Sov'raignety* to trace ;   2990
That ONE aboue the rest, should, (thus made weake,)
The *yock* of *Civill Iurisdiction* shake
From scornefull shoulders, raysd those *Men* aboue
Whom GOD hath called *Gods*, (how ere they proue

Exod. 12. 13 ;
22. 28.
In this *submission* lesse then *Men*,) to beare,   2995
In Princelie *Pow're*, His Royall Image heere,
Though therefore He *exemption* might haue pleaded,
And not beene *Caesar's Tributary* needed
To teach *obedience*, yet, to *Subjects* true,

Mat. 22. 21 ;
Rom. 13. 7.
Would giue to *Caesar* what was *Caesar's* due.   3000
    And, though hee might attaynd haue to a crowne,

Iohn 6. 15.
Himselfe made *Great* by throwing *Others* downe,
To voluntary *offers* giving eare
Of *such*, repining *Caesar's* yoke to beare,
As gladly would haue *Insurrection* made,   3005
Conspird by arms a bloodie *cause* to plead,
Yet did He flye ; and, (by *exemple* rare),
To solitarie *Desarts* to repare
Preferring, did all loyall *Subjects* teach
To shunne *Seditioun*, though a *Crowne* to reach.
Yea when His *life* was most vnjustlie sought,   3011
A *Weapon* to bee drawne He suffred nought
In His *defence*, but chuisd *Himselfe* alone
To *suffer*, rather than by *armes* oppone
The Lawfull *Magistrat*, so *authorize*   3015
Seditious men, for private *Injuries*
Persu'd by *Iustice*, who dare set their *face*
Against their PRINCE or *Deputs* in his place.
    Not of this *world His Kingdome* He profest,
To conquesse *rents* and *Lands* Him troubled least.
Men's *soules* alone He sought, and *these* to saue ;
No Prince by Him did *prejudice* receaue,   3022
By civile *challenge*, by pretended *right*,
By open *violence*, or secret *slight*.

Let *Church-men* follow as Hee did preceed,　3025
In *Imitation* of their LORD and *Heed*,
Or quite the false *pretence* themselves to call
His *Servants*, while with Him at *strife* they fall,
Proudly *practizing* what they contrare find,
Both to His *Mouth's* direction and His *minde*,　3030
For, (bee they sure), no TITLES of respect,
No rev'rend *Stiles* which *proudlings* so affect,
No name of *Fathers* in his *house*, no place
Of *Honour*, which so eagerlie they chace,
No *scugge* of PETERS chayre, no vaine *pretence*　3035
Of *powre*, by soveraigne *preheminence*,
No casting out of *devills* shall ought availe,
Preaching nor *wonders working ;* all shall faile
Proud *wordlings* from that dreadfull *doome* to saue :

Luke 13. 27.

I know you not ; with mee no part yee haue.　3040

Kings and rulers may learne their dutie by looking vpon Christ's purtrate in the Scripture.

　　As *Subjects* Him beholding humbled, see
A pearlesse *Patterne* of true *loyaltie*,
So *Kings* may looking on this KING of *Kings*,
Who proudest *Tyrants* in *subjection* brings,
Learne to be truly *Royall, Rule* as Hee　3045
To whom all earthly *Monarchs* vassels bee.

　　As *Subjects* prosper best, when to their *King*
They *Loyall* proue, and to his *Lawes* to bring
Obedience due no paynes *esteeme* too great,
The well to establish of His *royall* State,　3050
So *Princes* then, when *Subjects* good they proue
To IESUS CHRIST, a KING all *Kings* aboue,
His *Kingdome* seeking to advance, to *plant*
Relligion in Their bounds, thence to *supplant*
Contemners of His lawes, his *Throne* enlarge,　3055

Ezra 7. 23.

With noble *Artaxarxes* giving charge
That what enjoynd is by the GOD of Heaven
His House concerning, *Order* may bee given
It to *performe* with speed, *wrath* to keepe backe,
Which may the *Realme*, the *King*, his *Sonnes* o'retake.

Let *Kings* behold this KING, how *Hee* who stands
Nor by His *Subiects' wisdome, wealth,* nor *hands,*
Yet so doth seeke the wellfare of their *State,*   3063
As if, they weakned, hee could not bee *Great ;*
Behould, how Hee All such as dare injure,
The hurt or *Prejudice* of *His* procure,   3066
Foes to Himselfe professing : no *pretence*
Of fayned *friendship, show* of *Innocence*
Admittance finding to abuse His *Eare,*
All *Flatt'rers* false defended to draw neare,   3070
Whom Hee will, (on day,) to their endlesse shame,
(As if He them had never known,) disclame.

As DAVID than, to whom GOD's *Counsells* deepe
Revealed were, of this true KING the *Type,*
Looking vpon the *Prototype,* His LORD,   3075
His *Kinglie Carriage* did to His accord ;

<table>
<tr><td>Psal. 101. v. 1.</td><td>Learnd GOD His *Ioy* to make ; GOD's *Law* alone</td></tr>
<tr><td>v. 2.</td><td>His *Rule,* in *life,* and in *Relligion ;*</td></tr>
<tr><td>v. 3.</td><td>*Apostasie* and Apostats to *hate,*</td></tr>
<tr><td>v. 4.</td><td>And every *wicked* man, or *Meane* or *Great :*   3080</td></tr>
<tr><td>v. 6.</td><td>All such to *curbe : the Godlie* in their place</td></tr>
</table>

As *Favourits, Friends, Counsellers* to grace,
Raysd to *preferment,* in his *Eyes* to stand ;

v. 8.   GOD'S *foes* degraded, *rooted* from the Land ;
So let all *Kings, anoynted* from *aboue,*   3085
GOD for their *Portion, David's Lote* who loue,
Him who doth both *vnscepter* and *enstall*
Beholding, learne to *do the like* in all.

Every estate may
profite by looking
on Christ in the
Scripture.

Let every *Soule* in end, of what *condition*
Of *mind* or *case* of present *disposition*   3090
Of *Body, goods,* or *name,* of what *degree,*
Sexe, age, estate or *Ranke* so-ere they bee,
Seeke by the *eye* of liuelie *Fayth* to looke
On CHRIST, described in the sacred *Booke*
Of GOD's two *Testaments,* the *Mirror* true   3095
From whence alone reflects His perfite *view,*

And All in *Him*, (if rightlie seene,) shall find
For each *defect* of *Bodie* or of *minde*
Some seasonable *good*, some soveraine cure
To doe away in them *sinne's* spots impure.   3100
No *looke* on Him shall bee bestou'd in vaine,
For Hee in *Mercie* shall *looke* backe againe,
And from each *looke* shall liuelie *vertue* flow,
Which *difference* sufficient shall show
Twix CHRIST (aright) thus by His owne *Means*
        sought,   3105
And that deceaving, shamefull *Idole*, brought
In place of CHRIST, as CHRIST to bee *adord*,
And (now) is by deluded *soules implord*
For Christ, and *cald*, (what *blasphemie* more vile?)
By *Christ's* owne *personall* and proper stile.   3110

The particulare vses
of Christ's discrip-
tion in the Scripture
left to preachers.

Which things, as more than equall to my *strength*,
I leave to *Preachers* to informe at length,
Whose *Calling* is, (not in the *Bed* of slouth
Reposing), from the *Chayre* of sacred *Truth*
That LAMBE of GOD, by *Scriptures*, to point
        foorth,   3115

Mat. 13. 44.

That *Treasure* of vnestimable *worth*
Hid in the *Gospels'* field in *sight* to set,
Whence needie *soules* may lasting *riches* get,
CHRIST, *sacrifizde* for *sinners*, to present,
(By *preaching* of His *death* and *Testament*,)   3120
Vnto their *peoples'* eyes, by *vses* due
Quickning dead *soules* vnto obedience new.
        O, that not *Pastors* may a few bee found,

1 Cor. 3. 12.

Gold, pretious stones, who building on this GROVND,
With hearts right set, their *Maister's will* to know,
Him to their flocks may chieflie strive to show,
His Honour, and *safetie* of his *Sheepe*   3127
Preferring to what els the *world* doth keepe.

Christ a pattern
to preachers in a
speciall maner.

As CHRIST to All Himselfe a *patterne* gaue,
To *These* so chieflie *Charge* of *soules* who haue, 3130

Hee, not Himselfe *Intruding*, sent from HEAVEN,

Heb. 5. 4. As *Aaron* cald vnto the *Iews* was given,

To Them the *Gospell's* joyfull *news* to preach :

Thus in *God's House* no *charge at all* to teach

Place ought to haue, but *such*, (by GOD designd,)

As *warrant* doe from His *apointment* find, 3136

Iohn 10. 1, 2. And that in such None ought *themselues* to *thrust*,

But whom alone GOD daind hath to *entrust*

With His *Commission*, in His *worke to sweate*,

Found *Messingers* for His *Embassage* meet, 3140

Who, scorning *Means* which worthlesse *men* doe
  make,

By *doore* of lawfull calling *Entrie* take.

 The *charge* to beare of GOD'S *peculiar flock*

Thus when thrust foorth, the *Truth* of God Hee
  spoke,

Iohn 12. 29. Him in *Commission* given, and still did care 3145

Of all His *words*, *God's word* to make the *square*.

 No *sinne* Hee spard, Him No man's *face* did *feare ;*

Hee neither *whipt* in *spleene*, nor did forbeare

For *favour ;* so their *saftie* might bee wrought,

Men's *well* and not to please their *will* he sought.

Iohn 7. 18. *Glory* of men Hee *gloryed* not to get, 3151

Nor *Honour* to Himselfe Himselfe did set

To purchase, (though to Him was due by *right*

All *Glory, Honour, Majestie* and *might*),

To seeke GOD'S honour was his *maine intent*

Him who to *Labour* in His *Harvest* sent. 3156

 No curious *Phrase*, applause of *men to breed*,

(To *Ignorants* one with an vncouth *leid*,)

No *Eloquence* of *words*, no swelling *stile* '

Did from His mouth His *flock* of *foode* beguile ;

In all *Simplicitie*, in *termes* most plaine, 3161

His *minde* He *vttred*, to the *vulgar* braine

And *Iudgement* weake of *All* Himselfe applying

Eares had to heare, vpon His *charge* relying.

To further man's *Salvation* Hee did spare   3165
Paynes, nor by *night* nor *day*, nor *late* nor *ayre*.

Iohn 4. 34.
His *meate*, his *drink* it was, *soules* home to bring,
His Father's will to doe in everie thing.

Wordlie *Preferment, Honours, Titles, Place,*
Hee did not with ambitious *wordlings* chace,   3170
But vtterlie refusde, and lookt afarre
On what so ere his maine *Intent* might marre.

With things His *Presence* which did not exact,
Or from a better *worke* Him might destract,
Hee did no meddle, would no lay aside   3175
His *Calling*, matters civill to decide,

Luk. 12. 13, 14.
Though in pretence twixt *Brothers* peace to make
Vrg'd, Hee the *Iudge's* office did forsake.

His *Preaching* while Impugnd by *sinners* bold,

Heb. 12. 3.
Mat. 22. 15.
Mark 12. 13.
Luke 20. 20.
Hee suffred patientlie to bee controld,   3180
Not with the *obstinate* by *Iangling* vaine
To *tempt* Him set, and of his *words* to gaine
Advantage, Hee by *dispute* did contend :
Or *peace* Hee keept, or some few *words* did spend
Sufficient to *convince*, the *Conscience* check   3185
Of such as thus their *Envy* durst detect.

Luke 23. 2.
When as not *loyall* scandalizd, hee pleads
Fidelitie, in *suffring, doctrine, deeds,*

1 Tim. 6. 13.
Though KING of *Kings*, repining not to bee,
Heere subject to *Supreme Authoritie*.   3190

When to the Romane *Governour* accusd
As on whose *doctrins* false the world abusd,

1 Tim. 6. 13.
A *good Confession witnessing*, Hee stoode
Fast for the *Truth*, and *seald* it with His bloode.

To this His *Patterne*, perfitlie espyd,   3195
If true *conformitie* had beene applyd,
His *Vicar*, Him at least who steales this *stile*,
But from His *life* and *doctrine* doth resile,

Mat. 4. 8, 9.
Those Evill *offers* never had entisd,
Nor bad *condition*, by our LORD despisd.   3200

Nor should *ambitious* Men, puft vp with pride,
With *loue* of worldlie *Glory* led aside,
Haue turnd, their Earthlie *pompe* to entertaine,
CHRIST'S *Heauenly Kingdome* in a temp'rall *Raigne.*

Apoc. 2. 4.
Nor should the *Dragon's* taile haue drawne from
   Heauen,   3205
(By greed of *gaine,* and filthie *lucre* driven,)
So many *Stars* to *Earth,* and earthlie *wayes,*
Depriving both of *light* and *heat* their *Rayes.*

Nor should *vaine Men,* in damnable *pretence*
Of *Pietie,* with windie *Eloquence*   3210
And falsely cald *Philosophy,* haue dard
Themselues to *Preach,* of GOD the *Truth* haue
   mard.

Nor should such *Errors,* breeding onlie gaine
To blinded *Guids* of a deluded *Traine,*
Haue *Scriptures* made despisd, so farre suspect,
And *Toyes* and *Trifles* cary such *respect.*   3216
Strengthen, LORD IESUS, *and stretch foorth thine*
   hand
To ayde thy Seruants, for thy cause who stand,
And reddy are to suffer fyre and sword
For Thee, *thy* Truth, *and credite of thy* Word.
Sufficient Workmen *in thy Haru'st thrust foorth,*
Fitted for those pernitious Times in worth :   3220
Come clense thy Kirk, *discouer by degrees*
The Man *of* Sinne, *to All whose darkned eyes,*
Blind to discerne, yet can not truelie *see*   3225
Midst such a glorious Sunne-shine, *who is Hee.*
Thine owne deare Lambs *set free, who captiues lye,*
Which chains of Ignorance *and* Error *tye ;*
Iohn 14. 6.
That hence, (no more in by-paths led astray)
In seeking Thee, the Truth, the Life, the Way,
Their Crucifixes *faind they may disclame,*   3231
And of their Idols *and false* Christs *thinke*
   shame.

Amongst their hands, their hearts lift vp to Heaven,
Where Truelie *Thee to see by* Faith *is given,*
To All, that in the Means *ordaind by Thee,*   3235
With Souls right set, seeke in SINCERITIE.

Μονω δοξα θεω.

GAL. 6. 14.

GOD *forbid that I should rejoyce,*
but in the Crosse *of our LORD*
IESUS CHRIST,
Whereby the World is cru-
cified vnto mee, and I
vnto the World.

SONNETS

SONET 1.

While (mine owne glasse), vpon myself I looke,
Examining how (heere) my part is plaid,
Reading in conscience's accusing Booke,
Of pretious Time how meane account I made,
What hideous Formes my frighted Eyes vpbrade,
Reflecting from the Mirror of my mynd :
Abortiue Flowrs which in the blossome fade,
Most of my labours past, alone I find.
Eternall Ivstice, Thou who (vndeclynd)
To everie Worke proportions the Reward,
Pittie my folyes past : with Sprite refynd
So shall I praise Thee, who my paths repaird ;
    So from Egyptian Brick and Clay set free,
    My Songs shall only, only bee of THEE.

SONET 2.

Bvt while my Sprite aboue the spheares aspyres,
And from the World would separation make,
Myne Eyes repyning at my Soules desyres,
With Lot's fond Wife, relenting looks cast backe.
Thou, whose consuming breath her soyle did sacke,
All Lets, my flight which doe empeach, remove :
Wing my affection that in word, in act,
From Earth sequestred I may vpwards move,
There, where around Thee, Wisdome, Iustice, Loue.
Truth, Mercie with extended wings, abide,
With numbrous hostes all number farre aboue,
Of Sprites which in eternity them hyde :
    O lead me thither, thither make mee runne :
    Perfite thy worke, (Good Lord), in mee begunne.

SONET 3.

My wayes, my wandrings all to Thee are knowne,
No strength to stand (Lord) of my selfe I haue ;
I breath in bondage, so am not mine owne,
Emancipat to Sinne, so Sathan's slave.
No stinking carion, halfe consumd in graue,
My leprous soule in loathsomenesse exceeds.
Thy glorious Image how defacd I haue
While I record, my heart for horror bleeds.
Sweete Reconcealer, Thou who pardon pleads
To sin-chargd soules, which, faynting, groane for grace,
Thy Mercie measure not with my misdeeds ;
Thy wandring chyld, turnd home at length, embrace,
    Who brutishly mongst beasts, (with ackorns fed),
    Too long, a shamefull, swynish life haue led.

SONET 4.

O Three times happie, if the day of grace
In my dark soule did, (though but dimly), dawne ;
If to my strugling thoughts proclaimd were peace ;
If from mine eyes the vaile of darknesse drawne ;
If once the seed of true Repentance sawne
Made gushing streames leave furrowes on my face ;
Sinne's menstruous rags in pure transparent laune
Were chang't ; O then how happie were my cace !
So darknesse paths no more my feete should trace,
So ever on a quyet conscience feast.
Repentance planted so should vice displace,
So clenst from sinne, sinne's filth I should detest,
    Grace, Light, Repentance, inward peace I crave,
    Grant these, good Lord, for mee thy selfe who gave.

SONET 5.

Awake mee, (Lord,) from fancie's charming dreame,
My Sprit rowze vp from lethargie of sloath :
With doubled pace, O give mee to redeeme
My time mispent, the errors of my youth.
Hence let my taske bee thy eternall Truth,
Free from vaine fictions of distempred brains :
Grant what Thou addst vnto my years of grouth
Good seed may prove, cast on more fertile plains.
Set to the key of grace, tune all my straines
From lawlesse stryfe, fred from conceits prophaine,
Which poyson doe with gall the sweetest veines,
And, with the Sprit of lyes, most sprits enchaine.
    My sprit with thine inspire ; on wings mee raise.
    Lord, henceforth let my tongue sound foorth thy praise.

SONET 6.

Since that vast orbe, which doth the rest embrace,
More swift than thoght still whirls about times wheele ;
Since years' serpentine course, with speedy pace,
Doth a continuall revolution feele ;
Since houres still slyde, still life away doth steale,
Why then, my soule, heere art thou luld asleepe ?
As if on Earth's low stage were placd thy Well,
In streams of slyding pleasurs drencht too deepe :
Breake off thy dreame : from world's basse fetters creepe,
Thy soveraine Good with eyes vnsyld to view :
Ryse from earth's vaile to climbe that Mountaine steepe,
The only station of contentment true.
    Sooth no thy selfe, my soule ; shake of delay :
    Life's Flowre both spreidth and fadeth in a day.

SONET 7.

As waue doth waue, so day doth day displace;
Time's clock goes quickly : Moments swiftly slyde :
The longest Age scare doth a minut's space,
If with eternity compaird, abyde.
Yet Mortals, charg'd with madnesse, fraught with pryde,
Day-livers, dreame to see the world's last date :
Guyle held no guilt, craft they with craft doe hyde,
Sinne heap on sinne, deceat vpon deceat ;
No paine is spair'd to gaine the name of GREAT,
Prizde with contempt, aym'd at by few, is GOOD
But Ah ! and buildst thou vp a slipry state
With pressing vsury, with bribes, with bloode,
    Madde Man, yet dost not, neither wilst take heede,
    Thy Life ore hell hings by a slender threed.

SONET 8.

If Lines which Sphears in equall shares divyde,
But once the Center, twice the Circle touch,
Like slow-pac'd snails, why then still doe wee crouch,
Still craule on earth, on earth still grov'ling bide?
Let fayth our flight aboue Heaven's circuits guide
Where wee should dwell, redoubling our desires.
The Doue, no rest heere finding, streight retyres,
But in our Prison plac'd is all our pride.
As all the vast inferiour orbs of Heaven,
By proper pace, vnsensibly are rold,
But hurld about, with motion vncontrold,
Are by the Highest violently driven,
    O Mover first, let mee thy motion proue
    In grace, who rather retrograde than moue.

SONET 9.

A constant course, heere, Lord each creature keeps,
Not swarving from thine ordinance their ends :
Earth vnsustained stands, in showrs ayre weeps,
Fyre vpward, water to the Center tends.
The Sunne in his Ecliptick, mounts, descends,
Oblicklie runnes, with Tropics two confynd,
Whose course the years alternat seasons sends ;
Seas ne're transgresse the Limits thou assing'd.
But Man, in whom thy vive Character shynd,
That lytle World, of all thy works a Breefe,
Made Lord of All, of all hath most declynd
From thy obedience.   O tears !   O griefe !
    Man to the Angels whom Thou didst preferre,
    From his Creation's end doth only erre.

SONET 10.

My lif's fraile Barge, with an impetuous tyde,
Is on this world's tempestuous Ocean tost :
For me, as for our second Sire, provyde
A saving Ark, O Lord, or I am lost.
Or as thy people, (while proud Pharaoh's hoast
Seas overwhelmd,) through floods firme passage fand.
A Vessell weake, Mee save, at too much cost
Redeem't to bee depriv'd of promis'd Land.
As earst to Peter, Lord, streach foorth thine hand,
On liquid floare while as his fayth did faynt :
Let not betwixt mee and thy mercie stand
That I a sinner vile, hee liv'd a Saint.
    Thy Glorie greater, greater is thy praise,
    Mee a dead Lazare, from sinne's grave to raise.

U

SONET.

To the Blessed Trinitie.

Essence vnmov'd, whose Word made all things move,
Earth's pondrous Orbe midst Ayre who ballanst even,
By Discords sweete, who tun'd the ten-stringt Heaven,
God rich in Mercie, infinite in Love,
Light out of Light, O life who death didst prove,
Lost Earthlings to redeeme, depriv'd of grace;
Child full of wonder, glorious Prince of Peace,
Begotten, from Eternitie, aboue;
O Holy Ghost, sweete sanctifying Sprit
From both proceeding: All, in essence One,
Most sacred Triade: first and last alone,
Three vndividuall, Trinally vnite,
    Father, Sonne, Holy Ghost, God, One in Three
    And three in One! for ever blessed bee.
                       Amen.

END OF THE FIRST VOLUME.

PRINTED BY WILLIAM BLACKWOOD AND SONS.

CPSIA information can be obtained at www.ICGtesting.com
Printed in the USA
BVOW03s1416310314

349299BV00016B/974/P